PATRICIA HILLIARD

iUniverse LLC
Bloomington

GO TO LIBERTY

This is a work of fiction. All of the characters, names, incidents, organizations, and dialogue in this novel are either the products of the author's imagination or are used fictitiously.

iUniverse books may be ordered through booksellers or by contacting:

iUniverse LLC
1663 Liberty Drive
Bloomington, IN 47403
www.iuniverse.com
1-800-Authors (1-800-288-4677)

ISBN: 978-1-4917-1590-1 (sc)
ISBN: 978-1-4917-1592-5 (hc)
ISBN: 978-1-4917-1591-8 (e)

Library of Congress Control Number: 2014901905

Printed in the United States of America.

iUniverse rev. date: 02/06/2014

Contents

Chapter One

Eva Makes a Decision

From the beginning of its life, a bird knew it was a bird, and knew exactly what a bird should do. Eva watched as sunlight glinted off the metallic-blue wings of a tree swallow. The slim fast-flying bird arced over the fresh-cut grass with one wing pointed to the sky and the other pointed to the earth. Instantly, it turned like a stunt kite and circled back in the opposite direction. Eva walked toward the bird then stopped. She stood and watched as the bird merged with several other swallows darting back and forth over the park lawn.

Eva hugged herself and smiled. The birds were so beautiful. They flew so gracefully. How wonderful it would be to fly. Birds made flying look easy, made life seem so simple.

If only life could be so simple for humans. Eva was facing the complicated decision of what to do with her life. She was eighteen years old and needed to choose an occupation so she could earn money to buy life's necessities. She understood this. Mom had explained how important this is, but Eva wanted an occupation that was important, where she could do something for the greater good.

Was that too much to expect?

Eva looked around. Today, she was in a beautiful park at sunrise. Looking to the northeast, she saw the tall glass-and-marble buildings of New York City. Looking to the southeast, she saw the Statue of Liberty. Its torch gleaming in the morning light. On the path before her stood a small group of gardeners, their heads bowed as they gazed at the flowerbeds before them. The flowers were ragged and broken from last winter's heavy snow.

"Eva, can you stop bird watching and come help?"

Eva turned her gaze toward her mother, Colleen Kaufman.

"I'm coming," Eva said as she ran to join her mother. Colleen handed her a pair of rubber gloves in preparation for spring gardening. Their work today was voluntary; the beauty of the flowers that they planted would be their only compensation.

Eva stood ready now and waited.

From the group came a tall, big-boned woman. Eva watched her take a position among the gardeners. She lifted her shoulders and looked each one of them in the face. She looked at Eva, too. Eva watched as the woman's gray hair lifted in the gentle breeze.

"I'm Amanda Walters and I want to thank everyone here today. Your dedication and hard work is appreciated by the many park visitors from around our country and from around the world. We are able to garden here today due, in part, to the dedication of the Friends of Nature and their success in persuading the park management to let the community participate in beautifying the park."

The newcomers rested their hands on their hips. The experienced gardeners paused and leaned on their hoes.

"As you know, this area was once an industrial site. Railroads once crisscrossed where we are standing, but look at it now." She waved her arms around at the flower beds, lawns and trees, "Thanks to the Corp of Engineers and the Parks and Forestry Department, they moved the railroad ties away and planted grass and trees so that now we have this beautiful park. It's a place where people can come together to garden in harmony with nature. This is the Commons; this is the people's land. We must struggle to hold on to this, the land of the common people."

Eva was delighted to see the gardeners cheering and clapping their hands. She was impressed that the park meant so much to them.

"So let's get to work," one gardener called out, raising a gloved fist into the air.

Park employees began unloading tools from the back of a truck and gave them to the volunteers.

Soon the sound of shovels and spades clanging against the rocky soil gave a percussion beat to the musical laughter of the gardeners. This song of spring echoed throughout the park.

Eva had grown up in this metropolitan area, a place with lots of cement and sharp edges. The park was where people could return to soft earth, flowing grass and blowing leaves. When Eva joined the Girl Scouts, they went to the park every week to learn about wildflowers, trees and birds. Eva learned to identify these wonders of nature. She earned three badges. The thrill of this accomplishment sent her on a mission to learn more. That is when the park became her very special place.

Today, they were in the park for a new reason. Eva was not familiar with gardening and the tools it required. She picked up a hoe and looked at it, then she looked at her mother. Her mom had grown up on a farm. The joy of working in the soil was all over her face; in fact, a streak of mud had already painted her forehead.

"I'm so glad they've started a gardening program at the park," Colleen said. "I've wanted to do this for years."

Eva realized she was seeing something in her mother that she had never before known.

"Do this Eva, see, use the hoe like this," Colleen said as she jabbed the corner of the hoe into the soil tearing loose the stems and roots of weeds. Colleen then bent her tall thin body down to grab a clump of roots and shook the dirt out.

Eva bent down. Her long brown-hair, braided into a single strand, dropped over her cheek. She stood up and tucked it under her hat. She picked up the hoe and attempted to imitate her mom's actions. "How do I know which plants the gardeners want to keep?" she asked.

"Don't worry about it. What's coming up now is all weeds," Colleen replied.

Eva bent again to look at the small yellow flowers just beginning to form on a tall green stalk. They were bright, yellow, and sweet smelling. From her Girl Scout training, she knew this was wild mustard.

"But these wildflowers are so nice." Eva said, pleading in their defense. Why was Mom insisting that she tear them from the earth? To stall, she looked over at her older sister, Judi. Judi had found a less troubling and cleaner task doling out cookies and cups of water to thirsty gardeners.

"Nice easy job, Sis. You're doing your best, I can tell."

Judi wrinkled her nose at Eva. "An army travels on its stomach," she said. "I wanted to do my volunteering this way."

Eva smirked at her. Then seeing another plant that lacked flowers, she lifted her hoe and tore it out of the ground. Poor thing.

On this beautiful spring morning, birdsongs beckoned Eva from every treetop. Here a house finch, there a robin, next a delightful song from a song sparrow. She listened again to confirm its identity. The song rolled and twirled in the air. Yes, it was a song sparrow. Eva's interest had become a passion. She started with birds, but learned that their lives connect to plants and trees. She expanded her studies to include these. A day in nature was a busy time for Eva. When she heard birds singing, she listened and dedicated the bird's song to memory. When she walked past trees, she called out their names in her mind. She searched the meadows for new wildflowers she had never seen before. From this, she had gained a reputation as the nature expert in her scout troop. Being an expert set her apart from the others. She liked the feeling.

Eva thought about herself again. At eighteen, she needed to choose an occupation. Should she go to college? What should she study to be? She wanted a meaningful life. Why was it so hard for her to make a decision? The question kept turning repeatedly in her mind, nagging her, even in times and places where she should be able to escape for a little while.

"Eva, are you going to help with the gardening? You are so obsessed with birds."

Eva looked at her mom. A tree swallow dashed between them. There was just no explaining to Mom that she would rather pursue another avian wonder than dig up hearty yellow wildflowers from the face of the earth.

"I wish I had brought my bird book and binoculars today," Eva said. "We are so close to the river and on the fly-way during the spring bird migration. There could be some rare warblers coming through the park today. How did I let you two drag me out here without my binoculars?"

In the distance, Eva heard Judi laughing, "Really, Eva, you need to give up some of your weird hobbies. How are you ever going to find a husband or build a career?"

Eva frowned, "Judi, I like nature, but I'm not into finding a mate right now or building a nest. I think people should do more than just reproduce. I think we need to find meaning in life."

Eva saw a look of contempt on Judi's face.

"And what do you think life is about anyway?" Judi asked, "It's about mating and building a nest." She tossed her blonde ponytail with an arrogance that always irked Eva. Then Judi added, "You could learn from the birds you are always watching."

Eva sighed and looked at her big sister. Judi was always following the traditional ways, the normal way. Eva hated how Judi seemed to think this proved her superiority over Eva. All this just because Judi was older. Why should that even matter? Eva looked at Judi and wondered if Judi was really just a selfish, shallow person with no concern for others. How had the two of them turned out so differently? Eva knew she had to go beyond the limits. She wanted to fight the good fight for a worthy cause. With sadness, she was beginning to realize that most people were not interested in this challenge. They did not care about the greater good.

A large bright red bird flew into a nearby apple tree.

"There's a cardinal," Eva exclaimed. She was thrilled to see the bright red bird with its prominent topnotch. She saw Judi and Colleen laughing at her.

"Ok, so it is a cardinal," Judi called. She pulled the hair band out of her long blonde hair, and scooping it up again, refastened the band to refresh the ponytail. When she tossed her head, her hair whipped across her shoulders and sparkled in the sunlight.

"It's a male cardinal," Eva stated. "You can tell by its brilliant red feathers."

"So what?" Judi asked. She picked up some litter from the snack table and threw it into the trash bag.

The bright red cardinal tilted its head back and sang louder. Eva listened and watched. She wondered what the presence of this bird meant. Was the environment here better than elsewhere? Had the berry bushes blossoming nearby been the source of food that kept it alive during the winter?

Eva saw Judi looking at her and pointing. "That bird is singing for you. If only you were a bird, you could lift your wings and join him in the tree top." Judi laughed. "Then you would be in love, my dear sister.

5

Maybe if I fix your loose braid, your hair would look neater. You could finally catch someone's eye." She stepped toward Eva and reached for the braid that had fallen down again from Eva's hat.

"Leave it alone; I don't need any fussing from you," Eva said, moving away.

Eva looked up again at the bright red bird and frowned. She was not thinking of love. She had to be practical right now; she was still thinking about her career. If she knew what to do with her life, like a bird knows how to sing, then she would know the song of her own soul.

"Good morning ladies," came a greeting from Amanda Walters, the group coordinator.

"Good morning."

"You must be enjoying the sunshine here today in Liberty Park. We are glad you are contributing your time and energy."

Eva watched as Colleen stood up and leaned backward to stretch. "It's hard work, but it's a joy to do, much easier than my nursing job."

"We do appreciate everything you are doing," Amanda said handing Colleen a flyer. "Let me tell you about another activity here in the park. There's going to be a meeting soon. It's a public hearing about expanding the park."

"But this is such a big park already," Colleen said.

"Yes, we have over one-thousand acres here," Amanda responded. "But we live in an urban area that is so built-up and covered-over with concrete. You see that stretch of trees over there. That is not the park. It is industrial wasteland. Recently, a foundation donated it to the park. Come to the meeting. Help us decide how to convert it to parkland."

Eva watched with curiosity as her mother took the flyer.

"Oh, sure, you can count on us," Colleen said.

Eva laughed and signaled to her sister, "Here we go again, Judi. Mom is getting involved with something else."

Judi laughed. "Mom loves getting involved. Do you remember when she was president of the parent-teachers group?"

"I certainly do. Mom can't sit still and let her community go off track."

The daughters laughed, but their laughter soon ended in resignation. They knew their mom would expect their commitment as well.

"Tell me more about your family, Colleen. Two daughters? You are so lucky," Amanda said.

Eva looked up at Colleen who turned and looked back at her.

"Yes, I have two daughters. They may be going to college soon. They need summer jobs. I wish I knew where they could get some work. Eva, here, is the naturalist."

Eva stood proudly, expecting to hear more description and praise about herself, but Colleen turned to Judi. "Judi is my sophisticated lady. She's such a socialite."

Eva looked at Judi, who wore black tights and a sweater with sequins decorating the neckline. Then Eva looked down at her own practical jeans and sweatshirt. You could tell the difference between the two of them, right there. Eva looked at Amanda to see what kind of person she was. Amanda was dressed in baggy wool trousers and a bulky sweater with a jacket hanging open as if it were too small to zip closed.

"And your girls say you were president of the parent-teachers group?"

"Yes, I was."

"Good, we need activists like you. Our group is called the Friends of Nature, so come to the meeting and join."

"Ok, I guess we can do that." Colleen looked around at her daughters. "Yes?"

"Yes, Mom, we're in," Judi responded.

"It's decided. Now, let's get back to work," Eva suggested.

"Work? You've hardly done any yet today," Judi whined.

Eva laughed. She bent down and grasped the stalk of a plant at her feet. "Does this get removed?"

"Yes, everything here gets pulled out," Colleen advised.

Eva looked at the plant in her hands. It was amazing how the grass could grow such a resistant fiber out of soil, sun and air. Eva reached for a trowel and dug into the ground under its roots.

"Eva's more interested in saving nature than domesticating it," Colleen said. "She knows the names of trees, flowers and other plants, but only because they are the habitat of birds. She loves birds and can identify them by sight and sound."

"You know how to identify birds? Amanda asked. "What kind of bird is that over there?"

Eva gazed at the black bird sitting on a light post. "It's a crow."

"Very good," Amanda responded. "A friend of mine is teaching me about birds. He says we have two types of crows here in the park. There's the larger American crow and the smaller fish crow. We really have to hear its caw before we can be absolutely certain which it is."

The two women looked at the bird and waited. Soon it gave a caw, but it did not sound like everyone's idea of a crow.

"That's a fish crow," Eva declared.

"Very good. You do know your birds by sound. You should apply for a job at the park. They can always use people with knowledge about nature."

Eva felt Amanda looking deep into her eyes, as though Amanda had found something extra valuable in Eva. Eva turned and looked over at her mother.

"Where should she go to apply?" Colleen asked.

"Over there," Amanda said as she pointed to a building in the distance. "They hire young people for the summer to lead wildlife tours and assist tourists."

"Thank you for telling us," Colleen replied, "Eva, what do you think? I'll leave the decision to you."

Eva looked up at her mom. "I think I would like that. Yes, let me go there and try for summer work. It might be good."

"It's NOT for me," said Judi.

Eva saw a look of fear in Judi's eyes. She was ready to resist if their mother insisted that she do the same.

"I want to do something that pays very well, I really want to run my own business someday," Judi announced.

Eva frowned at Judi "Typical of my big sister."

"Well," Judi continued, "I could get into flower arranging as a hobby. But only as a hobby."

"Thank you, Amanda, for giving us this idea," Colleen said. "Eva might really enjoy working in the park." She turned to Eva. "This is very exciting, isn't it?"

Eva smiled with a sense of relief. Maybe there was a job she could do and enjoy.

After the volunteer gardeners finished removing the weeds, they raked the soil smooth. They dug holes for the sets and placed seeds in the rows. The sun climbed higher in the sky and, as it climbed, it burned hotter, making park beautification a daunting task.

"How is it that volunteering could be so grueling?" Eva asked her mother, looking up at her with sun-reddened skin. Could her mother not see how she was suffering?

"Let's have a snack and get some water to drink," Colleen said as she laid aside her tools. They went to Judi for refreshments.

After a short rest, they joined the other gardeners in the task of filling buckets with water. They poured the water on the pansies and daisies they had planted in the flowerbeds of the park.

"It will be wonderful to see how these grow and bloom," Eva said.

The summer held more promise than she had expected. After the gardening, she went to the park administration office, filled out an application and immediately got an interview.

"Do you come to this park often? Do you know your way around it?" The park superintendent asked as he looked at her dirt-covered jeans. "Looks like you joined our volunteer gardening crew this morning."

"Oh yes, I did and I know the park well," Eva replied.

"Besides gardening, what else have you done here?"

Eva told the superintendent about the many family picnics she had enjoyed in the park. She explained how she had earned her Girl Scout badges identifying birds, trees and wildflowers in the park. She stopped short of telling him about the many discoveries she had made. Her sister Judi had just laughed at these. Now, Eva wondered how the superintendent would react if she told him. As he browsed her application, she decided to take a chance.

"I've found three types of native American wildflowers in this park. I don't think anyone else knows about them."

She looked at the superintendent and waited.

He nodded, "Yes, I know about those."

"And I saw a rare bird nesting in the park. It was a yellow-crowned night heron."

She saw a look of amazement appear on the superintendent's face.

"You saw the nest? Are you sure? The County Bird Watchers Association was reporting the bird as a sighting, but no one has reported any nesting of that bird here in the park."

"I can tell you where the nest is. It's in that part that's all grown over and has no paths."

"You were in that part? The public is not supposed to be there. That land was just recently acquired. The yellow-crowned night heron is nesting there? This is good news. I'll look into this. Listen, you're hired. You can start to work next Saturday," he said.

When Eva heard these words, she felt as if she could fly.

Chapter Two

The New Land

Sunrise was the best time to go bird watching. To be in the wild at sunrise meant you had to get up before sunrise. Amanda wished that were not true. She was scheduled to meet Dan Murphy today. Her alarm clock had gotten her out of bed, but it hadn't convinced her body that it was time to get moving.

When they set the date for their bird walk, Murphy had teased Amanda, "You mean you would give up the chance to see a bald eagle, just to lie in bed?"

Amanda grumbled, "Well, I guess I can always sleep in some other time." In her heart, she knew that sleep would still beckon as a more desirable alternative.

"Fine, we'll meet in the park on Thursday morning. Bring your binoculars and your camera, if you have one."

She had binoculars, but her camera was not that great, just a small family camera for portraits. When the morning came, she tossed it into the bag with her binoculars and a small lunch—a sandwich, a bottle of juice and some homemade cookies. She climbed into her small economy-car and drove to the park.

The sun was just coming up over the horizon above the sprawling city of Brooklyn, across the Hudson River in New York City. As she drove down the New Jersey turnpike, the sun glinted off the torch of the Statue of Liberty that stood in the harbor.

Amanda's thoughts drifted back to yesterday's gardening. The Kaufman family was a delight. Colleen and Judi were good recruits to the gardening program, but Eva was amazing. She was about the age of Amanda's own daughter Stephanie. Just like Stephanie, Eva had an interest in nature. When Amanda looked into Eva's eyes, it was as though she were seeing her daughter again.

Amanda's car glided along the winding turnpike exit ramp where the road led her to a parking lot. There she saw Murphy standing next to his bike at the bike rack. Amanda watched as Murphy bent over one of his open bike panniers. He stuffed his bike helmet in and pulled out his camera and those huge lenses he always carried. She turned off her car's engine, grabbed her bag and locked up.

"Hey, Murphy, I'm here. You didn't think I'd get here, did you?"

He looked up at her. "Well, what else do you have to do with your life right now? You don't have a job; nobody wants to hire you at the age of fifty-six, so you can hang out with retired folks like me. Come on, we've got to get over to the water and look for the harbor seals."

"But Murphy, seals aren't birds."

"I know that. Don't you think I know that? But harbor seals are a splendor you don't want to miss."

Together with their arms full of equipment, they walked across the parking lot and stationed themselves on a park bench.

They gazed for some time out across the water at the distant rocks, searching for the rock-like forms of the harbor seals.

"Now see that. Is it moving? By golly, I think it's moving," Murphy declared.

Amanda searched frantically along the rocks with her binoculars, but saw no movement.

"Over there, see, look under . . . . Oh, I know, look under that tower over there on the shore line and then look down to that rock just beneath."

"Oh, yes, I see it now. That's a harbor seal?

"Yes, right here in New York harbor. No one really knows how much nature there is in this place. They think only humans live here. What would keep the animals away? They were here before humans. That's what makes me crazy. People have this attitude. They think nature is out there somewhere, someplace else on another continent."

"Well, Murphy, we need to teach people about the wildlife in their own community."

"Yes, well it reminds me of a story about the people who live downtown near here. They believe ghosts haunt the old railroad terminal. They tell a story about a lady in white who cries out in the night, but it's really just a barn owl screaming. They never thought it could be an owl."

"Speaking of the park," Amanda said, "Did you get the park newsletter? Did you see the article about the acquisition of more land for the park?"

"Oh, yes, I saw that. It worries me."

"How can that worry you, Murphy? It's a great opportunity to have a bigger park in our community."

He frowned at her. "Come on, let's go look for warblers on the trail behind the nature center."

They picked up their gear and hiked across the parking lot to the trail that led to the nature center. The sun had climbed higher and its warmth was radiating through the treetops. Spring migration was in full force and the warblers, some of the tiniest birds in the world, were flitting crazily among the tree branches.

"Look over here," Murphy said, pointing. "Yellow-rumped warblers. Look again, I see a cardinal."

"All I see are robins; they are everywhere," Amanda said as she turned to the left and right. "Where do you see warblers?"

"Up in the trees, oh my, look at that. It's a black-throated blue warbler."

"Where, oh I see it, oh wow, I didn't know they flew through this area."

"Of course they do, that's my point. People just don't know what kind of wildlife exists here."

"So Murphy, what did you think of the article about the acquisition of the new land? There's going to be a public meeting to decide what to do with that land."

Amanda peeked through her binoculars and waited for Murphy's response. He was silent for a long time before he finally responded.

"I know. I saw that. That's what worries me."

"How can you be worried? It's a positive development for the park. We can now have more wildlife areas, more ball fields, gardens and more picnic areas."

"That's the problem," he growled. "I don't want more ball fields or picnic areas. When they create wildlife areas, all they do is put bridges and boardwalks into the sanctuary of nature. Soon all those idiot humans will come tramping through with their noisy kids, their radios, their garbage and their flash cameras. They will drive the wildlife away." He hung his head in a sense of doom and defeat. His face looked sour.

"But Murphy, it's the only way we have of preserving the land. Otherwise, the company that gave up the land will sell it and turn it into a shopping mall or parking lot. Murphy, I can't believe you. You keep pointing out that people know nothing about nature, yet here is an opportunity for children and adults to learn about nature in their own community and you want to . . . . what? Oppose this? Murphy, you aren't going to go to the public meeting to oppose this are you?"

Amanda was exasperated. Years ago, she and Murphy had been partners in the struggle to save the big Sycamores on Main Street. They had stood up in city council and argued that the town would lose its beauty if all the big trees were removed. The council had pointed out that the trees were twisted and maimed by the city's own habit of chopping away branches that came near electric lines. This had left many trees with big empty gaps in their middles. The council wanted to remove the big old trees and start over with shorter trees, like spring-blooming Red Buds and Dogwoods. These trees blossomed in spring and never grew tall enough to get into the electric power lines. It could save the city money on tree trimming and storm damage removal.

Whether the outcome was good or bad, Amanda and Murphy had succeeded at saving the big old trees that they had walked under as children on their way to school.

Over the years, they had collaborated in many battles, including the biggest battle of their lives: the creation of Liberty Park. Amanda could not believe that Murphy was now going to veer away from their usual way of thinking concerning the park.

"The park, is after all, a park, Murphy. It's for the people. I think this can be resolved painlessly. When I go to the meeting, I'm going to be in favor of wildlife, gardens and picnic areas. It is not impossible to make these things compatible."

"That's what you think," he growled. "Come on, let me show you what that area looks like. Obviously it's going to be destroyed someday."

Amanda followed Murphy across the park to a hole in the fence. Near this hole was a rusty sign hanging by one corner that said "DANGER: NO PUBLIC ACCESS." Apparently, this was Murphy's secret entrance into the forbidden area.

Dan Murphy was a highly regarded member of the County Bird Watchers Association (CBWA). He acted like his membership and his passion for birds gave him a license to go anywhere a bird could be seen.

"Listen Amanda, for years I've been monitoring this area. You see, I usually hide my bicycle in the tall reeds over there." She saw him look back at her to be sure she was paying attention. "But today I'll share this sanctuary with you because I have to convince you how important it is. You'll see what it's like. We cannot let this be destroyed."

Amanda watched as he moved his sturdy arms and legs to push through bayberry and autumn olive. With no paths to make entry easy, nature had guarded this forgotten and secret place. Murphy smiled and looked around. Amanda smiled. She could see that he was delighted to have this private little world.

"I have seen a spectacular array of warblers among a grove of wild cherry trees right here. Black-throated blue warblers, American redstart, ruby and golden-crowned kinglets and even the red-eyed vireo," he explained. "In the blackberry bramble in the center of this land, I've seen hundreds of cardinals, blue jays and goldfinch as they hopped from the berry bushes up to the branches of those massive eastern white pines. It's the perfect habitat."

Amanda looked around and tried to identify the trees. There seemed to be many tall cottonwood and willow oaks. Virginia creeper vines climbed through the tree branches; there were just enough of them to bring more berries to the birds, but not yet choke out the growth of the trees.

"You see that tree over there," Murphy pointed. "I've seen Coopers Hawks and Red-tailed Hawks sitting and watching for rabbits. This land is not abandon; nature loves it."

Amanda struggled through the bramble. She looked down at a big pink loop in her knit sweater. A thorn had caught and pulled out a long trail of pink yarn. She winced.

At last, they came upon a small brook bordered by silver maple trees. Amanda paused in the shade and looked out at the wide blue sky. She felt like a small helpless creature held between heaven and earth.

"Come this way," Murphy called.

She stepped forward, tripped over a root and fell face first into the little blue stem grass. Now seeing the strands of grass close up, she observed the red and gold colors of the stems with just a hint of blue at the very base of the stalks. She loved nature—or so she thought, but she liked it a little better groomed. A trail would be great to have here, she thought.

Amanda got up and brushed seeds from the knees of her pants. She followed Murphy until they returned to the opening in the fence.

"This is a beautiful place. We need to preserve it," she said. She thought of how northern New Jersey was cluttered with thousands of little houses and stores. Whole towns crowded, border to border, against each other so that it was impossible to tell where one town started and another ended. There was a crying need for more open space, more parks for people to relax and enjoy the natural world.

Murphy pushed the branches over to cover his secret passage in the fence.

"See how beautiful this land is. They will destroy all this, Amanda. Remember my words. All humans want to do is put up more buildings and clear more lots to park their cars. That's all they care about. By the way, I checked all the big trees in there. There were no bald eagles here today. So, I apologize for that."

Amanda shrugged.

"Yet, you have to admit," Murphy continued, "it's so beautiful here, I don't know what I'll do if it's destroyed."

Amanda looked at his face. He had a scruffy gray beard that looked like the bramble she had just passed through. He was a grumpy old man, but right now, his eyes indicated he could cry like a baby.

Chapter Three

A New Park Employee

Eva rushed out of the park office and ran to the car where her mother and Judi were waiting.

"Mom, I got the job," Eva screamed as she climbed into the car. Eva lifted her hands and proudly displayed two tan shirts. The shoulders had patches with a tree symbolizing the Park Service.

Colleen looked at the shirts as Eva displayed them. "Oh, honey, I'm proud of you. Eighteen years old and you have your first real job."

Judi looked at Eva and wailed, "My sister has a job. I can't believe my little sister is going to make money and I'm not. I must go out and get a real job. I can't live with this shame."

Eva saw the look of anguish on Judi's face and laughed. "You've been out of high school nearly two years, Sis, you're twenty. You should be working in a real job by now."

"I've had lots of real jobs. I just quit them because I wanted a variety of experiences in retail," Judi protested. "Now I'm looking for something more challenging."

Eva was thrilled. She felt she had outdone her sister. This was going to be a great summer. Working in the park, she would be surrounded by birds, trees and wildflowers. She was going to have a great summer.

On the first morning of her new job, Eva posed in her Park Service uniform. "How do I look?"

"Let me get the camera," Colleen said, pulling open a drawer. "Now Eva, stand over here, step to the right. Ok, hold it there."

Eva posed one way and the next as Colleen took several shots. "I can't believe you're growing up so fast."

Eva smiled. "Wish me luck on my first day."

"I wish you all the luck in the world," Colleen said.

"You may need it," Judi added. "Watch out for the stinging bees and wasps."

Eva dashed out the door and looked up to see her mother and sister waving to her from the window. She skipped down the sidewalk to the train that would take her to her first day on the job at Liberty Park.

It was a beautiful spring day. Sunlight sparkled through the train windows; the wheels of the train clacked as it moved along the track. Out the window, Eva could see fresh green grass and even more trees covered with shiny new green leaves. All these things came together in a collage that would be stored forever in Eva's memory. At the Liberty Park station, she disembarked from the train and walked the narrow gravel road that led to the park's main office.

It was a very modern looking office with several computers and phones. Park visitors were standing at a counter browsing flyers about current park events. When Eva stepped through the door, she saw a group of young people like herself. The office staff led them to the conference room. After they were all seated, a man in another type of park uniform stood before them. "I'm Curtis Elliot, supervisor of summer seasonal employees."

Eva watched him scrutinize each one of them. "As seasonal workers, you are hired to assist in maintaining the park. You are also to advise park visitors on the use and enjoyment of the park."

Eva listened, eager to understand what Curtis expected of the summer seasonal workers.

As Curtis walked back and forth, Eva estimated his age to be about twenty-six years old. He had a wide, well balanced face and happy brown eyes. His hair was short and curly. He was a tall man with broad shoulders. He waved his tanned, muscular arms in the air as he spoke. His hands looked powerful, yet gentle enough to hold the rarest of native wildflowers. He had a sense of humor, too, that made everyone laugh. Eva thought he was great. She wanted him for a friend.

"As you know, this park is here to give urban dwellers contact with nature. Do they always appreciate it? No. Why not? Because they don't always understand it. That is your role; think of your experience in this park and share it with our park patrons."

A fellow seasonal raised his hand and Curtis pointed to him.

As they talked, Eva stood, thinking of her experience as a Girl Scout. She wondered what kinds of experience the others had. She turned to one of the other young women standing next to her and whispered, "Have you ever been a Girl Scout?"

"No," said the young woman. She pulled her baseball cap down over her eyes, and moved away from Eva. Eva shrugged and turned back to Curtis.

"Now, I'm going to take you on a tour of the park," said Curtis. "Climb into the van outside and let's go."

As they climbed in to the vehicle, a guy with a name tag that read "George" handed them each a map of the park. Eva sat down in the van and unfolded her map to begin following the tour. She did already know a great deal about the park, but she was curious what in particular the Park Service would emphasize as important in their day-to-day work. When Eva glanced up from her map, she saw her fellow seasonal, the one in the baseball cap, seated next to her with her chin in her hands. Boredom poured out of her eyes.

The van circled around the park to the various locations. First, they were shown the picnic sites and the flower gardens, then the boat launch and favorite fishing spots, next they went to the playgrounds and, at last, the lawns where the summer concerts were held.

After the tour, they were given a list of frequently asked questions and the answers they were supposed to use. Next, they were divided into teams and given a radio to report any trouble they saw. Eva expected to be matched with one of the other seasonal workers, but was surprised and delighted when Curtis singled her out.

"Eva, you and I are going on foot patrol around the picnic areas. Come with me."

Soon Eva and Curtis were strolling down Liberty Walk toward the main picnic area.

With the noonday sun overhead, park patrons were busy under the shade trees cooking their barbeque. The smell of meat on the grill filled the air, but so did the smoke from the charcoal. It was so thick that Eva wondered what it was doing to the air quality of the park. How many forests had been cut down to make the charcoal? The excitement of a summer had done little to remove the lessons Eva had learned in her high school environmental classes.

"Now here's what you do as a customer service rep, Eva. When you see something like this or someone complains to you about a problem, you radio a report." Curtis pointed to the overfilled garbage can at the end of a picnic table. "We need a clean-up over here at table eight." He pressed the buttons on the radio that soon crackled a response, "We'll be there in ten minutes."

Curtis moved on and Eva followed. They soon came upon two more garbage cans that were spewing dirty paper plates and sticky cups onto the lawn. Several food wrappers blew past them in the breeze. They called on the radio to report yet another need for cleaning. Eva marveled at the amount of garbage that had accumulated. Then she looked around at the people sitting at the tables and realized that they were generating even more garbage. Oh yes, over the years, her own family had held picnics in this park, but she had never realized that the little bit of garbage they had created was a small part of a growing trash heap. For the first time, she realized how huge the garbage problem was. There were hundreds of picnics going on from noon to dusk all summer long in this park and thousands of other parks around the country. A simple picnic by a few people and the planet was wrecked by little things like plastic bottles, forks, spoons and plates. Eva felt over-whelmed.

"Now, Eva, take this radio and walk the trails. Assist park patrons with directions. Try to help them or call for help." He placed the radio, a contraption she was not very familiar with, into her hands. He waved good-bye to her and walked away.

Eva knew she had to do her best, even though she felt unsure of herself, so she waved back and smiled before turning and heading down one of the trails that led away from the picnic area.

It was a relief to be on her own. She looked up and saw the green leaves of the trees waving in jubilation. The swallows swung low through the air, coming close to her to have a good look at the new park employee. Eva laughed to herself. She had an important job to do and she wanted to do it.

The park was vast. From Liberty Walk you could see much of New York Harbor. The Statue of Liberty stood, holding her torch up high, welcoming the tourists that gazed at her from the top of the ferries.

Eva decided to follow the main trail that would take her ultimately to the Grove of Remembrance, a memorial flower garden for those who had died in the attack on the World Trade Center. As she walked, she saw a little girl sitting alone on a bench. In her hands, she was holding a plastic cup. Eva wondered why the child was alone.

"Hello," Eva said as she approached the child. "Are you having a good day in the park?" She expected a cheerful response from such a lovely little girl, but the child was in an uproar.

She flung her cup across the sidewalk and yelled, "No!"

"Hey, there's no need to litter. You don't want the park to look all messy, do you?"

"I don't care,"

"You don't care about nature and the beauty of the park?"

The little girl looked at Eva with eyes full of belligerence.

"It's all full of bugs."

"The park? Full of bugs? But bugs are our friends. They help . . . ."

"I don't care. It's all full of bugs. My juice cup is all full of bugs."

Eva ran to retrieve the cup and saw that it did, in fact, have a beetle inside. She knocked the bug out.

"It was only a lady bug," Eva said.

"Well, that's a bug."

"Well, I know, but you don't have to worry about all bugs. Some are nice."

"Phooey, I don't like bugs."

Eva stood next to the child holding the cup. The little girl quickly reached out and knocked it from Eva's hands. It flew into the grass again. Eva retrieved it and tossed it into the garbage can. She looked at the child in wonder.

"Where's your mommy?" Eva asked.

Suddenly a woman appeared, "Come on Trisha, let's go."

Eva looked up and saw the mother take the girl by her hand. Eva offered a polite smile that the mother returned in kind as she led the child away.

Eva watched them disappear behind the Hawthorn trees. She sighed; how was she supposed to help park visitors appreciate the park if all they saw were bugs they didn't like?

Eva turned and wandered down another trail. Here she found a balloon caught in a small tree. It was almost too high up to reach, but Eva felt it was important to remove it to help save the environment. She was determined to find a way to get it down. She jumped and reached, first with one arm and then with both. What a park this was: litter on the ground, smoke in the air, balloons in the trees—what made her think that working in the park was a job that had anything to do with the joy of nature? Was it her job to protect the park from the patrons?

Finally, after a high leap she retrieved the balloon from the tree. She burst it and stuffed it into her pocket.

"I won't let the negative side get to me," Eva promised herself. She then strolled along the trail, trying again to enjoy the day.

Up ahead she saw a man jogging. She watched as his arms moved back and forth against his sides. His muscular legs pumped his nearly naked hairy body closer and closer to her. As the distance between them shrank, she wondered if she should greet him, or how she should greet him. She wanted to hide. Then suddenly he went down.

The jogger had tripped and fallen. He needed her help.

She rushed to him.

"Are you hurt? I have a radio here if you need help."

The man grimaced and clutched his knee. Eva saw the bloody scuff on his knee.

He looked down at his knee. "Oh no, I'll never make the race. I've got only four more weeks to train."

"I can get you help." Eva suddenly felt very important. Now she was rescuing a marathon runner.

The man sat down on the grass and breathed heavily. "Well, it's not so bad," he said. "These things always hurt more than they should."

"You need first aid," Eva said. "I'll call the police. They have first aid kits to help you."

She looked at the buttons on her radio. How was she to do this? Press the red one and talk, isn't that what they said to do? Eva spoke into the microphone. "I need some first aid assistance here on the south end of Freedom Way."

The radio crackled. "What kind of assistance?"

"First aid, I'm with an injured jogger."

"An officer will be there shortly."

Several minutes passed.

"I should have my own first aid kit," the jogger said. "But I was so sure this would not happen today."

At the bend of the road, Eva saw a police car approaching. She stepped out and waved.

"What's the problem?"

"A man has fallen and cut his knee. He needs first aid."

The officer pulled the car over and came with a small medical kit. Soon he was dressing the injury.

"Thanks for your help."

"That's what we're here for," Eva explained.

The police officer assisted the jogger to his feet.

"I think I can make it home. I'm not hurt too badly, but thanks, again," he said looking at Eva. She waved good-bye as he limped down the trail.

Eva was amazed at the kind of day she was having. She had just rescued someone. How amazing. She strolled along the trail now making good time. Returning to the Grove of Remembrance, she saw another group of volunteer gardeners planting marigolds and petunias. Eva smiled thinking of her own experience with gardening at the park. "Enjoy," she said to them as she headed down the trail. Soon she was at the historic railroad terminal. She stopped to lean against the gates at the end of the pier. Out on the harbor, the waves were gleaming in the bright sun. Sailboats and ferries were plying the waters. Across the Hudson River, skyscrapers rose up from the island of Manhattan like crystal stalagmites.

The brilliant sun filled Eva with confidence. She was lucky to have this job. Would it be possible to spend her life working in a park? She could share her love of nature with the people of the world. Fantastic!

From the pier, Eva walked back to where the tour buses were dropping off more park visitors. Eva watched a woman get off a bus and look around. At first, the woman seemed lost, but then she walked up to a tree and began examining its bark. Eva laughed. She was curious why, with all the wonders of the park, this woman was looking at a typical park tree.

"Good afternoon," Eva said to the woman.

"Oh, and a good afternoon to you, too."

"Do you need any help? Do you have any questions?"

"Well, yes, I was just wondering, I'm from Kansas and I have seen so many of these trees from the bus window. They are up and down almost every street. What kind of trees are they?"

"Oh, those are sycamores," Eva said and went on to explain, "You will see a lot of sycamores in cities because they are very tolerant of air pollution. They are a very hearty tree."

"Sycamores? Like the tree Zacchaeus climbed to see Jesus?"

Eva paused and wondered. Would sycamore trees in the old biblical world be the same species as these sycamores? She did not know. She tried to imagine someone climbing up a sycamore with the bark falling off at the touch, she wondered how anyone could believe this tree was easy to climb.

"Oh, it's an indirect descendent," Eva said, hoping this answer was not too far from the truth.

The woman gazed up at the tree with a biblical proportion of belief.

Eva laughed and strolled away. What a strange job this was. Eight hours a day being helpful to people and protective of the park. You couldn't find a better job.

With a look at her watch, Eva realized it was getting close to lunchtime. She headed back to the park office where she joined the others to eat and share stories about their first day on the job.

Now having some experience with what the typical day would be like, the other new employees were starting to act friendlier. Eve saw the one in the baseball cap she had tried to talk to earlier.

"I'm Eva. How was your first day?"

"My name is Sally Denton. My first day was great."

"Oh, that's good. I had a great day too. I rescued a jogger and identified a tree for a tourist. Curtis and I reported a lot of garbage overflow. I can't believe how much garbage there is."

Sally laughed, "Sounds like you had a really busy day."

She pulled a small packet of peanuts out of her lunch bag and ate them with some raw carrots, an apple and a can of cola.

Eva opened her lunch box to the chicken and lettuce sandwich her mother had packed for her.

"I'm a vegan," Sally announced.

"What's that?"

"I don't eat anything that comes from an animal. I work to protect and care for all animals."

"Oh, I see," said Eva. "Well, I do eat some meat and cheese. You know, there are domestic animals that humans have bred specifically to be eaten—like chickens, pigs, cows."

"You have no respect for life if you eat animals," Sally said. Her self-righteous indignation shocked Eva. They continued eating in silence.

After a while, Sally asked, "Where is Curtis?"

Eva looked across the lunchroom. "He's gone."

Sally smiled, "You know what I did today? I snuck off to the restroom and hid there. I read my romance novel. Ha, nobody caught me. This is going to be an easy job. You don't really have to do anything in this job if you play it right." Sally slurped down the last of her cola drink.

Eva gasped. "You didn't do anything? I could never do that. I used to be a Girl Scout and we had this pledge. It went like this: *On my honor, I will try to serve God and my Country, to help people at all times and to live by the Girl Scout Law.* I guess that's why I felt good about helping that jogger or helping that lady who wanted to know about the tree."

"Oh, you really are such a goody-goody Girl Scout," Sally said and stuck her tongue out at Eva.

Seeing bits of carrot on Sally's tongue, Eva sneered. "You may be such a good vegan and don't hurt animals, but you could use some table manners." Eva caught a piece of lettuce that was slipping out of her chicken sandwich. "You also need to learn to do an honest day's work."

"Ha, I want to take life easy. I don't want to work hard. If you don't work hard, you don't need a lot of food energy."

"Meaning, I guess, that you don't have any energy because you eat carrot sticks all day?"

"Meaning this job doesn't pay me enough for what they expect me to do."

Eva grimaced at Sally, but said nothing. Already they had used up fifteen minutes of a thirty-minute lunch break. When lunch was over, Eva cleaned up the table, including the mess Sally made, and threw the garbage into the can. "More garbage," she thought as she looked down at what had accumulated from six employees during just one short lunch break. The garbage can lid dropped shut. Eva looked over at Sally.

"Come on, Sally, let's get back to work, if you are capable of doing that."

"Not me, I'm too smart for that."

After lunch, the new summer employees lined up for their next assignments. Curtis sent Sally to do litter pick-up. He sent Eva to enter data into the computer at the park office.

By the time the day ended, Eva felt tired. She had made a daylong commitment to doing the best she could. As she walked the gravel road back to the train station, she discovered a baby bird and gently placed it in a small bush, giving it some protection until the parent birds came to guard it. When a park visitor asked how to get to the Statue of Liberty, she politely gave directions—in spite of the fact that she had clocked out of her first day on the job.

Chapter Four

The Threatening Storm

Amanda always looked forward to the meetings held by the Friends of Nature. Sometimes they were orderly discussions about issues and points of view. Sometimes they were dull meetings with lots of legal and technical terminology about different aspects of the park. Still, it was a great opportunity to meet with friends and get in touch with what was going on in their lives.

The meetings were held at the Hungry Fish Restaurant, Bait and Tackle Shop, a two-story building that had much to do with food and fishing. It was a seafood restaurant with added features. When you entered, you were greeted by an original old-fashioned sea diver's suit that looked like a knight's shining armor. The main room was filled with chairs and tables covered with red and white plaid tablecloths. Above the door, leading to the next room, was a bright blue and white fish mounted on a plaque and labeled *Atlantic Bonito*.

In that room Charlie Vern, the owner, set up a store and sold bait, hooks and fishing rods to local fishermen. The shelves of the store had a small supply of such basic necessities as gloves, hats, pocket knives, charcoal and accessories for cameras. The large refrigerator in the corner of the store contained both boxes of bait for fishing and packages of frozen meat and seafood that was cooked and served in the restaurant. Outside the Hungry Fish was a gas tank where Charlie sold expensive gasoline to desperate tourists.

When Amanda entered the Hungry Fish on Saturday morning, she went under the *Atlantic Bonito* into the store where the chairs were arranged in rows at the side of the room in preparation for the meeting. The roaring noise of multiple conversations filled the air. People stood around with cups in their hands. Amanda looked for and found the large aluminum pot that was used for coffee and tea. After she made a cup of tea for herself, she noticed a small table behind the row of chairs that held plates of pastries and fruit. She went there to have a look and told herself to stay away, but as she passed, a chocolate covered donut tumbled into her hand. What could she do? She carried it off to a chair where she sat down next to Gary Russo, president of the Friends of Nature.

"Amanda, I'm glad to see you're here today. You are one or our best fighters for the cause."

"Oh thank you, Gary, I try," Amanda said, holding up the delicious donut.

Amanda knew there was a certain amount of civility to get through at present, but she wanted to be sure to let Gary know that Murphy might be bull-headed in the wrong direction on the issue they were going to discuss today. The park newsletter had indicated that there was a possibility of "mixed use" for the newly acquired land. Even though the meeting was to give everyone a chance to express his or her preferences, Amanda was worried its progress would be disrupted.

"Ok, we're calling this meeting to order," said Steve Crawford, the park superintendent. He nodded and Charlie Vern closed the door. "Now, George Medford of the State Department of Parks will give you a presentation of what the state sees as possible for this additional land that was donated to the park. Please keep in mind, this does not mean we are making final decisions at this time. We do want to hear from the community. If you know folks who want to comment, but could not be here today, let them know they can still comment. Just take a copy of this letter and it explains how to submit comments to the state."

He began passing out the letter as Mr. Medford approached the podium. On the back wall, ordinarily a white cement block wall, a slide show appeared, coloring their view with images of the park as it presently looked and how it could look.

The crowd of about thirty-five people nestled into their wood chairs and clung to their cups as curiosity and hope fixed their gaze on the presentation.

Amanda noticed that Murphy had not yet come to the meeting. She sipped her tea and mused. Maybe he was not going to come. Very strange, she thought. It was not like him to be passive about an issue that held so much concern for him.

From her purse, Amanda pulled out a pen, then she tore free a piece of paper napkin. On it she wrote a note to Gary.

> *Gary,*
> *Murphy opposes ball fields and gardens. He only favors nature preservation—NO boardwalks or paths—too many people.*
> *—Amy*

Gary took the note and then nodded at Amanda. The presentation went on for half an hour and finally they arrived at the time for comments.

"My name is Colleen Kaufman. I'd like to see more nature trails created, but I feel sorry for the girls in this community. My daughters loved to play soccer. Over the years, we had such a problem trying to get a field so their team could play. We need soccer fields for girls."

Amanda saw Colleen's daughters quickly sit up with pride. Judi's ponytail swayed as she looked around the room for support for her mom's comments. Eva gazed around the room shyly while she re-braided a strand of her hair. A few girls in the back of the room started to cheer, but cut it short when the park superintendent looked in their direction. Amanda winked at Colleen, then mouthed a "Thanks for coming." It was good to know the park community was still growing.

For a moment it looked like the meeting would move on to the next speaker, but Ms. Kaufman began to speak again, stuttering. "Bbbut even though I'm for soccer fields, I love nature very much."

Someone in the audience groaned loudly.

She continued, "I want all children to have the opportunities to appreciate nature like I did when I was growing up in the country." Colleen pressed her shoulders back to regain her confidence. "City people don't get to enjoy the sound of bird song in the morning or the smell of fresh air. The park is the only place to experience that—at least a little bit—there's still the air pollution, though. So I'd like the land to be used for . . . . well, like it said in the newsletter, for "mixed use" so that we can have it all. I think we can do that."

Colleen sat down. Now there was much fanfare from the girls at the back of the room. This cheer leading event inspired Eva and Judi, who started waving their hands and smiling. Amanda caught Colleen's attention again and pointed to the young women in the back. The two older women shared a laugh over the exuberance.

The superintendent pointed to another raised hand. The audience turned in the direction of the next individual to make a comment.

"I'm Sheila Cramer and I . . ."

Suddenly the door burst open. In came Dan Murphy. As the door banged shut behind him, he stomped toward the small table at the back of the room, knocking an empty chair out of his way. As Ms. Cramer retreated to her seat, another woman rushed to the small table and removed the pastries. Murphy placed both hands on the now empty table as if to hold himself up.

"I'd like to say something to this community," he yelled.

"Sorry, Murphy, a lady here had her hand up," said the superintendent.

"I'm going to say something anyway," Murphy interrupted. "I don't want any of you to lay a finger on that land. It is wildlife habitat and it should **not** be destroyed. There are so many birds and wild animals on that land and if you put so much as one trail there, you will drive the wildlife away. And if you put a ball field there—that is the most sterile of land use and it will destroy everything."

He pounded the table with a fist.

"That's all I have to say."

Amanda turned to see Murphy glaring at everyone in the room. He scowled at them with hate flaring out of his eyes. He bent over the table, holding the edges with his hands, bracing himself as if he were preparing to withstand their assault.

"Ok, thank you for your opinion, Murphy," said the superintendent. He looked across the room at Ms. Cramer, but she nodded that she no longer wanted to speak.

A tall man with dark hair stood up next. He was dressed in old blue jeans, wearing heavy work boots and wearing a black jacket with large bold silver letters on the back, Steel Workers Union.

"My name's Ed Wilson, Steelworkers Union Local 583. I worked for B & L Foundries for twenty years and like so many other workingmen in this community, I was pushed out of my job. So I think this here company owes this here community something." He paused and looked around the room.

Amanda smiled at him. He looked like a cowboy in one of those old movies who was about to lift his guns and give them a shoot-out.

"I can tell you—it's a fact—that land out there has toxic waste buried under it. The whole damn place, excuse my language, needs to be dug up and hauled away."

The audience gasped. Dan Murphy was quick-frozen. Ed Wilson continued.

"If you don't clean up that land, you will be responsible for contaminating all the people who go there. It's toxic. I know. I used to work at B & L Foundries. I know what was dumped out there. B & L doesn't want you to know what was dumped out there. Why do you think it's been fenced in for all these years? It's toxic. Poisonous. I'm telling you. The whole place needs to be dug up and hauled away."

The crowd broke into a roar.

"Calm down, calm down everyone," said the superintendent.

Dan Murphy stood and looked at Ed Wilson.

"You mean to tell me you think that whole area should be dug up? Hauled away?"

"It's poisonous, man, don't you get that? There's cadmium, chromium, lead, mercury. I know, I was on the safety committee of the union. Workers were being poisoned every day from that stuff. Your precious wildlife is being poisoned by it too. If you want to save nature, that place needs to be completely dug up and hauled away. Did I make myself clear?"

The audience roared. Colleen gasped. Her daughter's eyes filled with fear.

"Ok, ok, can we bring this meeting together again? People, you can express your views, but we need to give everyone a chance to speak. Please raise your hands," said the superintendent.

The audience quieted and looked around expectantly.

Amanda looked at Murphy. His bewildered expression made it seem as if he were having a heart attack. She knew that losing the wildlife area could kill him. Still, if the land was really that contaminated, what else could they do?

"Yes, my name is Cathy Armano and I teach here at the elementary school. I do wish the school children here could get on a bus and be in a nature area with just a short ride. As it is, they have to travel long distances so they only get to go once in the school year, if they even get to do that. You know, the experiences children have with nature can lead them to a better understanding of science. We all know how important science is to our nation. So I hope that this land is made a local nature preserve for the children's sake."

Cathy looked around the room. Seeing Colleen, she addressed her.

"Ms. Kaufman, I also understand a need for soccer fields. Perhaps we need to put pressure on the schools to give girls equal time on the sports fields that the school system already has."

Amanda saw all the issues clearly. She felt sympathetic toward the girls. They needed a soccer field so they could practice and get exercise. Amanda also believed that all the children of the community should have the experience of nature and a chance to understand science in action. Then too, an old guy like Murphy should have a wildlife area to enjoy the birds. Amanda felt pivotal, as if the whole conflict circled around her and she had to lead them to a reasonable agreement. Could they plan the use of this new land in a way that would make everyone happy? She raised her hand. It was her turn to speak.

"The park is receiving a very large amount of land. I'm sure we can accommodate everyone's expectations. Of course, some of it will need special care to make it safe. We don't want children or wildlife to become ill. But we must remember, we have to work together on this project. Promise me you can do that?"

She looked around the room again. Some people nodded, some looked at her with raised eyebrows. The children jumped from their chairs and cheered. Only Murphy shook his head in disgust.

The superintendent stood to address the meeting. "We aren't here to debate this tonight, we are here to listen, but it looks like we've run out of time. Thank you for your comments. For those of you who did not have a chance to speak, here are some forms you can fill out and return to the state." He pointed to the forms on the table.

Amanda sat down in her chair. The meeting had ended so abruptly. Murphy had done just what she was afraid he would do.

She watched as the superintendent said a few words to the other state officials. Soon they were all bidding everyone farewell and heading out the door to their cars.

"What do we do now?" Amanda asked.

Gary Russo immediately acted in his capacity as president of the Friends of Nature. He waved his arms in the air and pleaded, "Everyone please stay here and join us for a lunch and discussion. We need to talk further."

He directed those who were willing to stay to take a seat at the large round table in the corner. Amanda decided to support his effort by coaxing Murphy to take a seat. Soon Colleen, her daughters and a few other new recruits went to the big oak table and sat down. The waiters came from the restaurant side and took their orders. After this, they looked to Gary for guidance.

"Now we've had our public meeting with the Parks Department. They have had a chance to hear what the public has to say."

Amanda looked up at Gary. He was a levelheaded, smart young man. He had a degree in environmental science and taught in the local college. Amanda was glad he was so sensible. In the politics of this group, she had always counted on him to help counter some of Murphy's belligerence.

"As the Friends of Nature, we have to demand that the state run tests. We can't ignore what that steel worker said." He nodded to Ed Wilson who had joined them at the table. "There are probably lots of toxins in the soil."

Murphy glowered, "If the Friends are in favor of digging up any of that land, I'm quitting this group."

"Murphy, stay calm," Amanda pleaded. "It may be necessary to remove some contaminated soil. Think too of the wildlife, you don't want them poisoned."

Gary continued, "Once we get the government's reports on the toxicity of the soil, we can know which part of the land has to be dealt with. It may be that only certain small areas need to be remediated."

"Remediated? What kind of word is that?" Murphy barked. "You mean dug up and hauled away? Nature has taken that land back and made it pure again and now you want to come along in all your scientific glory and dig it up and destroy it."

"Murphy," Amanda begged.

"Listen Murphy," Gary said, leaning toward him. "We have to come to a consensus. We need a plan of action we can all support. This is not a debate over whether to dig it up or not. We must apply science to this problem. We can make the park a better place for wildlife and humans. Humans don't always destroy; we have the power to make amends. I'll prove it to you. I have a magazine article that shows what they've done in other areas. Let me go get it. It's in my bag over there." He stepped away from the table and retrieved his bag.

"That's not the same. It's not what nature wants," Murphy protested.

"It sounds good to me," Amanda offered, trying desperately to tip the scale in Gary's direction.

Some of the other Friends of Nature nodded in agreement with Amanda.

"Colleen, I liked your comments in support of "mixed use," Amanda said. "We need to be reasonable about this." She then gave Murphy a meaningful poke in the ribs.

Colleen sat up and looked toward her daughters, "Oh, I hope I said good things; I think we can work something out. I grew up in the country, spent my summers out in the sun and climbing trees. I can't believe how city kids, my kids—they grew up in the city. I was glad to give them the social experience of city living, but the city's got horrible air pollution from all the traffic. We had to drive for hours to get to the country and fresh air. This park was our only hope."

"Air pollution, yes," Murphy laughed. "You would get more toxins in your lungs from breathing the air on Main Street than from the toxins in the soil on the new land."

Gary laughed, "You have a point, Murphy."

"Thank you, sir." Murphy looked around the room, "I have an idea too. Let me give the Friends a tour of the new land. See it for yourselves. Nature has solved a lot of the problems that Mr. Wilson here caused when he was busy dumping barrels of sludge on the ground as a worker."

Ed Wilson glared at Murphy. "I didn't know what I was doing at first," he said. He turned to look at the others. "I was just doing my job, trying to earn an honest living and support my family."

"Sure you were. Do you want me to get rid of this poison, boss? I know where I can dump it," Murphy jeered.

Amanda watched as the two men clashed, but she was impressed with the way Ed Wilson held his head up and gave the community a feasible explanation. She smiled at Ed as he continued.

"When I joined the union safety committee, I learned what poisons we were working in EVERY DAY. And don't be so high and mighty, Mr. Murphy, each one of us in this society is responsible for the pollution that we breathe, eat and drink. Don't we all drive cars? Don't we all want to turn up the heat in winter and burn the lights all night? For this, our world is exploited and ruined. We share the cause of this problem. Now that I understand that, I want to bring a change to it."

Amanda saw a look of approval on the faces around her. "We're glad to have you as a member of our group," she told Ed. But then, Amanda saw a look of disapproval on Murphy's face. Meetings were so tricky.

Amanda thought for a moment. Maybe by supporting Murphy's idea of a walk through the new land she could bring him in as an ally. She looked at each of the Friends' faces wondering if they would be too fearful to visit the new land. She raised her hand to speak.

"Murphy has made a proposal. He wants to lead our group on a walk through the new land. He took me there last week. It is beautiful. Who would like to go and see what the land looks like?" Amanda asked.

"You have to see it. Then you can appreciate what nature has done there. It's a miracle," Murphy explained.

"Yeah, I'd like to see that miracle myself," Ed scoffed.

Amanda looked around the room. There sat Eva. Her eyes were wide with either fear or wonder.

"Eva," Amanda called, "what are your thoughts?"

Eva swallowed nervously, "Well, I just realized that I have been on that land."

"What?" Colleen asked, "How did you get there?"

"I didn't even know that it was contaminated. It looked so beautiful. That's where I saw the Yellow-crowned Night Heron nesting. It's a rare and endangered species." Eva looked around the room, "I was learning about birds so I could get my Girl Scout badge. And I thought, what an incredible bird, it would make me look like a professional birder."

"Eva is good at identifying birds," Amanda explained. "So I think, Murphy, you have some competition."

"It is a rare bird, very rare," Murphy responded. "Endangered too. So, you've seen the nest?" He gasped in disbelief, "Not just the bird, but the nest? Where? You have to tell me. How did you find it? I've been all over that place."

"Last spring, I went through a hole I found in the fence. I was following a prothonotary warbler. I went deep in. There was a marsh with a big tree. I saw a pile of sticks on the end of a tree limb. There was this large weird bird in it. I studied it. It had a big white cheek patch. I looked in my bird guidebook. I'm pretty sure it was a yellow-crowned night heron."

"Eva, you are a girl of adventure," Amanda gasped, "You give me hope."

Eva smiled.

"She took a risk," Murphy said, "but she made a major discovery, it was well worth it. That's what life's about."

Amanda looked to Colleen. "Your daughter is a dedicated naturalist."

"You see this proves it," Murphy announced, "the land is not so toxic. Nature has reclaimed her own." Murphy sat up in his chair and looked at each person attending the meeting, "Who is interested in coming with me for a walk in the new land?"

"Count me in," Ed Wilson said. "I haven't been on that land in years. I would really like to know that the toxin has not done as much damage as I've feared."

Amanda watched as Colleen and her daughters put their heads together.

"Ok, Amanda, we'd like to see it. Especially since Eva's already been there. We'll wear boots to protect us. We want to see this land."

Eva laughed, "I told the superintendent of the park about it. I think he gave me the job because I knew about the nest."

"Oh, you did get the job?" Amanda smiled at Eva. "And you'll be working in the park all summer? I'm so happy for you, Eva,"

"I'll have to test your bird identification skills," Murphy said. "If you're really good, I can introduce you to the County Bird Watchers Association. I'm a member of that group."

The Friends agreed to meet with Murphy. They set a date for the tour.

Gary held up his magazine and handed it across the table. "Here, Murphy, read this. It will give you hope." Without even looking at it, Murphy took the paper and laid it aside.

"Now, let's get started planning what we are going to do with this park land." As Gary spoke, he propped his notes against the sugar jar and looked around the room. Before he could say another word, the busy staff of the Hungry Fish delivered the food to their table.

Amanda made a motion to move discussion of their plans to the next meeting. "That will give us a chance to see the new land before we make decisions." She watched as Gary shrugged. He laid down his pen and picked up his fork.

Chapter Five

Eva's Cry for Justice

"Mom, I just don't understand why people let those factories dump all those toxic chemicals into the ground," said Eva as they left the meeting and got into their car.

Eva sat in the front across from Colleen. Judi sat in the back. Eva watched as Colleen turned the key and listened to the car's engine. It had been having problems lately. Finally, the engine ignited. Colleen shifted the car into gear.

"Now we can go to the grocery store," Colleen said, "I don't know how we'll get groceries if this car breaks down."

In the front side mirror, Eva saw fumes coming out of the tail pipe. How horrible it was that the car was now burning oil and giving off so much smoke.

Judi sat up and leaned over the front seat. "Mom, really, we need to tell Dad about this car and get a new one."

"We're fine with this car," Colleen stated. "Your dad is busy at his job right now. I can handle this."

"Then, let's get it to the shop for repair," Judi whined.

"We will, after I get my next pay check."

Eva heard the conflict. Why was Mom not willing to tell Dad when there was a problem with the car? Of course, he was miles away on the other side of the world. He did consulting work, but that was no reason to leave him out of their family troubles. It seemed Mom wanted to prove she could do well without him. Eva looked at Colleen.

"Now, to answer Eva's question," Colleen began

"What question?" Judi asked.

"Why did they dump the toxic chemicals into the ground?" Eva explained.

"Oh, fine. Let's not talk about getting a new car, something we could be proud of," Judi grumbled.

"Yes, well, back in those days," Colleen said, as she stepped on the gas pedal, "people didn't think there was a problem with dumping like that. They believed that nature would break down those chemicals and reabsorb them."

"That's what Murphy thinks," Eva said. "Could he be right? Could it be possible?"

They were driving down the tree-lined road that led them out of the park. It was a beautiful sunny afternoon. A large black and yellow butterfly glided out from the trees at the side of road. It drifted over the car's windshield and into the grove of trees on the other side. Judi gave a squeal of delight. Eva watched hoping the delicate butterfly would survive the near collision with their car. From the way it continued to drift along, Eva declared it a survivor. She returned to her concern about the dumping. What was so important to them that they did not care?

"The factories could have used those waste chemicals to make something else, couldn't they?" Eva looked intently at her mother.

"My dear, to hire scientists to figure out how to re-process those chemicals would have cost so much money."

"It would have given people jobs. Now look at how much money will be spent to clean it up," Eva argued.

"Well, in time, companies realized the need to do that," Colleen explained.

Eva knew her mother was trying to calm her. Why was it necessary to remain calm? Why silence her anger and disappointment? All Eva wanted was for society to do the right thing. Mom acted like the world was full of ignorance, greed, hypocrisy and lies—and it was just to be forgotten or ignored. Somehow, work your way past it.

"Look Eva, the world is changing. Maybe your generation will save the planet from the terrible things of the past. When I was growing up, we worried that the United States and Russia would declare war on each other. Everyone feared they would blow up the entire planet. I'm just glad that didn't happen. You can't even imagine what that was like. For so many years, we lived with that fear."

Eva heard this and moaned. Clearly, something had to be done. "I want to dedicate my life to saving the earth. I want to protect it. I want to stop this insanity and make the earth wholesome again for all people and animals."

"Oh hooray for you," said Judi, "I think people just worry too much. There are so many good things in this world. Why worry about anything?"

"Ahh! You exasperate me, Judi," Eva said, amazed at how she sounded a bit like her mom. Then she began to wonder if that was where she got her attitude. Why hadn't it rubbed off on Judi? Was Judi more like Dad?

They left the park and joined the busy streets where the exhaust from their automobile mixed with the exhaust from other automobiles, large trucks and buses. Eva multiplied this in her mind with every city she could name: Washington, D.C, Chicago, Los Angeles, London, Paris, Madrid, Sydney . . . . How could life go on in spite of all this pollution?

Yet, life went on.

On Monday, Eva got up early, put on her park uniform and went to work again with Curtis, Sally and all the other seasonal employees of the park. The weather was getting hot and humid. The parking lots were filling with cars. Tourists asked the same questions that yesterday's tourists had asked.

Today's assignment was to understand the park's rules concerning dogs. The seasonal workers were to remind people to obey the rules.

"Dogs must be kept on leashes."

Curtis was standing in the playground. He had just asked some dog owner to put his dog on a leash. The man immediately did so and walked away. Eva secretly believed they obeyed Curtis because he was tall and a man, so he had more respect. She wondered how they would have responded if she had asked them to put their dog on a leash. She was convinced the world would not listen to a small young woman.

Soon it was Eva's turn to remind the next offender. She saw a middle-aged woman with a free running toy poodle. Eva stepped forward and politely reminded the woman. The woman bent down and put her dog on a leash. It was amazing. Eva smiled. But wait a minute, it wasn't her own power that the woman obeyed, it was the badge on Eva's shirt and the power of the Park Service.

Unfortunately, that positive response was misleading. From then on, no one even cared about the power of the Park Service. Every park patron told Eva:

"My dog doesn't bite."

To some people, the freedom of their dog seemed more important than the safety of their fellow humans. Eva heard the statement over and over again. *My dog doesn't bite.* She was becoming quite discouraged. The authority of the Park Service was being challenged.

The afternoon heat was also eroding Eva's patience. Passing the Nature Center, she decided to monitor the pond. The shade of a nearby tree and a cool breeze helped her regain her strength. She thought about this strange job. It was not really a hard job to do physically, but it certainly was emotionally draining.

She watched the ducks on the pond. What a beautiful life they were living. The little yellow ducklings were paddling about behind the adults. There were several species that Eva could recognize: mallards and gadwalls. An American egret dropped from the sky like an angel and began wadding around in the water. It cocked its head to the side, searching for fish it could stab with its bill.

Suddenly a dog dashed into the pond. Eva recognized it as a spaniel, a breed known for its love of water—and its love of duck hunting. Flushed from their tranquility, the ducks began frantically calling and fluttering their wings. The egret lifted up and flew away. The dog pursued the beautiful male duck with the bright green head. When Eva saw its teeth wrap around the duck's neck, she screamed. Startled by the scream, the dog turned toward Eva, letting go of the duck's neck.

A voice called the dog from the other side of the pond. The dog paddled back to the shore and ran to its owner. Eva watched as the owner welcomed it with joy.

Eva marched over to the dog owner and confronted her.

"How could you let your dog do that?" Eva screamed.

"My dog didn't do anything."

"Your dog disrupted these wild ducks and nearly killed one, you idiot."

"I'm not an idiot, my dog enjoys playing in the water."

Eva saw Curtis running down the path toward her. "Eva, what's happening?"

Eva turned to him. She felt the rage boiling up in her. "One of the ducks nearly got killed by this dog."

Curtis turned to the park patron, "Excuse me, dogs are supposed to be on leashes. We will call the park police if you don't put your dog on a leash."

The park patron bent down and put a leash on the dog.

"Ok, there, he's on a leash," said the park patron. "I don't know what's happening in this country, but it seems like they're taking everyone's rights away—all for a damn duck."

"Let's go sit down and talk, Eva," Curtis said sternly.

They went to the nature center and sat on a bench overlooking the newly planted scent garden. A cool breeze came in from the harbor. Eva felt it and tried to calm herself.

"This is a park and things do happen that we don't like," she heard Curtis say in a scolding tone, "but you cannot scream at people. A park is human habitat too."

Eva hung her head. "I understand," Eva said, hoping to hold back the tears that were welling up in her eyes. They rolled down her cheek and now she felt silly crying. She wiped them away with the back of her hand and looked up. She saw sympathy in Curtis's face.

"And I understand how you feel about the duck. Luckily, it was not captured or injured. We can only remind people not to break the rules."

"And what would have happened if the duck were killed?" Eva asked.

"Well, that's illegal and we would call the police and prosecute. The dog owner could be fined for killing wildlife without a permit."

"Can't they be fined for letting their dog run loose?"

"Well, yes, but the park police are busy with more important matters. Now let's go to the picnic sites and check on the garbage."

As they rode in the truck to the picnic sites, Eva pondered why people did not follow the rules. Did they not care? Did they think the rules would not be enforced? What if the police arrested people for not keeping their dogs on leashes? Was it too expensive for the police to do this? Curtis had said the police were busy. *No time to write tickets! It cost too much for something so minor.* There was always an excuse. All through her childhood she had been told, "Don't make excuses." Now here on the job, she found excuses, and more excuses. Everything was excused.

The picnic site was crowded with children, elderly and adults eating and dumping garbage. Plastic containers gooey with oil and syrup tumbled out of the garbage cans. Paper was mixed with metal, burnable plastic was mixed with plastic that had the potential to be recycled. As Eva and Curtis walked around and surveyed the mess, park patrons stopped them and told them of their concerns.

"We were looking forward to coming here for a picnic, but there is so much garbage around. Why can't you get someone to clean it up?"

Curtis radioed for help from Maintenance. Eva was beginning to realize they were overwhelmed. The budget only allowed the hiring of a few people and never enough to really get the job done. When the trucks came to empty the garbage cans, Eva watched as the heaps of paper and plastic were all dumped into the same wagon and carried away. Was any recycling going on here? If not, what excuse were they using here? Not enough money?

It was a crazy thing this money. There were people with too much of it and people with too little of it. There was never enough to do the job right—to hire more workers, to do the recycling, to remediate the toxins, but everyone wanted everything to look good and function well.

The sun blazed down on their backs as they moved on to their other responsibilities. Tourists needed directions to restaurants and ferries, teachers needed wheelchairs to help disabled students, truck drivers wanted to know where to deliver the new rakes and shovels and bags of grass seed that the park needed for maintenance of the lawns.

At the end of two weeks, the superintendent handed the park employees their paychecks. It was the first paycheck Eva had ever gotten and she felt proud. All the way home, as she rode the train, she studied the small slip of paper. Deductions for taxes, deductions for medical, deductions for her old age. After that, it was all hers—a real paycheck.

"So what are you going to spend your pay on?" her mom asked.

"Music, books and, I don't know, some of those fancy soaps and shampoos?"

Her mother nodded.

"Beauty supplies? You?" Judi asked. "What about all those bottles you'll need to recycle? You could do without beauty supplies. After all, you want to protect the environment, don't you? Think of that poor duck. If it swallowed a bottle cap in search of food, it would die a horrible death. I can't believe my sister, she's so full of contradictions." Judi smirked. "As for me, I'm not worried, I will tell you plainly, I want money and the good life. I don't care what it takes."

"Or what it destroys," Eva countered.

"Enjoy your beauty supplies, sister," Judi laughed.

Eva frowned. How could she avoid being part of the problem?

Chapter Six

In the Spirit of Nature

"We had a great meeting today, dear. I can't wait to tell you about it." Amanda Walters said as she hurriedly climbed the stairs. She carried her cup of tea and went into the room that once was her daughter's.

"Yes, dear, we had a very good meeting. I think you would be proud of me. I took a stand in favor of gardens, soccer fields and wildlife. Isn't that great? All of your favorites."

The walls of the room had dozens of pictures of Stephanie Walters—from the time she was a baby to the time she was a young lady in her third year of high school. Amanda looked up at Stephanie dressed in her favorite party dress. That was such a lovely dress too, covered with the delicate images of iris. Stephanie loved flowers, especially iris.

Dolls, large and small, sat on the bed like an audience waiting to hear Amanda's report about the meeting. China teacups and saucers, decorated with red roses, were arranged on a small table in the corner ready for tea. From the tops of the lavender curtains, pink paper fuchsia blossoms draped down over the windows. Through those windows, Stephanie's flower garden could be seen in the yard below. Amanda had kept that garden just as Stephanie had planted it many years ago.

"Now, dear, as I told you, Murphy is going all the way for nature. He doesn't care what girls need or want. But I know the young women do deserve a field to play ball. There's no reason to oppose that. The land can bring benefits to people and wildlife. I think this works out fine."

Stephanie Walters was not really in the room. She sat next to Amanda in her thoughts. She looked up at Amanda from the past.

Stephanie had loved soccer and was forced to travel long distances to reach a playing field. This traveling created all kinds of problems. The school board members had said that the school system was large and expensive to run. Consequently, they purchased cheaper buses that had the minimum safety requirements. With children on board, why hadn't they gotten the best buses with all kinds of safety devices? The corporations had forced tax abatement from the politicians. The property owners were angry about tax increases and were not willing to pay one more cent of taxes to maintain the school system and its transportation needs.

Even when the children wanted to experience nature, they had to climb on the school buses that merged with the high-speed roadway of commerce. Sadly, this is how Amanda's daughter had died—a class trip to a campsite where a double-tandem truck had collided with the school bus near the off ramp.

Stephanie had loved trees and was looking forward to seeing the Appalachian forests. She begged her mother to let her go on this fieldtrip. Amanda re-lived the phone call, then the scene at the hospital. If only there had been a nature trail closer to home, they would not have had to travel so far.

Amanda tried to soften her pain with a promise. Standing over Stephanie's grave, she swore she would work to make life better and safer for children, especially girls. She would do this by bringing nature closer to home. When she heard about the creation of Liberty Park, she joined the effort to make it a reality. She was glad to see that the park was gaining more land and could accommodate all the children's needs.

She sat quietly in the room now, looking out the window at the wind blowing the weeping willow tree's branches. If nature could be brought into the cities, making the cities more livable, there would be no need to transport children far away just to get a breath of fresh air or hear a sparrow's song.

Amanda shook herself out of her pity. She realized she needed to be rational to succeed. There were other arguments to consider. How much of the world's resources were burned up so that people could move back and forth to places they could have experienced closer to home—if only the natural world in their communities had not been destroyed.

Amanda finished her tea. She thought of Colleen's two daughters. Eva was Stephanie's age just ten years ago. "So Eva got the job at the park. How wonderful," Amanda whispered. "And she's found a rare bird nesting in the park. I have to do whatever I can to encourage her. She is the park's new guardian angel."

Again, Amanda thought of the meeting. The conflict between Murphy and Ed over what to do about the toxins was disturbing. Yet, she had been able to keep a balance. What was so dangerous? She had been to that land and it was truly beautiful. It would be a shame to destroy it in the name of remediation. Most incredible of all, Eva had been on that land and had discovered the rare bird. Amanda remembered how this had impressed Murphy very much. But what was the big deal about a rare bird? Amanda stared out the window. "I'll give him a call right now and find out."

She went downstairs, put her cup in the sink, and then made the call. "Murphy, Murphy, are you there? I need to know, what's the big deal about the rare bird? Get back to me as soon as possible."

She turned back to the sink and washed out her cup. The phone rang.

"The big deal is it's rare. You don't see these every day. I'd love to get a picture of it. A picture of the bird in the nest would be even more incredible. I'm going out there again today to check the location Eva mentioned."

"But Murphy, you said at the meeting that it is also endangered. Does that mean it's going extinct? Why?"

"Loss of habitat. The bird is a shore bird, but it needs trees to nest in, and good-sized trees, too. We're not talking about a robin, this is a bird that stands above the height of my knee. Listen, I'm headed out there right now. If you have any more questions, contact the Audubon Society."

"Will do," Amanda stated. Being a park activist could be very interesting. She was learning more about birds. She called the Audubon Society.

"My name is Edgar, how can I help you?"

Amanda went into the details about the park and the endangered bird.

"Well, technically, you don't have a rare bird, that would be a bird that is not usually seen in your part of the country, like a bird that blew in on a hurricane from Florida or high winds from Nebraska. The yellow-crowned night heron is a New Jersey species, but it is listed on the endangered list because there are so few."

"Oh, I see," Amanda responded. She wondered why Murphy hadn't made this clear.

"Where did you see this bird?" Edgar asked. Amanda told him the location in the park and told him the problem with that land. She went into the details about converting it to official parkland and the toxins.

"You know there are laws that protect endangered species. The land they nest on cannot be disturbed. I'm telling you this because it may help you with your work protecting the land from development. We find that many times, contamination is used as an excuse to put in a golf course or a sports complex."

"Oh, no!" Amanda explained, "We want to preserve the land, especially the area where the bird is nesting. We do want some ball fields and flower gardens, but we'll be careful not to disturb the heron."

Amanda heard a laugh over the phone before Edgar continued, "This is new, an endangered species on toxic land. I've only worked with endangered species on pristine land."

Amanda admitted to the irony. Edgar continued, "Another thing you might want to consider is that there are endangered plants also that are protected, but I don't think you would find many of them on industrial land. Maybe you could find some plants, like reeds, that are actually absorbing the toxins and neutralizing them. I'll send you some information that you can share with others. Give us a call if you need any help."

They signed off with each other and Amanda laid the phone down in relief. She raised her hands and clapped them over her head. "We have an endangered species to protect and the law is on our side. There are plants that can clean the soil. Oh, I can't wait until I tell Murphy. Maybe we won't have to dig up the land after all."

Now, Amanda began plotting. It was something she loved to do and she had been doing it for years. She had two bird experts: Murphy and Eva. Where would she get a plant expert? She checked her email and found the information that Edgar had sent her. One link had a list of botanist in the state. Amanda ran her eyes over the list. There was one listed under Liberty Park. His name was Curtis Elliot. He was also a supervisor at the park. Amanda wondered if Eva might know him.

A plant expert might be able to tell her if there were endangered plants too. This would also help protect the land. Amanda hoped Curtis would know which plants were already cleaning the soil. Amanda gave Curtis Elliot a call.

"Hello, is Curtis Elliot there?"

"Curtis speaking,"

What luck! He answered the phone. Amanda explained to him that the Friends of Nature needed a study of the plant life on the new land that the park had acquired.

"We at Park Service are already talking about doing that," he explained. "We had a meeting just this morning."

"Great," Amanda cheered. "Let me tell you, the Friends are taking a tour of that land next week. Why don't you come with us?"

"Ms. Walters, the public is not supposed to be on that land."

"Oh, well, we just wanted to see it."

Curtis laughed, "Look, I'll authorize your trip and I'll go with you. I've been wanting to focus on that area for some time, and now that it belongs to the park, this will be a great opportunity."

Amanda was relieved. She didn't realize how restricted the public was. That crazy friend of hers, Murphy, had not respected the rules of the park when he led her into that site weeks ago. She had almost made a terrible mistake letting the Parks Department know about their tour. They could have been arrested. What luck that she had made the call. Now they were getting an authorized visit to the new land.

What a great day. Who would think that an endangered bird and an endangered plant could help them protect the new land? Doing good work for the cause always made her feel like her life was still worthwhile.

Amanda gave Murphy a call. If he were already in the park, he was probably out of range. She left a message. "Murphy, we have another person joining the tour. He's a plant expert and he'll let us know if there are any endangered plants to protect as well."

Amanda laughed as she ended the message. Here was a man who didn't want humans treading on his beloved nature sanctuary. Yet, leading a bird walk was the only thing that put a smile on his face.

When the day arrived, Murphy was one big happy boy leading the Friends of Nature and Curtis Elliot on an adventure into the new land.

"Now, here's where we enter," Murphy explained to his followers. "It's basically illegal for the public to go in here. But, today, I can take you here to see the miracle of nature."

Amanda saw Curtis look at Murphy with surprise.

Murphy looked up at him and said, "Curtis here is the weed man, he's going to tell us a lot about the plants and how the land can be preserved by weeds."

"Let me clarify," Curtis said, "As an employee of the Park Service with a degree in botany, I'm here to assess the plant life and determine if any of these plants are improving the soil beyond the need for remediation."

"Whatever," Murphy grumbled.

The adventurers proceeded to follow Murphy through the hole in the fence.

Amanda had dressed for the weeds this time, leaving her pink knit sweater in the closet and wearing instead a jacket that would not catch on the briars. Colleen followed Amanda with her two daughters, Eva and Judi, trailing behind her. Curtis Elliot followed them, stopping to observe the plants on the ground.

Pausing in an open field to look around, Murphy and Eva scrutinized the trees for birds. Amanda watched Curtis examine the trees themselves. He reached for a branch and looked closely at the bark and leaves.

"What made you take an interest in plants?" Amanda asked him.

"My grandmother, mostly. We were poor and she used to make all kinds of concoctions with various medicinal herbs. Whenever I got sick, they'd give me these medicines. Peppermint for stomach aches. Rosehip tea for colds. I began to wonder what plants they used and how those plants grew and changed the world. I got so fascinated by it."

"Oh that's great, so when you look around here what do you see? What does it tell you?" Amanda looked at him with respect for all that he knew about the plant world. She studied the expressions on his face as he studied the different leaves, stalks, and stems.

"Well, let's see. There are some native trees here. I see the cottonwood trees and the eastern white pine,"

"That's good, right?"

"Yes, but there are also some non-native trees. Those are black pines from Austria."

"What about that tree over there?" Amanda asked.

"That tree is an ailanthus or commonly called tree of heaven. There's another non-native, the mulberry. They are both from China."

"There are trees here from around the world?" Amanda asked bewildered. "How can this be?"

"Mulberry was brought here to establish the silk industry. But the Chinese weren't stupid, they gave the American's the wrong tree and the wrong "silk" worm. So the silk industry failed here in the U.S. Those tall reeds over there are probably from Australia."

"Here's the mockingbird," Murphy said as he pointed to a gray bird happily eating the berries of the mulberry tree.

"Are mockingbirds natives to this area?" Amanda asked.

"Yes," Eva responded.

"And they are eating a non-native plant?" Amanda asked.

"There you go," Murphy called. "Don't make it complicated."

They moved along through the tall grass as Curtis gave them an explanation.

"During the 1700s and 1800s, shipping companies would fill an empty ship with dirt, called ballast, to keep it upright in the ocean during storms. When they arrived in the Americas, here in the New York harbor, they emptied this ballast and then loaded up with raw materials like wood and marble. In the ballast soil, there were seeds and roots from around the world. These seeds were released into the wild here on this land where they began to grow. So, because of this, many of the trees, shrubs and grasses are really from far away. I've found only a few native American wildflowers in this entire park."

"You mean we're really looking at the plants that are mostly from Asia and Europe right now, and not the natural world of the Americas?" Amanda asked.

Curtis laughed. "You would have to get far away from a seaport before you would see any quantity of native plants. If plants could talk, they would tell a story of how they have traveled with humans. For example, the native American people had corn, squash, beans, pecans, maple syrup and potatoes. Europeans learned to cultivate these and took them back to Europe as new food sources, which they desperately needed. After all, that's why Europeans got on those boats and risked crossing the ocean. They were in search of food and new sources of wood. In Europe everything was being devoured."

Amanda smiled. She liked the simple way that Curtis explained things.

"Europeans brought cabbage, beets, rutabagas and parsnips to the Americas. Plants have been traveling on the backs of humans for a long time. The plants in our community are a mix from around the world, just like the various ethnic groups of people who now live in this area."

"And what does that have to do with preserving this park?" Murphy grumbled.

"We would want to clear out any of the non-native plants," said Curtis.

"But you are saying that might be most of the plants here?" Murphy asked.

Amanda saw trouble brewing.

"Murphy, please, Curtis is just here to make a survey of what is growing in this area."

"But the birds and animals have adapted to these now, you can't just dig them all up." His face twisted with anger.

Everyone sensed Murphy's changing mood. They moved on in silence. With the human voices quiet, the birds began singing.

As she walked, Amanda puzzled over how the land could now be destroyed by their own good intentions.

Curtis approached a cluster of trees and then looked up at them.

Colleen and her daughters wandered apart as they stepped into an open meadow. Suddenly a large bird swooped down between them and glided over the grass.

"Oh, look at that," Murphy called. "It's a northern harrier hawk. It could be nesting here. I've never seen one so close. But you must understand, if too many people come here, the hawk won't return."

They stood and watched the large brown bird glide over the meadow with its wings outstretched. A defining large white spot could be seen at the base of its tail.

"That white spot is the identifying mark. The female is brown; the male is gray. This one is female," Murphy explained.

Eva pointed out the disk-like eyes peering through the weeds in search of rabbits or mice. "The disks help with hearing and vision," she whispered to Amanda.

The bird lifted into the bright blue sky and disappeared. They continued their walk. Murphy pointed to song sparrows and brown thrashers and showed everyone how to identify them.

Amanda and Colleen soon drifted into a conversation that caused them to lag behind the others.

"Since being in the Girl Scouts, Eva has taken such an interest in flowers and birds. I told her she should have a career working with nature. Her job at this park is a great start. Thank you so much, Amanda, for suggesting it to us."

"Oh, I'm glad to have helped. And what does Judi like?"

"My two daughters are so different from each other. Believe it or not, Judi is good in math and loves to entertain."

"Oh that's very good, too."

They watched as Curtis bent and examined some plants on the ground. He picked a few leaves that he placed in a small box that he was carrying.

"What are you finding, Curtis?" Amanda asked.

"This is incredible. I've just found some native wild geraniums. I can't imagine how this could happen. How could they have survived? Some wild violets are here too. We will have something to preserve."

Murphy looked at Amanda and then grumbled, "Thank goodness, I was worried he'd not find a thing worth saving."

Amanda nudged Murphy and sighed.

"Ok, everyone, we're finished with our adventure," Murphy announced. "If anybody tries to convince you there's nothing here of value, you let them know the truth." His followers smiled and thanked him for the tour. He then led them back through the secret gate.

Colleen, Eva and Judi waved good-bye and climbed into their car. Murphy brought his bike out from the weeds and peddled off.

Amanda turned to Curtis and invited him to lunch with her at the Hungry Fish. "I'd like to hear more of your thoughts about what you saw today," she said.

"Well, certainly," Curtis responded.

Inside the Hungry Fish Restaurant, they sat near a window and ordered something cool to drink. It was still spring, but the air was warming nicely.

"Well, Amanda, there are a lot of non-native invasive plants. They are mixed in with the natives. So I would suggest pulling and cutting in hopes of allowing the natives to expand their growth. I don't want to see the place entirely dug up. Some of those reeds could be absorbing toxins out of the soil already. I hope we only need to cut the reeds and haul them away, leaving the land without much disturbance."

"That's good," said Amanda. It was what she wanted to hear. She would tell this to Murphy so her old friend could calm down and continue to work with her and the Friends of Nature.

"The next big event in the park is Earth Day. Are you coming Curtis?"

"Of course, I'll be there. I'll be at a table for the State Botanists Association explaining biotic succession. That is how the land changes if it's left to re-grow on its own. First, you have the pioneer species of plants, then come the next type and so on until over a long time, you get the old growth forests. We'd need another 500 years for the trees in this county to be as big as they were when the Europeans first came. Have you ever seen the paintings by the Hudson River School of painters? They painted during the 1800's, back when there was still a lot of wilderness."

"Oh, I've seen some of those paintings. They make you aware of what it used to look like back then. When I was young, I remember there used to be farms in this area. They are all gone. Now, there are just houses, shopping centers and highways—not even much industry anymore."

The food was served. They ate in silence for a few minutes.

"I look over at Ellis Island from our park here. Our community has such a diversity of plants and people. Yet, we are all working together on the park," Amanda said. "That's what makes me feel good about our country." She smiled at Curtis, then she continued, "I always find people's backgrounds to be so interesting. Mine is German and Irish. I was just wondering, what is yours?"

Curtis looked up at Amanda. "On one side of my family, there is Afro-American and Irish. On the other side of my family, we're Delaware of the Lenape. My grandparents lived in the state of Delaware."

Amanda gasped, "You are one of the original people."

Curtis smiled, "Well, some part of me is."

"But we're all Americans now," Amanda said confidently. "And we all love our park."

"Yes, we do," Curtis agreed.

When they departed, Amanda knew she had made a new and valuable friend at the park.

Chapter Seven

Going Shopping

Even though it had been fun teasing Judi, Eva was happy for her when she got a job. Judi now worked at the Hungry Fish Restaurant, a logical place to put in an application for work, since they had gone there so many times. Judi was hired as a food server and cashier. She was delighted to have a job where she could keep her eye on the money. Today, with both sisters having the day off work, the young Kaufmans decided to spend their hard-earned income at the local shopping mall.

They dressed in their best casual clothes, donned a purse and hat and then ran down the street to the train station. The new commuter train took them directly to the mall entrance.

"Remember when we used to have to beg for money to go shopping?" Judi asked.

"I remember, and we had to beg for a ride as well."

"Now we can go on our own." Judi said, sitting back in the seat to relax.

Eva smiled with satisfaction and looked out the window, "I love the train."

"I love having my freedom," Judi declared. "I can't wait until I'm totally on my own."

"Well, I know what you mean, but it scares me sometimes. You see in the news all the terrible things that can happen to young women."

"Just stay out of bars late at night, date only competent, career-oriented men, and never have more than two alcoholic drinks," Judi stated in her classic "big-sister" way.

"That's all it takes?" Eva asked. She looked over at her sister and laughed. Sometimes Judi was funny with that "know-it-all" expression on her face.

"That's all, dear Sissy. I've read that advice in all the best women's magazines. They are easy rules to follow."

Eva leaned back in the seat and wondered. Would the day ever come when Judi was wrong?

The train pulled into the station and the young women got off. The bell clanged and the train pulled away.

They entered through the wide doors of the shopping mall. A smell of perfume and plastic and leather filled the air. The high ceilings made Eva feel like she was entering a palace. In this world, everything was new, shiny, sophisticated and designed for convenience and pleasure. The music enchanted, the lights beckoned, the crowds roared with excitement. Eva and Judi joined the flow of eager shoppers with high hopes and great expectations.

Everywhere Eva looked, there were clothes, appliances, electronic devices, toys, furniture—everything you could dream of and no mother to stop you from making your own choice. Now, with a job and a paycheck, Eva felt like she had the independence and the power she always wanted.

As the two young women wandered between the shelves and racks, the fast loud music seduced them, the lights tricked them, the grand design of the mall teased them with promises, but Eva felt like the limits of her paycheck scolded her. She looked at her sister, the expert shopper. Judi was scurrying about trying on one dress after another, one pair of shoes after another, one hat, bracelet or ring after another.

Within a few hours of looking, touching and trying on clothes, the glamour faded for Eva. She felt disappointed. This world promised things that were just a little out of reach. Eva began to see it as a huge accumulation of stuff that people might buy, but who could buy it all? Where did this stuff go when it lost its luster or failed to function?

Eva looked around at her sister. Judi had two large shopping bags, one hanging from each elbow. Eva had none. What had she intended to buy at the mall? She tried to remember. Oh, yes, she needed a better, more comfortable pair of shoes to wear at work. She was on her feet a lot and needed something durable and functional. By now, they had walked through most of the stores in the mall, but Eva was never pleased with what she saw. It seemed like everything in this place was designed to amuse or entertain—even the shoes were less for wearing and more for show.

It took yet another hour before Eva finally purchased what seemed to be a practical pair of shoes. She carried her one purchase in a plastic bag and trudged along behind her sister. Judi marched forward now with her two large shopping bags on each elbow, her purse around her neck and two smaller shopping bags dangling from each wrist. She had found bargains galore and had purchased numerous scarves, dresses, hats and rings. Eva looked at her with disgust. Judi would spend her whole paycheck and not save a thing for college. Eva wanted college and the promise of a better life; a career doing something in which she could believe.

"I'm exhausted," Eva said. "Can't we sit down somewhere and rest."

"Rest? But you only bought one thing," Judi said looking at the one bag in Eva's hands.

"Oh, and look at you, you've been buying like things were going to disappear," Eva said, sighing. "I don't know why I thought going shopping with you would be fun. Oh, I just realized what I'm facing here, we don't have Mom with us to counter-balance. I've been dealing with Judi in full-force shopping mode." Eva gave an exhausted huff. "I'm hungry. Can we go somewhere to eat?"

Eva gave a pleading look at Judi who rolled her eyes, "Now you're hungry?"

They looked around at the fast-moving crowds, the busy store windows and jewelry kiosks in the aisles. Judi pointed, "Look, there's a pizza shop. Let's go there and sit down. It's not too crowded yet."

The two young women made their way into the pizza shop and found a table. They ordered pizza with onions, mushrooms and peppers. Eva smiled. Pizza toppings were something they always agreed on. Soon, it was placed before them. The heat and aroma filled the air.

Judi picked up a slice and held it. Eva put a slice on a paper plate and waited. She looked at Judi. "We should tell Mom how easy it is to come to this mall by train. She'll like it."

"Mom loves her car," Judi responded, "I wish she'd get a new one. Or get that old thing fixed. All she has to do is call Dad and ask for the money. His job pays so well."

"But Mom likes to be independent; she wants to provide for us, too," Eva explained. "If it were up to me, I'd say we should send the car to recycling. Mass transit is better for the environment."

"Oh, don't start the environmental stuff now, we're not at the park. We're at the mall."

Eva lifted her slice of pizza—it should be cool enough to eat by now. As she bit into it and chewed, she looked at Judi.

Why were the two of them so different? Where could these differences have come from? Eva munched and thought back to the days when they were more like a typical family. Mom and Dad always had differences of opinion. They didn't fight, but they frequently disagreed. Eva remembered the old saying, "opposites attract." This must have been what brought her parents together. It certainly did nothing for the bonding of two sisters. Then, Dad got the consulting job that sent him traveling thousands of miles away to distant countries. He was gone for months on end and the disagreements seemed to disappear.

"So, you are only buying the shoes? Nothing else?" Judi asked, nipping the end of another slice of pizza."

"I finally got what I came here for," Eva responded. "I don't need anything more."

"Well, as I see it, dear Sis, there are certain things a woman needs to have. Don't you want to look at the lipstick? Lipstick gives color to your face; it makes you look pretty. And nail polish? Let's go see what new colors they have in the nail polish section. How can you feel like a real woman? I would be lost without my makeup."

Obviously, Judi wanted to look at a few more things, but Eva didn't want to give into her right away. Eva held her hands up as though to display herself better.

"I'm the natural woman," she said. "I don't need any of those frills. I am what I am. I think I look quite nice. I'm healthy, strong, energetic, happy—well, most of the time. I have clean clothes and they have nice colors."

"But you are so plain," Judi complained. "I showed you that pink dress and you wrinkled your nose at it."

Eva felt like she was turning boiling red inside, but trying to stay cool blue. "Oh, excuse me," she responded. "I'm saving my money for college. I'm a Plain Jane who would rather have an education than a dress—a dress that will go out of style in a week, if it lasts that long."

"I don't know how we could be sisters," Judi said. She looked at Eva in disbelief.

"Yes, I know, and as neat as you are with your hair and fashions," Eva countered, "you are a slob at home in our room—clothes on the floor and all over the chairs. I'm hoping you **do** find the job or man of your dreams soon—and move out. Then I'll have the room to myself."

"Oh, yeah? Well, I'm eager to go into the world," Judi said, waving her hands to display her pink painted nails. "My dear sister, you can have the room. You'll probably be living in it for the rest of your life— you, Mommy and Daddy will live happily together. You're on the path to being a lonely old lady, dear Eva. But don't worry, I'm sure you'll do great works. You can save the tufted titmouse from extinction. Won't that be grand?"

"Oh, don't be ridiculous," Eva said laughing, "I'm not going to stay with Mom and Dad forever. After all, I'm going to college. When I graduate, I intend to travel and see this beautiful planet."

Eva wondered if what she had just said would actually come true. At any rate, it was a great way to end the stupid conflict.

"So be it." Judi announced. "Now let's talk about something else that's important. Dad's birthday is coming up soon. We need to buy him a gift."

"A gift? Our father travels all over the world advising chemical companies. He's seen the shopping malls of Dubai. What kind of gift could we buy him?" Eva asked.

"Something that shows we think of him," Judi responded.

"I don't know what that would be," Eva said.

"A travel clock? A suitcase for his computer? A musical card with our picture in it?" Judi suggested. She was always good at gift shopping. "Oh, yes, perfect, we could get an updated portrait made of us, dressed in our best. He could show it to his colleagues."

Eva thought of her father and wondered if that is what he would like.

"We so rarely see Dad anymore. Judi, do you realize that?"

Judi looked blankly at Eva.

"What do you mean?"

"For the past seven years, Dad has had to travel for his job. At first, he used to come back and spend weeks with us. Now, he's gone for months, and when he comes back, none of us seem to have time for him. We don't get together like we used to. I feel like our family is falling apart."

Eva stirred the ice in her glass. There was only a little juice left and she tried to decide if she should get another one. Judi took a napkin and wiped the grease from her hands.

"I'm sure everything is ok," Judi responded. "Dad should be retiring soon and he and Mom can go to that place in Arizona to live. Dad will play golf and Mom will be busy bird watching. Arizona has fantastic hummingbirds. She'll love it."

"I think we should go out to dinner together as a family. We need to show some interest in Dad," Eva suggested. "Ask him questions about his job, about his life. That might mean more to him than a gift. Do you realize, Judi, how little we know about the man that helped to create us? Ever since he got this job where he travels—I think I was eleven years old when he first got the job, I feel like we lost him. He only has time to be with us a few weeks a year and during vacations. I don't know how Mom endures it. Sure, Dad is bringing home lots of money. That meant you and I had everything we needed and wanted in high school, but who is he?"

"He's our father," Judi responded.

"Well, I know that, but we don't really have a sense of his personality. He is Father, but that is a role."

As Eva spoke, she realized that Judi was nervously tapping the table before she turned to gaze across the busy mall. This meant Judi did not want to discuss the topic. Eva waited in silence. Judi finally turned back to face her.

"And Mom is a Mother and that is a role," Judi responded. "So what?"

Eva saw a look of discomfort on Judi's face. Yes, it was Judi's belief that if everyone in the family just stayed in place, no one would have to face what was happening. Yet Eve always wanted to see the real world and what she saw was that they were no longer sharing their lives with Dad.

"Why do you always talk such nonsense?" Judi asked. "Life is simple. Moms do what moms do. Dads do what dads do. Women wear make-up and fashions. Why do you have to question everything? Do bird's ponder whether they should fly south for the winter? No, they just do what they do."

"I guess I'm trying to figure out what's happening . . . with our family."

"What's happening? Nothing is happening."

Now, Eva was afraid that Judi would start with one of her big-sister lectures. This was not what she wanted; she wanted an honest discussion. The realization that their parents' marriage had little or no substance was beginning to worry Eva. The fact that Judi was getting so emotional meant she felt it too. That's how Judi was. Obviously, Judi did not want to admit to something this scary, but Eva felt they needed to pay attention. Their happy family was reaching a turning point.

"Now that we're getting older and soon to be on our own, I worry about Mom and Dad," Eva explained. "They were our examples of what we can do with life. Would you want to be married to a man that you would hardly ever see? Like Mom is?"

Judi looked down at the empty, grease-smudged paper plates on the table.

"I know what you mean about that. I have thought about it. I want a man who can earn his income locally. A marriage should be a partnership. When I marry someone, I want to be with him."

"Me too," Eva replied. "I'm glad Dad got this job. It paid him really well. That's great. If he ever retires, he and Mom should be able to have a great life together. But, it is strange. He's been gone so much over the years. I worry sometimes that he may be seeing someone else."

Eva saw a look of disappointment on Judi's face.

"I worry about that, too, sometimes," Judi said. "But that's just the way their relationship is. They talk on the phone all the time. You know Mom, she's so busy. She's always been involved in lots of community activities. Maybe she will get more active with the Friends of Nature. Everything's fine. Mom's so independent. She and Dad have been going on like this for years. We have nothing to worry about."

"I know, but I worry anyway," Eva responded. "When we both leave, she'll be home alone most of the time. I only hope that Dad will retire and take Mom some place special, so they can be together. Like that place in Arizona. But, somehow, I don't believe Dad could live such a different life from what he's used to. And neither could Mom."

"I do hope they stay together," Judi admitted. So many parents split up after the kids leave home, Eva. My best friend Cathy Somers told me her parents are getting a divorce. I don't want that to happen to our parents. They have taught me to believe in marriage. To see them split up makes me wonder what it's all about. Why bother getting married if it means nothing in the end?"

"I know, Judi, that's my point. What is love, what is marriage? I have to say, I don't really understand adults," Eva said. Finally, she had gotten Judi to talk about something she felt they both needed to share. They smiled at each other.

Judi picked up a napkin. "Being an adult is a strange thing. I'm looking forward to it, but it scares me, too. That's why I think you have to stick to the rules," Judi said. She blotted her lips delicately with the napkin, "Here are the rules: Get a job, get a man, buy a home, have kids, get old and stay together. That's the way it's meant to be. That's what brings satisfaction in life."

"Some people are doing things differently," Eva reminded her. "They aren't buying homes or having kids. The world's population is huge, why would you want to contribute to that? And if love does not last, then marriage is just for those who want to raise children—for the experience of having children."

"I believe there is greater security in going with the flow, doing what most people do," Judi responded, "It's natural."

Eva saw a persuasive look in Judi's eyes. Her use of the word "natural" was to convince Eva that Judi was right, but no, Eva saw through it.

"It's natural because the birds do it? Right, Judi? I'm for nature and doing the natural thing, but what is natural for humans? Over-populating the earth? Are you planning to have a child every two years because you don't want to use birth control? What is natural?"

Eva felt cruel now. She was pressing her light-minded sister with some hard, thought-provoking questions. Judi twisted her lips in disgust, and then she burst out with her answers.

"Look Sis, I'm for tradition. We should do what most people do with life. We have to find husbands, Eva. It's important. I've already got more experience than you. I've had three boyfriends already. But you haven't had one. You need to work harder on this. I don't want my sister to be a lonely old woman."

"Oh please, what is this? A boyfriend contest?" Eva replied. It was disappointing. Once again, Judi had turned their discussion into a contest.

Eva felt the sting of her sister's criticism. For some strange reason, she thought of Curtis at the park. No, no, she would not even mention Curtis to her crazy sister Judi. Judi would read all kinds of things into it. "Well look, Judi, I'm out there in the world working right now, so I'm sure my life will change."

"I'm sure it will," Judi said as she sipped the last of her drink. "So we've decided that a portrait of us would be the best gift for Dad. Yes?"

Eva felt a jolt. Had Judi just changed the topic? Of course, she had. That was her way of getting her way. But the idea of a portrait was a good idea. Now, if Eva could just push Judi into getting the picture taken today. That would be an accomplishment.

"Yes, of course" Eva responded. "We should get our picture taken soon."

"I'm not ready for a photo session today," Judi protested. "Let's just check on the cost. Look, there's a photography studio right over there. Let's go talk to them. We can set up an appointment."

Eva grabbed her purse and her single purchase of shoes. "Yes, let's find out what the prices are and then we'll make a decision." She looked at Judi. Her shopping bags had enough clothes for a full afternoon photo session for a top fashion model. Eva smiled with a devilish glee as she helped Judi pick up her shopping bags. Together they walked across the mall.

Chapter Eight

Earth Day

Every spring, Amanda looked forward to the Earth Day celebration. This year they were lucky to have sunshine and a clear sky. At the park, all the nature groups and vendors had set up their tables and exhibits. Soon families and friends came in search of something green, something growing, and something that truly represented their love of the Earth.

Curtis Elliot had put up posters along the edge of his table showing the biotic succession. He laid out booklets about trees and shrubs and how to care for them. In several buckets of wet sand on the side of the table, he had hundreds of starter trees—saplings—to give away to anyone who came to his table and showed an interest in planting a tree.

Judi and Colleen were at the park's volunteer gardening table. Today they were giving away packets of flower seeds that were sure to grow—sweet peas, four o' clocks and sunflowers. They were trying to persuade the community to get involved in gardening. They sat across the aisle from Eva, who was at the Park Service's table handing out brochures with a map and the history of the park.

Amanda was busy setting up the table for the Friends of Nature. She laid out sign-up sheets with several pens and a bean-counting game where visitors could guess the number of beans in the jar and win a prize. This year's prize was a set of tickets to a concert in the park.

Gary Russo was pacing back and forth in the aisle with a clipboard and pen in his hands. He was eagerly looking around for anyone he could talk to about the goals of the Friends. He knew that the success of the organization depended on how many people he could get to join.

Soon a folk band started singing and playing mandolins. The smell of roasted vegetables and fried onions and sausage filled the air as the restaurant vendors started cooking. More and more people poured through the gate. As the aisles filled, children skipped and dodged among the adults who sauntered from one table to the next. Artists painted flowers and stars on the faces of little girls. Teachers instructed boys on the building of birdhouses. Teens guided little children in the making of necklaces out of nutshells and wood beads.

From the Friends' table, Amanda watched the crowd for more than an hour. Soon, another friend came to staff the table. Amanda stood up and stretched. "I just want a chance to see what else is here today," she explained.

"Certainly, take your time."

Amanda strolled away.

The pavilion, which had been a large railroad and ferry terminal in the 1800s, had a large opened door that let a steady breeze blow through. Sun filtered down from glass panels in the roof. Amanda was thankful that they had this building for Earth Day. Last night there had been heavy rain and she had worried that people would be discouraged by the storm. But now, the place was full of people. The excitement of the crowd lifted her like a wave. She saw the faces of so many different nationalities and cultures. There were people of all ages. Older folks were still clinging to their winter jackets, while the young were already displaying their skin to the cool breezes blowing in from the harbor.

The crowd meandered through the lines of vendor tables loaded with trinkets and prizes. One table in particular had captured a lot of attention with its display of live lizards, turtles and snakes that children could pet. Amanda also noticed a very sturdy table holding some big cages with their doors hanging open. Nearby, a man and woman walked about in a ring displaying two huge birds on their arms—one an owl and the other a hawk. The crowd watched in amazement.

Next to these large birds sat Murphy at his own table showing off his photographs of wild native and migratory birds. Amanda was pleased to see that he had attracted a small audience.

"Wrens usually hold their tails up in the air, like this. See? Now the brown creeper looks like a wren, but it holds its tail down, against the tree surface like this. See?" Murphy looked up at some older children who leaned forward and noted the difference in the birds' tails.

Amanda strolled along thinking how wonderful it was to have this festival. How great it was that people could come together and celebrate spring. As she walked, she came upon a series of very colorful signs at a very long table. She moved closer to have a look. A woman greeted her.

"Hello, I'm Barbara Harrison of the B & L Foundation."

Amanda shook her hand, but was overcome by a strange thought. What was the B & L Foundation doing here on Earth Day?

"Come see our display. We want to introduce the public to the variety of things we believe can be done with the land at Liberty Park. You can also go inside the tent there and see a video of *Our Dreams for the Park.*"

Amanda looked at the pictures. They had not been taken in the park, but were enhanced images of what the park could become. She entered the tent and sat down among fifty other viewers who waited for the show to start.

"Good afternoon ladies and gentlemen. We've invited you here today to see our *Dreams for the Park.* This will give you an opportunity to see what great potential exists for this resource donated by B & L Foundation, and what can be done to make these newly acquired acres a sparkling gem in our community."

On the screen was the image of Barbara Harrison looking spectacular in a glittering suit of green polyester. Music played and the icon of the B & L Foundation floated around on the screen as ribbons of color formed rainbows. Silhouettes of birds flew through fluffy white clouds.

"Hello, I'm Barbara Harrison. As you may know, B & L Foundries has donated forty-five acres of land to Liberty Park. Our foundation, the B & L Foundation, is our tax-exempt organization. With this foundation, we are ready to contribute funding for the development of the land. Let me be your host and introduce you to our dreams for this park. Our dreams will bring to the community all the liberty that we seek here in Liberty Park."

Amanda watched as iridescent pictures appeared on the silver screen. Beautiful bright purple and pink flowers appeared against a soft lavender background. Suddenly the image of a sparkling glass and steel castle appeared. The audience gasped.

"Yes, ladies and gentlemen, Liberty Park could be the site of a grand botanical garden. Just like the famous New York Botanical Garden."

A swirl of green leaves, trees and blue sky led them to the next scene: a luscious green garden, and from it arose a unique spiral architecture of sparkling glass and silver. The audience gasped again.

"An international hotel," the screen version of Barbara Harrison exclaimed. Lights shined on her as she talked.

"And now for some fun . . ."

Suddenly pictures of laughing children, their faces showing through large splashes of water. Then the words "Olympic Pool," "Tennis Court," and "Jogging Track" flashed across the screen.

"A Sports Complex," Barbara's voice announced.

The crowd cheered again. Some of the men stood and whistled.

Amanda's heart fell into her stomach—how were the Friends of Nature going to stop all of this? They could never convince the public that a small bird in the weeds would be better than a ritzy hotel or glitzy sports complex.

The crowd continued roaring with approval. Then the floating icon of the B & L Foundation reappeared and again the screen version of Barbara Harrison stepped into the center of the stage. She gave her closing remarks and the music grew louder.

Amanda knew she was staring at the ENEMY. As she hurried out of the tent, she brushed past the real-life Barbara Harrison and ran into the crowds to find her dear friend Murphy.

"I've got to tell you something. You must go to that table over there—the big long table and go into that tent. You have to see what the B & L Foundation wants to do. You have to see it."

She began to explain all that she had seen.

"I don't want to see that. I'm staying out of that tent," he said. "You see, I knew it was coming. Now do you agree with me? We have to do something powerful. I think maybe even extreme!"

"No, Murphy. We can't do anything extreme. There must be another way, but we must do something. I'm going to tell Gary and the Friends."

"Are you ridiculous? The Friends won't do what really needs to be done. I thought you were a fighter. All the years we've been together in this struggle. Now, I can't put up with your namby-pamby silly ways, Amanda."

She looked at him in shock. She cared about him. They had been the best of friends, almost partners in crime, though they had never done anything criminal. Now he sounded like he was going off the deep end.

"Well, Murphy," Amanda hissed, "if you're going to be that way, so be it. I've got to get back to the Friends table and be sure that they know what B & L Foundation wants to do with our park."

Amanda made her way back to the Friend's table. Her head was spinning and her heart was pounding. Around her, the voices of her community filled the air. Earth Day went on with all its merriment.

A deep sadness filled Amanda. It seemed like the sun was setting on the park she once knew and loved.

In Stephanie's room that evening, Amanda pondered her fears, considered her weaknesses and strengths and tried to make sense of what she had experienced that day in the park.

"Dear daughter, I know I promised . . . but some people are too powerful to confront. All my life I've tried to be a good person, do the right thing, be kind and all that. But being an environmentalist is just too much for me. I can't take the pressure anymore. I can't take the risks."

Tears rolled down her cheeks. She pressed her face in her hands. Worries consumed her. With her life dangling so close to the edge, this was not the time to take risks.

Amanda thought about her situation. She was over fifty. She could find nothing but part-time jobs. Those jobs, that came and went like sunny days, did not even bring in enough money to maintain the house her husband had left to her. She could not risk standing up to a big corporation for something as small and insignificant as a park. They had such powers of retaliation.

She thought about her other sources of income. She did make a little money renting out a room to her nephew who was going to college. Unfortunately, the money he paid went to cover the property taxes. If the taxes weren't paid, she would lose the house and her daughter's room. During past summers, she had held yard sales where she sold furniture she no longer needed. This money was used to pay the heating oil bills to keep her home warm in winter. Life was so much of a struggle and now, with a corporate entity about to consume the park, she would have no place to go to that gave her hope, no escape from the constant anxiety over money and her own survival.

She looked up at Stephanie's picture. "I told Gary about the Foundation and what they want to do to our beloved park," Amanda continued. "He said we're going to keep on fighting." Amanda thought of the small stipend Gary Russo had been paying her for her work on the membership committee of the Friends of Nature. This stipend paid for her weekly groceries. If they kept fighting, they would need her more in the Friends' office.

She looked out the window of Stephanie's room. A large gray cloud covered the sun. Sorrow came over her. What's the sense of living when you have to struggle so hard to survive? This great society had promised so much in the early days of her youth. But now she was seeing, at the end of her life, that its past luxuries had deadly repercussions. She had lost her husband to cancer from smoking. She had lost her daughter in an automobile accident. All her life she had lived for them and now they were both gone. The only thing left was this old house that was falling down around her—and her grouchy old friend and neighbor, Murphy.

"Maybe Murphy's right," she said to the picture of her daughter on the wall next to her. "What kind of a future do I have anyway? I might as well go out in a flame of glory. What would happen if I stepped beyond and did what people aren't supposed to do?"

She turned to the opposite wall and looked at the picture of her husband and daughter standing side-by-side.

"I'll see you soon, my dear ones."

The next day she called Murphy.

"Ok Murphy, I've been thinking over what you said yesterday. I see your point. We need to do a little more than the Friends of Nature will likely ever do."

"Great. I knew you would come to your senses. So, here's my plan. Let me come over and talk to you about it. I don't want to talk on the phone—just in case the government is listening to the phones."

Amanda's blood curdled. This was it. She was going to go beyond the legal limit. Soon Murphy was at her door. They sat down in the scruffy lawn chairs in the backyard.

Murphy presented his plan by first detailing his philosophy. Amanda could not follow it. Instead, she thought about the big wood lawn chairs they were sitting in. The chairs should have been taken in during the winter. They were flaking paint. Amanda did not have the strength to haul them in. Now, she wondered why she had been so captured by the Adirondack style. Peter, her nephew, who grew up on computers, had no clue how to do anything in the physical world. It was hopeless to ask him to help her by either painting the chairs or bringing them in for winter.

"So to make this happen, we need to know Ms. Harrison's schedule. I suggest we hang out near her office at the B & L Foundation and watch. I suspect she likely does the typical "nine to five" routine of office workers. We'll see how many days a week she works."

"What do you mean by hang out?"

"We'll sit in the car, sit low in the seat and watch for her. Once we establish her schedule and where she goes, we plan our attack."

"What kind of attack?"

"There's lots we can do. We can confront her away from her place of safety and intimidate her."

"That won't do any good. It'll just get us into trouble," Amanda countered.

"If we do this to her, she'll quit," Murphy explained. "The B & L Foundation will hire someone else and we'll harass that person until they get the point."

"Murphy, this won't accomplish anything." Amanda was slipping away from her earlier resolve to take risks for the cause.

"It will work; I've done it before."

Amanda leaned her head back in the lawn chair and pondered his suggestions. She was curious where the B & L Foundation office was located and what sort of house Barbara Harrison lived in. It wouldn't hurt to just stake out the place and see what they could learn.

"I'll go with you Monday and we'll have a look. Just a look," she told him.

"See you Monday at 7:30 in the morning."

"That early? We aren't trying to see bald eagles."

"Nope, we're looking for the endangered corporate vulture who feeds off the destruction of sacred habitat." Murphy laughed at his description of Barbara Harrison.

He rose from his chair to go home, but then he fell back down into it again.

"Why did you buy these stupid Adirondack chairs? I can never get out of them."

Amanda laughed. "Ok, I'm selling them in my next yard sale."

After Murphy had departed, Amanda made some dinner and tried to catch up on her reading. But his crazy scheme kept intruding into her quiet time. She tossed and turned in bed that night and worried about the outcome.

Monday morning came clear and sunny. Amanda had hoped for rain or some kind of weather that might discourage their investigation. They arrived in the parking lot of the B & L Foundation. Soon after, Barbara Harrison's car arrived and they watched as she got out and went to the office.

"Ok, she's in at nine o'clock so I'm sure she'll be out at five o'clock," said Murphy. "We'll come back at that time and follow her home."

"Fine, we'll do that."

Amanda and Murphy parted ways for the day and then returned to see Barbara Harrison coming down the stairs in the late afternoon. She got into her car without a clue that she was being watched. When she pulled out of the lot, Murphy waited just long enough to allow a car to go ahead of them before following close behind.

They went up the ramp to the turnpike and joined the rush-hour traffic.

"We'll probably lose her on this highway," Amanda mused.

"No, we won't. I've been trained on how to monitor people. I did security work years ago and I still know all the tricks."

Murphy swerved the car in and out of traffic. Amanda gasped and clutched the handle while tugging several times to be sure that she had actually fastened her seat belt. Now she was glad that the weather was clear and the roadway was dry. She even hoped that the drivers surrounding them would be wary of these two gray-headed old folks bullying their way down the highway in Murphy's beat-up old truck.

Finally, they saw Ms. Harrison turn into the driveway of a beautifully maintained home that looked like it came from a high-priced real estate magazine. The house's architecture displayed the charm of bay windows in front. The second floor had regular windows with small balconies holding decorative flower vases. Along the sidewalk to the house, hedges were neatly trimmed and ornamental pines stood like butlers waiting to greet their master. The winding gray stone staircase led to the entrance, a bright red door with a bronze knocker.

"Well, she lives in a nice place," Amanda said as she gazed upon the well-designed ambiance.

"I figured she did. I'll bet her husband is probably the Chief Executive Officer of the B & L Corporation. That's how all these executive types do it. They put their wives and kids in key positions inside the company to keep an eye on the money," Murphy explained.

"And so now what, Murphy?"

"Now we know where she lives. Now we can take action."

"What kind of action?"

"You think you know me, but you don't know what I'm capable of."

Amanda was silenced. This was a side of Murphy she had never seen. She did recall that he had mentioned a time when he used to do security work, but who would have thought it had something to do with harassing people?

"Murphy, tell me, just exactly what do you have in mind."

"Well . . . . it depends on how much we need to scare her."

"Let's go home now. We need to discuss this further."

"Amy, let me take you out for dinner. We're partners in action again. We can think while we eat and talk when we get home."

Amanda never liked to turn down an opportunity for a free dinner. She consented.

He started up the truck's engine and they drove back to their own neighborhood where they stopped at a popular diner and ate. During their dinner, they had civilized conversation, mostly about the migration and nesting of neo-tropical song birds, but once they settled into the Adirondack chairs in Amanda's backyard, Murphy shared his complete action plan.

"Here's what we do. When the B & L Foundation makes a move to do something that we don't like, we follow dear Barbara home and flatten a tire on her car. The first time we do it, they may not suspect anything. The second time it happens, they will realize that they are being punished for what they are doing. By the third time, B & L will know for sure. That's when we have to change our tactics."

Amanda listened and kept her fear to herself. Murphy was crazy. Now that she knew his plan, she knew she would have to take responsibility for stopping him.

"I don't know, Murphy. Maybe we had better save these tactics for when we get really desperate. Promise me you won't do anything until we reach that point."

"Aye, ok, I can hold off a little while. But remember, I'm your big gun. So when the nicety-nice tactics of the Friends of Nature don't work and you need to give 'em a big scare, you let me know. Meanwhile, I'm staying out of sight. You got it?"

"Great, Murphy, you just stay out of sight until I give you the word."

Amanda felt some relief. Maybe Murphy was beginning to scare himself back into sanity. Surely, he did not want to spend his retirement in prison. He wouldn't be home to fill his backyard bird feeders if that happened to him.

"Ah, this reminds me of an old girl friend of mine," said Murphy. "She made me so mad once, I used an old BB-gun and shot the windows out of her car. That really gave her a scare. I wonder where I put that old BB-gun. It could be in the basement somewhere."

Amanda looked at Murphy. "I didn't know you could be so evil."

At that moment he was not bird watching, yet a big smile came over his face.

Chapter Nine

Politics at a Picnic

Eva and Judi were struggling to carry a large plastic picnic cooler between them. It was heavy, stuffed with meat, melons and other goodies. They stumbled along, nearly twisting an ankle or two as they crossed the lawn to their chosen table. When they set the cooler down for a rest, Eva looked up and saw Amanda waving.

"Amanda! Amanda! Come join us."

"Oh, Eva, it's you. I was just waving to the lady in the harbor." Amanda called.

Sunlight blazed across New York harbor where the Statue of Liberty caught the light on her gleaming torch. Amanda waved again at the lady and smiled up at her as if she were seeing an old friend.

"We're having a picnic. Why don't you join us?" Colleen called.

"Well, that's a fine idea, but it's still morning. You have a few hours before lunch time."

"We're starting with breakfast. Don't you think it's a great idea? Breakfast in the morning sun?" Colleen responded.

"Come help eat some of this food," Eva yelled. It was her day off and she was trying to enjoy it in spite of all the work that picnics always create. Judi was now setting bottles of orange juice on the table to hold down the green tablecloth in the steady harbor breeze.

"We have all kinds of muffins, biscuits and breads, too. We have melons." Eva announced.

Amanda strolled over to their table and sat down. The variety of foods provided an adventure in eating. She put a few biscuits on a paper plate.

"This is my favorite place in the whole park," Amanda said. "What a view of the harbor and the Statue. Listen, I have to tell you about something I learned from the Audubon Society. Maybe Eva can help me with this."

They gathered around her ready to listen.

"A guy at the Audubon Society told me that if an endangered species—like that yellow-crowned night heron that you found nesting, Eva—is on anyone's land, it is protected by law. They cannot destroy the habitat because it could harm the bird. Did you now that?"

Eva shook her head. "I just identify birds as a hobby. I didn't know they had laws protecting them."

"What we have to do is document the location of the bird. We need a picture proving that the bird exists and where its nest is."

Eva looked at Judi and Colleen and smiled.

Amanda continued, "My buddy Murphy has gone out several times with a camera, but he still can't find that bird."

"I might have just been lucky," Eva explained. "Besides, I saw the nest two years ago, it may not be nesting there this year."

"But I thought I read somewhere that birds always come back to the same location," Amanda said, looking to Eva.

"I've heard that, but it's never a certainty," Eva said, "Sometimes they change nest locations to avoid predators."

"Could we try to find the bird this year and document it? It would help protect that land."

Eva pursed her lips and looked at her mother. Colleen frowned, "Amanda, I don't think this will work and I don't really want Eva going into that area on a regular basis."

"Well, it was just an idea," Amanda said. She shrugged, "We'll let Murphy pursue that possibility. He needs something to keep him busy."

Eva laughed. She liked Murphy and wondered if he was Amanda's boyfriend. How nice it would be to have a boyfriend that was interested in environmental issues. Eva poured some juice into a glass and considered Amanda's next suggestion.

"Another thing I learned is that endangered plants can be used to protect the land as well. Just think of it Eva, if you saw an endangered lily it could help keep the Foundation from putting up a hotel or sports complex there. We have to use all our resources to protect this sanctuary."

Eva nodded, "I see what you mean."

Judi picked up a large spoon and dipped out some fruit salad into a bowl. She handed the bowl to Amanda. "Try some of this."

Amanda smiled at Eva and then turned to Judi. "This fruit salad looks good. Did you make it yourself, Judi?"

"I did, Amanda. It's all natural—no preservatives."

"Very good," Amanda said. She settled herself better on the picnic bench and lifted a spoon to eat. "You know, when I think of all the good things we've done in the park, I wonder whether the land in the new area will look like this in years to come."

"Sometimes," Eva said, "I wish I could just see into the future and know what will happen." Eva took a bowl and dished out some fruit salad for herself.

"But we can't see into the future because we have not yet made it," Amanda cautioned. "The future is not already written. We make choices and they affect nature. I believe that humans do have some control. What I worry about is just which humans will have that control and what they will do with the environment: exploit it further or preserve it?"

Eva listened to what Amanda said. "I want to do whatever I can to help preserve it."

"Very good, Eva," Amanda responded. "You know I'm an old-time activist. Murphy and I fought to save the trees on Main Street. Maybe because we heard the birds singing in the trees, it made us care about the environment. Maybe that's what made me become a nature lover, and maybe that's why I taught my daughter to love nature." Amanda thought of Stephanie.

"Where's your daughter now?" Eva asked.

"She passed away in a terrible car accident," Amanda said.

"Oh, I'm sorry," Eva said. The horror of it filled her heart. How terrible that someone as nice as Amanda should have suffered like this and to lose a daughter must have been even worse. Eva looked at Colleen who turned to Judi. Judi looked back at Eva. Eva felt the silence between them as though a fog had formed. She hurried to break through it. "You have done so many important and beautiful things for our community. You saved the trees; you helped create this park."

"Later, I helped campaign for the new rail project. I'm glad I did, because it's great. It's just like the old trolley cars the town used to have before the automobile took over the world."

"What was it like being an activist?" Eva asked, leaning closer to Amanda. "Did you ever get into trouble?"

"Well, you know, life is a work-a-day world. The activism stuff was something I did every now and then. You can't really earn a living with it, but life sometimes demands that you set aside time for activism. No, I never got into trouble. In some ways, my activism opened many doors for me."

"I see," Eva said. It was amazing to talk with someone like Amanda who had a determined spirit and felt dedicated to causes she believed in. Eva looked at Colleen and then back to Amanda. She compared the two. Colleen helped in her community, but it was in a more acceptable way. Amanda had stepped beyond, not quite over the edge, but very close. She had taken some risks. Eva wondered what would happen if you totally dedicated your life to a cause. She gazed at Amanda with greater respect.

"Eva, I'm passing the torch on to you," Amanda said, lifting her arm with a quick glance at the Statue of Liberty, "Our environment needs more young people to dedicate themselves to protecting it."

"Passing the torch? Like that torch?" Eva asked pointing to the Statue.

"Yes, like that torch. It's a big torch I'm passing on to you," Amanda laughed.

"It's a big torch, I don't know if I can lift it like she does." Eva replied, laughing. She shook her head in doubt.

"Well aren't you the chosen one," Judi said, dropping her spoon into her empty dish.

Colleen looked at Judi, "Our Eva might just be the one to take the challenge."

Amanda stood and stretched her arm in the air, "Take the torch Eva."

Eva was about to reach up when she heard Judi call out.

"Oh, look, Eva." Judi nudged Eva and pointed to a spot across the lawn. A rabbit had appeared from under a hedge. The women quietly watched as it hopped along the fence, paused, stood up to view the picnic area, so crowded with people and their pets, and then turned and hopped back into its leafy hiding place.

Amanda sat down, "Just think of all the small wild animals living here. How will they survive the plans that we humans are making for their home and habitat here in the park?" Eva smiled at Amanda. Talking with her was always inspiring. They got beyond the usual chatter about shopping that so many people focused on. Eva looked over at her sister Judi, but she did not say a word for fear the conversation would drift into mediocrity.

"You know, Amanda," Colleen began, "I'm glad the park got this new land." She sipped some orange juice. "But with all the toxins to clean up, I'm wondering how long it will take, what should we do and what exactly will happen?"

"Colleen, after what I saw on Earth Day, I don't know what is going to happen. Did you see that exhibit by B & L Foundation? They have the money and the power to get what they please. The Friends of Nature will have to fight even harder to succeed with our plans for the park. I'm afraid that the government may think that since cleaning out the toxins is necessary and expensive, it might be better to go with the big money-making ventures that the Foundation is proposing. With those proposals, the government will get tax dollars in return."

"Oh, I know," Colleen responded.

Amanda nibbled on a chunk of banana, then continued. "The Friends are suggesting simple things like gardens, wildlife observation and ball fields. All of these will need some funding to cover the cost of maintenance, but they will be less expensive to maintain," Amanda explained.

Eva and Judi looked on solemnly.

"I saw the Foundation's exhibit," Colleen said, "The B & L Foundation wants a sports complex and a botanical garden. All these things are great, but the community will have to pay to use them. The average cost for a family would make this inaccessible to many families in our community."

"We know this is true, but does the state know that?" Amanda continued, "What scared me about their Earth Day exhibit was the audience. They were cheering as if this was what the general public wanted. Somehow, we have to prove that the Foundation's proposals are not really what the people in this community want."

"I'm the public and I want gardens, ball fields and nature walks. I want children to grow up with an appreciation of the world beyond the shopping mall," Colleen stated.

Judi sat up startled, "What's wrong with shopping malls? They create jobs."

"But are they good paying jobs?" Eva challenged.

"What can we do to prove that our community does not want what the Foundation wants for the park?" Amanda asked.

They sat silently munching some strawberries and looking deep into their thoughts for an answer.

"I'll bet they paid people to go in there and cheer for their plan," Eva suggested.

Judi looked at her and grimaced, "Leave it to my little sister to be so suspicious."

"I know what we can do," Colleen said. She leaned forward on the picnic table. She looked both ways to make sure no one else was listening in on their discussion. "I think we need to start a petition campaign. With petitions, we can show that we have the public on our side. The more signatures we collect, the more proof we will have."

"That's a good idea, Colleen," Amanda said. "Let's do that. I'll talk to Garry Russo about a Friends of Nature petition campaign."

They smiled at each other with a sense of satisfaction. They now had a plan of action.

The sun was high in the sky. All around the picnic area, numerous families had arrived with their picnic baskets. Their table settings and food displayed the various cultures and countries they were from: Poland, China, India, Puerto Rico, Pakistan, Dominican Republic, the Philippines and Haiti. Grills were set up and charcoals lit in preparation for lunchtime cooking.

Children of the various nationalities ran back and forth through the playground exploring the possibilities and screaming with excitement at the sliding boards and self-propelled rides that were available to them.

Eva and Judi cleared away the breakfast waste from their table and put it into the garbage cans. Eva stood and looked into the garbage can.

"I never realized how much garbage people create until I got this new job at the park."

"So what, we put some garbage out. We're just like everyone else," Judi teased. Eva watched as one of her fellow park employees soon came and emptied the can. She waved to her co-worker and apologized for the litter.

"It's a job," the worker said, gathering the waste into the truck and driving away.

"See," Judi scoffed at Eva, "It's a job. Everyone wants to do something to earn money." Eva shrugged as she sat down at the picnic table.

Some house sparrows raced around the legs of the table, quickly grabbing crumbs and hopping away. The birds had learned that humans were a source of food. Eva listened to a catbird hiding in the shrubs, talking to itself. A mockingbird was sitting at the top of a nearby tree, singing a variety of songs from various bird cultures. When a crumb fell from a table, every bird in the area lunged for it.

"Oh look, there's Sally. She's here today too." Eva said. "Let me go talk to her and ask her to join us."

Eva ran across the lawn to the parking lot where her co-worker, Sally, was busy re-arranging small plastic bags in the trunk of her old used car.

"Come join our picnic," Eva said and pointing back to the table where Amanda, Colleen and her sister Judi sat.

Sally smiled, "Of course, I'll join you."

As Sally reached up to close the trunk, Eva realized that the bags were filled with dry cat food.

"Why do you have so much cat food in your car?" Eva asked.

"It's for a project I'm involved with," Sally explained.

"What kind of project?"

"I feed the homeless kittens and cats in the park," Sally explained.

Eva laughed, "You've got to tell me more about this." They walked to the picnic table. Eva introduced Sally to Judi, Colleen and Amanda. Soon they were all sipping tall glasses of iced tea.

As the sun began to drift downward, the shade from an oak was beginning to cover their picnic table.

"So how do you like working for the Park Service?" Amanda asked Eva.

"I like it, but some days I'm doing things that aren't what I expected."

"That's the case with any job, but what surprised you?"

"I spend a lot of time trying to get people to put their dogs back on leashes, pick up their litter, that sort of thing. I thought I'd be doing bird and wildflower tours."

"And you, Sally, what do you think of working in the park?" Amanda asked.

"It's ok, but I wish they would listen to me when I give them ideas."

"Ha, don't we all wish they'd do things our way," Amanda said.

Eva turned to Sally. "So tell us about your project feeding stray cats."

"Well, I belong to the Animal Protection Group. It's my responsibility to take care of the cats in Liberty Park. You see, we have meetings every Thursday and we report on the areas we're assigned to cover. Mine is Liberty Park, so I bring dry and canned cat food for the poor unfortunate stray kitties. You know, they would have died this winter if I hadn't come out here and fed them. I had to come out in some really bad weather too, but I knew they would need food. Last fall, some of us came out and built little houses so the cats wouldn't be forced to sleep in the cold wind. Our organization was trying to get the park superintendent to help us, but he wouldn't do it."

When Eva saw Sally looking to her for approval, she had to turn away. Eva was horrified. She thought back to the incident of the dog chasing the duck. She felt very protective now of the wildlife in the park. What a shock that she was getting the details of yet another menace to wildlife from her co-worker, a fellow park employee. How could Sally work in the park and defy park policy at the same time?

Eva looked at her mom who was frowning with disapproval. Judi was snickering and turning away. Amanda was looking at Sally with an expression of concern.

Sally continued, "Can you believe this? The park superintendent told the park employees to take away our little houses. They said we weren't allowed to put them here and we weren't allowed to feed the homeless cats. How can they say they are for protecting animals?"

Eva did not know what to say. She was trying desperately not to scream at Sally the way she had screamed at the park patron about the dog. Then she wondered what Amanda would do; she loved the park as much as anyone did.

Amanda smiled at Sally. "I think they like to take care of wild animals that are native to this land, not abandoned house pets."

"Wild animals? House pets?" Sally stammered, "What's the difference? They are all animals?"

"Wild animals can take care of themselves, if we don't destroy their habitat and introduce predators like house cats," Amanda said calmly. "Feral cats are a problem we humans have caused; really Sally, those kitties should never have been abused nor should they have been dumped out in the wild."

Eva let out a sign of relief. Amanda had given a gentle explanation of her own views, allowing her to avoid confrontation with Sally, her co-worker.

"We are trying to find homes for the cats," Sally explained, "but the longer they stay out here, the wilder they get. It's so difficult to take care of them. I spend a lot of money each week on cat food for these dear babies. So now I've started asking friends and family to make donations to me so I can keep up my work."

Eva saw Colleen put her hands on the edge of the picnic table as if to brace herself against the possibility of being asked for funds.

With Amanda nearby, Eva tried to be diplomatic but a little sarcasm seeped out of her. "Oh Sally, I was just going to ask you to donate money to save the birds." Eva gave a nervous laugh. "Sally, you'd be better off catching the cats and removing them. Some people in the Parks Service want to kill the cats. The cats do destroy the wild birds. There are birds in the park that are endangered and could become extinct. Don't you care about them?"

"Of course, I care. I care about all animals and all of nature. I'm trying to find homes for these cats. Sometimes I take sick kitties home and bottle-feed them. They get worms in their heads and I squeeze them out and put medicine in. I care. But I don't think the other park employees are doing the right thing. Why did they take and destroy the box houses we put out in winter?"

Eva saw Colleen look at Amanda and smirk. "People these days definitely have different attitudes about animals. When I was young, I used to spend my summers helping my Aunt Mary butcher, clean and pack chickens. We used to catch the chickens with a hook, lay the chicken over a tree stump, and then chop off its head with a hatchet."

Sally gasped and stared at Colleen.

"After that we would pick up the chicken's body and put it in a tub of boiling water. This made it possible to pull the feathers off really easy."

Eva watched as Sally pressed her hands to her ears, but Colleen did not notice and continued her description of chicken butchering.

"After we pulled the feathers off, we'd cut the chickens open and pulled their guts out with our hands."

Judi and Eva listened to their mother's tale with curiosity. It seemed brutal but realistic. Eva wondered how Sally was taking it. She looked in her direction. "Oh, no, Sally's fainting."

Amanda looked at Sally, too, and quickly took her by the arm and began fanning her with the package of paper plates.

"Be strong, my dear, different people have different ways."

Eva opened a bottle of apple juice and handed it to Sally. She took a sip.

The smell of charcoal was in the air. Around the picnic tables, people began putting raw slices of meat on the grill.

"I think I'm going to have to leave, but thanks for the juice."

"I guess you won't be staying for lunch?" Colleen asked.

"I guess she won't be" laughed Judi, "We're planning to have grilled chicken."

"Oh, that's it for me," said Sally.

"Wait," said Eva. "We could make a donation to your cause. I think we should contribute some cans of cat food."

Eva saw Sally stand and wait for the donation, but then Judi jumped up. "Yes, let's donate some cans of cat food. What flavor, Sally? Chicken-flavor?"

Eva fought to keep from laughing. Judi could be so mean.

Sally sneered, "Ok, I get it, cats are carnivores." She gathered her hat and sunglasses. "I'll see you tomorrow at work, Eva."

"See you tomorrow. Nice talking to you."

As Sally turned to leave, a homeless man approached the table.

"You lovely ladies look like you're having a fine day. I wonder if you could help a kind gentleman such as myself. Could you spare me a little something? I would appreciate it and God will bless you."

Eva found a spare muffin and gave it to him. Sally gave him the small change she had left in her pocket. He blessed them then headed down Freedom Way.

It was early afternoon. Some tall Cottonwood trees at the far edge of the picnic area were blocking the sun and casting a welcomed shadow. Colleen spread the pieces of chicken that had been marinating in sauce onto the grill. Eva and Judi lifted from the cooler a large bowl of green salad, topped with chopped red peppers and bright orange carrots. They put it on the table. Amanda assisted by placing fresh napkins and utensils at each place mat. Soon they were feasting from meat to vegetables to fruit.

"Now let's work on our petition," Amanda said.

Colleen found the bottom of a pie box to write on.

"Whereas," Judi said and giggled.

"Whereas this park is dedicated to the people and . . ." Amanda declared.

Eva listened and marveled at how Amanda could pulled the words out of her head. They bantered back and forth until they got their ideas set. Colleen put the final changes on it and then offered to send it to Gary Russo for consideration at the next meeting.

So this was the process, Eva thought. They had come up with a plan of action to counter the B & L Foundation. Now they would work at getting the petition signed. Eva wondered what would happen next.

Chapter Ten

In Need of a Rescue

A few weeks passed before Amanda saw Sally again. Amanda had just finished exercising with a group that met regularly in the park. As she walked toward the rail station, she saw Sally's car parked along the road. Any other time she might not have thought about it, but having met Sally, she was curious how the feral cat salvation project operated.

"Sally, hello, I guess you're taking care of the babies? I like cats too. I wish I could do more for them."

Sally looked up from the tray where she had just dumped some canned cat food—fish flavor. Amanda saw apprehension turn into friendliness.

"Oh Amanda, it's you. Yes, I just finished doing my run here for the little kitties."

"But I don't see any kitties," Amanda responded.

"Oh, they hide. These are cats that have been abused by their owners or others in the owner's family. They are actually afraid of people. I can understand them. They are hurt and scared."

"You told us about the houses you put out for the cats. Where do the cats stay now?"

"Over there. See?" Sally pointed to a small brown box tucked into the tall grass. "Come with me and I'll show you the work I do."

Amanda got into Sally's old raggedy-looking car.

"How did you get this car?" Amanda asked.

Sally laughed. "An old boyfriend gave it to me. It has brakes and runs well, but I don't take it out of the neighborhood. He gave it to me to keep me from reporting him to the cops." Sally drove them around to each site. There were four in all, spread around different parts of the park. At times, they could see the adult cats. There were grays, tigers, and some pretty calicos.

"How did you get into this kind of rescue work?" Amanda asked Sally.

The young woman leaned back in the car seat. "I don't know, I joined the group three years ago. I just wanted to get a pet. I love cats. I got six of them. Unfortunately, I was evicted from my apartment for having too many animals. I took care of them, but the landlord said I didn't. But I really did."

Amanda comforted her. "I'm sure you did take care of them, my dear."

"I had to give my cats away and go live in a homeless shelter. Then I got the job at the park and could afford a small room, but it's expensive."

Amanda was amazed at how all these young women reminded her of her daughter Stephanie. Stephanie loved her domestic cat, but she loved wild animals, too. Amanda wondered how Sally would react to seeing the wild animals of the park.

"Sally, when you are finished with this, I want to show you the wildlife viewing area. There's lots to see there. It's amazing how the wild birds and animals take care of themselves."

"Ok, I guess I can go there with you."

When Sally finished her tasks, Amanda instructed her on where to go.

When they arrived, Amanda pulled a small pair of binoculars out of her purse. "Here, we can use these. It always helps."

They walked down the marsh trail that was bordered by Red Cedar trees. They stopped at an overlook and scanned the surface of the pond.

"There's nothing out there," Sally said.

"Oh, my dear, there is. Of course, there is. Your mind hasn't been trained to see what you are looking at."

Amanda searched the shoreline and found a Great Blue Heron.

"Look at this," she exclaimed, "You won't believe such a big bird can exist in our community." She handed the binoculars to Sally.

The tall long-legged blue-grey bird held its head up, displaying a long neck that made it possible to see over the tall grass. The bird moved forward, curved its head over the water, and then extended its bill like a dagger ready to stab a fish.

"What is it doing?" Sally asked.

"It's searching for food. All wild creatures fill their days looking for food and protecting their young."

Sally handed the binoculars back to Amanda. Amanda put them up to her eyes again.

Sally sighed. "I find it really hard to believe that wild animals care for their young. They are wild creatures; what do they know? Even human parents don't always care for their young."

Amanda heard these words spoken in such a listless way as though Sally carried some burden of sorrow. She lowered the binoculars and looked at Sally. Yet the young woman looked back at her with no expression as if what she had said was a truth known by everyone.

They moved on along the trail.

Now Amanda was wondering what it really meant. *Even human parents don't always care for their young.*

"Let's walk over there," Amanda said. They now stood at a different angle and viewed the pond again.

Amanda drifted into her thoughts. As a parent, she had done everything for her child and still her own child had died young. Had she failed in some way to protect her daughter? What if she had flatly refused to let Stephanie go on that trip? Kept her from potential danger. But life has its risks, you can't hold back from living.

A pitiful cry filled the air. Under a big shade tree on the grass was a tiny baby bird. It raised its head. It looked around and cried again. The two women were drawn to it.

"You see here," Sally said, "look at this little baby. Its parents have abandoned it. Now we have to rescue it or it will die."

"No, Sally, see over there. The parents are calling to it. See that one on the tree branch, it's calling."

"How do you know **that** is the parent?"

"Come on, let's stand back and watch." Amanda looked up into the tree and spotted the nest. She pointed it out to Sally.

"The baby bird must have fallen from there."

Amanda saw Sally bend down and scoop the little bird into her hands. They stood head to head and looked at it. The little bird had such tiny feet. Its small claws made no mark on her skin. Its wings flapped, but with no feathers, it failed to fly. It tucked its head in between its shoulders and screamed louder, aware that it was in even greater danger. The parent birds flew back and forth barking their warning chirps at the human intruders.

"Sally, we can't take that little bird home, we would be taking it away from its parents. See over there, they are angry at us. The parents are so worried that you have taken their baby. Put it here under the bush if you want to protect it."

Sally lowered her hands and spilled the little bird under the shrub. It instinctively began to climb up into the branches. The two women stepped back and watched as the parents, two big red-breasted robins, swooped down from the tree toward the calls of the chick.

"We rescued this baby bird," Sally stated. "It would never have found its way to safety without us."

"Well, ok, my dear, but you see the parents were keeping an eye on it and they would have protected it. Their biggest threat comes from feral cats. The birds will use their bills to pick at stray cats or any animal that might try to take their chick. Wild creatures do take care of their babies. But humans make it difficult when we let so many stray cats and dogs run wild."

Amanda spoke, watching how Sally might react.

Sally was quiet.

After a few moments, they walked further down the trail. Soon they saw a great egret and later a snowy egret.

"Let me share with you the story on the snowy egret. This bird almost became extinct. Back in the 1800s, people were killing them for the feathers to decorate women's hats. Then they passed laws to protect the bird. The snowy egrets have been thriving ever since. So you see, Sally, humans can do the right thing and make the world a better place."

Amanda looked into Sally's face and was surprised to see total boredom.

What could have caused this? Amanda wondered if she may have over-stepped that delicate border between teaching and preaching.

"Amanda, I'm hungry. Can we go over to that restaurant in the park?"

Amanda agreed to go. They climbed into Sally's car and stopped at the Hungry Fish Restaurant.

Inside, they took a seat at a booth and began considering the lunch specials that were written on a chalkboard next to the kitchen door. When the waiter came, they were surprised to see Judi, Eva's sister.

"Oh, Judi," Amanda exclaimed, "you got a job here? How lucky for you. I suppose you are trying to earn money to go to college."

The two young women nodded at each other, and then Judi answered Amanda's question.

"College? Me? I don't think so. Now that I'm done with high school, I just want to find a business I can advance in to make money. My sister Eva wants to go to college, but not me."

"I see," Amanda said, smiling politely. She and Sally both ordered sandwiches. When their sandwiches arrived, they ate and made small talk about the décor of the restaurant. Then they selected dessert.

Sally ordered a small pie, a fruit drink and a package of cookies. Though tempted by the sweets, Amanda settled for a banana instead.

"Let's take our dessert out," Sally suggested.

Amanda nodded in agreement. They went to the cashier to pay.

"I don't have enough money," Sally whispered.

Amanda wanted to tell her to put the cookies back, since their wrapping made that possible, but she didn't want to be confrontational with Sally. She looked in her wallet and realized she had just enough money to pay for it all.

They took their dessert and climbed into Sally's car. She drove them to a shady parking space and stopped.

Amanda nibbled on her banana as she watched Sally devour the pie. When Sally opened the cookies and offered them, Amanda decided to have a few.

"You remind me of the lady I stayed with one summer when the state child protection agency took me and my sister away," Sally began. "They put us in this foster home and the woman was really nice. She had cats. That's probably where I got my love of cats. You remind me of her."

Now Amanda was beginning to understand Sally. "And you remind me of my daughter. She passed away in a bus-truck collision, but she loved nature and kittens too." Amanda said. "Sally, how old are you?"

"I'm twenty now."

"If you were younger, I would adopt you as my daughter."

The two women laughed at the idea.

"If there is anything I can do for you, Sally, you just let me know. I have a big house with nice rooms. I charge really reasonable rent."

Sally looked at her with a hopeful expression, so Amanda continued. "If you need a place to live, please let me know."

"I could use a cheaper place to live. The rent that I pay now is so high. I can't even afford to get the oil leak fixed in my car."

They sat in Sally's old dented car and looked out over the landscape of the park. The recent rain had turned the grass bright green. The leaves on the trees were shiny and new. A promising breeze playfully climbed in through the open car window.

As they sat munching cookies, they watched a group of men enter the park with tall fishing poles in their hands. The men walked to the dock and set up their fishing expedition for the day. They swung fishing lines into the water, and then set the poles in holders attached to posts along the shore.

After a while, Sally started the car and drove to the other end of the park. There, they watched tourists boarding the boat to see the Statue of Liberty. Male joggers with long muscular legs ran by in their baggy shorts, sweat dripping down their shoulders.

"The park means so much to so many people," Amanda said.

"It does," Sally agreed.

"I have an idea," Amanda said as she brushed some cookie crumbs out the window. "Why don't you come over to my house right now and have a look at the rooms I have available."

"Oh, Amanda, that's a great idea. Let's go."

Amanda directed Sally on the location of her home. Soon they were walking through Amanda's house. They climbed the stairs. "Here's the best room of all and you could have it," Amanda said as she opened the door.

It was a large room with pretty curtains in the windows. There was plenty of floor space in the room, even with a large bed and dresser still there. As Amanda looked around the room, she remembered the furniture that used to be there but was sold to pay last winter's heating bill.

"I could fit the little bit of furniture that I own in here easily," Sally stated.

"Great, and don't worry, I charge reasonable rents," Amanda promised again. They discussed the details and Sally agreed it was very reasonable.

"Let me show you the room across from yours. It used to be my daughter Stephanie's."

Amanda swung open the door and Sally looked in at the many dolls that crowded the small bed. The tiny table and tea set under the window still looked as though they were ready and waiting for a tea party.

"Here are the pictures of my daughter," Amanda said as she pointed to the wall. She turned and looked at Sally and then looked at the pictures again. Then she looked back at Sally.

Here was another young woman with so much potential. But unlike Eva, who had a happy home, Sally needed someone on her team. Amanda knew she could be that person. How nice it was that Sally had blue eyes, just like Stephanie's. Her hair, parted in the center, hung straight down, forming yellow ribbons that swayed every time she walked. If this was not Stephanie, did it matter? Amanda knew she was looking at a young woman who needed some help.

Sally looked back at Amanda and the two women smiled at each other.

"I wish you were my mom and I had lived in a place like this. That would have been great. I would have had the life I was meant to have."

"We could pretend," Amanda suggested. "Let's create a past that we could share. Let's pretend what it would have been like."

"Good idea, that would be a fun game," Sally said laughing.

"But first we need to make some tea. I'll heat the water." Amanda went to the kitchen, filled the teakettle with water, and put it on the stove. On a tray, Amanda put the lemon, sugar, small milk pitcher and all the adult-sized cups and saucers they needed for a "pretend-a-new-life" tea party.

Soon they were sitting in Stephanie's room at the little table.

"I would pretend that you walked me to school every day and sang to me," Sally said.

"I would do that my dear, and I would dress you in the prettiest clothes of any girl in the school."

"Oh, that would have been great. I always felt rejected in school. Besides pretty dresses, I never even had any dollies," Sally said.

"No dollies? Oh dear, take your choice of dolls. All these dolls are now yours because you are my new daughter."

The "pretend-a-new-life party" brought them to making plans on how and when Sally could move in. They began to put the plans into effect that very day by cleaning the spare room. A few days later, Sally started bringing boxes of clothes and shoes to fill the closets. Soon came her few pieces of furniture and her radio and small television.

The next day, Amanda discovered that Sally had taken over the kitchen.

"I hope you like vegan cooking," Sally said. She was wearing an apron and had oven mitts over both hands. The aroma of good food filled the room.

"Well, it smells great," Amanda said. "If you want to do all the cooking, that's ok with me."

Suddenly the side door opened and in came Amanda's other tenant, her nephew Peter.

"Wow, what's that good smell?" he asked. "It smells like home cooking and I don't detect any meat smell at all. Amanda, are you becoming a vegan?"

He stopped short when he saw Sally.

"Oh, Peter, this is Sally. She's renting one of the bedrooms upstairs," Amanda explained. She saw a spark of interest fly between them and laughed. "And you are right, she's a vegan cook. Maybe I'm going to become a vegan. Meat has been a little tough on my digestive system lately."

"Peter, why don't you join us? I cooked enough for a vegan-loving army. Well, let me see, would vegans even be in the army? Have a seat."

Sally put an extra plate on the table across from her own. From that time on Amanda could not get a word in. The two young people hit it off fantastically.

Amanda was surprised to learn that Peter was also a vegan. She had always wondered why he never joined her for dinner.

The three of them passed dishes of vegetables and grains around and ate until all the food was gone. Amanda introduced them to a bottle of wine that had been given to her as a gift. She left them to expand their friendship and went upstairs to bed. She fell asleep listening to the sound of their laughter.

Chapter Eleven

Genetic Diversity

Ever since Eva had heard from Amanda about the endangered species law, she had wanted to go back to the new land and see if she could find the yellow-crowned night heron and its nest. She knew her mom would not want her to go there. She remembered seeing the sign on the fence that denied access to the public due to industrial contamination. Nevertheless, Eva had already been there twice. Once by accident when she was working on her scout badge. She had pursued the night heron into that area. The second time, when she had gone on Dan Murphy's tour. What was the problem with going back again?

She came up with a plan. If she could get up just thirty minutes early every morning, she could get off the train, go over there, and have a look. If she did this every morning for a week, surely she would get a chance to see the bird again. This species of bird would be roosting in the old trees early in the morning. That would be the most likely time to find it.

Eva thought of Amanda. There was no doubt in her mind what Amanda would do. Eva decided to put her own plan into action.

She leaped out of bed early. She got ready for work and then picked up the backpack she had prepared the night before. In it, she put her binoculars, bird and flower field guides and a small camera that Judi had given her for her birthday last year.

When she went to the kitchen to eat breakfast, her mom was already there.

"You're up early," Colleen noted.

"Well, I really love my job, Mom. I can't wait to get there," Eva said and saw the proud look on her mom's face. Eva wished she could share her plan, but already knew Colleen's opposition would prevent her from going.

Getting the backpack out the door without a lot of questions from Mom was the next problem. She decided to follow through on her usual morning preparation, hug her mother good-bye, and then pick up her backpack, so that Mom would not notice. As it turned out, by the time Eva was ready to leave, Mom was sipping her coffee and watching the latest news.

As Eva made her way to work, she thought about her plan. If all went well, she would get into the sanctuary, see the bird, snap a few pictures—time dated, of course, to show everyone when she took the photos. She'd be back out of the sanctuary in time for her day on the job. It would only take about thirty minutes.

She got off the train, walked down the trail, and entered the hole in the fence that Murphy had showed her. As she pushed her way through the bramble, she thought of the other bit of information Amanda had given her. Laws protected endangered plants and the land they grew on. If she could find some of these plants growing on the new land, her discoveries could put a legal stop to any excavation of the soil. The nice thing about plants was they stayed in one place, making them a lot easier to find and return to for proof of their existence.

Eva bent down and slipped under the branches of some maple trees. Maybe she should be a botanist, she thought as she walked along. No, she didn't want to limit herself to just plants. She really liked birds and animals, too. Maybe becoming a naturalist was the best choice. It would combine all three. She could use her knowledge to teach children and adults how to appreciate nature. Maybe she could spend her life working for the Park Service. She looked up at the blue sky. It sure was a beautiful day. She made her way to the place where she had seen the yellow-crowned night heron several years ago.

Soon she was standing exactly where she had stood before. A big willow tree that had fallen down helped her remember the spot. She wandered around looking between broken branches and standing trees. There were American crows, and brown thrashers. She even scared a flock of snipe out of the tall grass. But she could see no heron. She only had fifteen minutes left before she had to be at work.

Feeling disappointed, she turned around and headed back. She couldn't help making a quick stop, here and there, to examine the size and shapes of flower blossoms, leaves and stems. She knew from her high school science classes that the Earth was not always a friendly place to live and grow, yet some plants had always found a way to live in those barren places. She reasoned that this was probably why even the contaminated land in the park was lush and green. The plants had adapted.

Suddenly Eva had a realization. Genetic changes could cause deformities, but some changes could also create **advantages** that would help plants survive. Instead of finding endangered species, could genetic changes have created new species of plants? Amanda said they had to use every means they could to protect the land. Could these plants, with their genetic diversity, have adapted and could they now be detoxifying the soil?

When birds landed nearby, Eva looked at them closely. She looked for any genetic deformities that might have occurred from eating berries and bugs from contaminated plants. As much as she probed and searched, she made no startling discoveries. This was good in many ways, but it was disappointing. She really needed more time to do this study effectively. She would have to come back tomorrow.

She moved on across the meadow.

As she strolled through the tall grass, she saw a truck in the distance moving through a section of the new land. What was it doing there? She quickly bent down and hid behind a shrub.

The truck stopped and two men came out. They went to the back of the truck and began unloading cut tree branches. On the side of the door was a sign that said, "B & L Foundation." After the men had emptied the truck, they climbed back into the cab and drove away.

When the truck was well out of sight, Eva went to the pile of branches to examine them. The branches were from deciduous trees. Their broad leaves were wilted and sap was dripping out. Some pine branches were also included in the heap. Those branches were not wilted, but covered with a gray-green dust. Eva looked closely at this strange coating on the needles. She had seen plenty of healthy pine branches before and knew these were likely to be diseased. Could this rubbish contaminate the other trees? Curtis would probably want to know about this dumping.

She looked at her watch. If she ran like mad, she had just enough time to get to the park office to clock-in for work. She took off at a run; her backpack added a strain to her efforts. Questions kept going through her mind. Why was the B & L Foundation dumping diseased tree branches on the new land? Could it mean that B & L knew this whole area would soon be gone?

When Eva arrived on the job, she signed in. She was on time, but completely out of breath.

"We're going down to the diabetes walk fund-raiser," one of the other park seasonal workers explained to her. "Come on." They headed out the door.

Eva was soon busy handing out park maps, giving directions to tourists, telling dog owners to put their dogs on leashes and struggling with park patron's complaints about garbage. She had to put her discovery about the dumping by B & L Foundation aside. Hour after hour, she watched for Curtis and waited for him to appear so she could tell him what had happened that morning. By the end of the day, she learned that he was not even scheduled to work that day.

The week wore on. Eva continued to remind herself that when she saw Curtis, she needed to tell him about the dumping of the infected pine branches. The longer the mold was allowed to remain there, the greater the chance it had to spread. By the middle of the week, she finally heard Curtis' voice on the radio. Her heart leaped. He was back in the park.

Unfortunately, he was assigned to take special guests on a tour through the park. She knew it would not be appropriate to interrupt him when he was doing this. The two of them didn't cross paths for the rest of the day.

As time passed, Eva began wondering if what she saw was really of any concern. Maybe it meant nothing and she was just becoming "all wrapped up in herself" like her mom sometimes said she was.

Under the bright hot sun of summer which drained her energy, and under the pressure to be patient while performing trivial tasks, Eva also began to have doubts about working in the park. She wondered how useful this work was in pursuing her career as a naturalist. She was doing nothing that had any connection to birds or plants or educating anyone. As she walked down the trail, she saw another little girl crying. She hoped this experience would be better than the last one.

"What's wrong, honey? Where's your mama?"

The little girl looked up, looked around and burst into tears. Unlike the last time, this time no one stepped forward to claim the child. Eva took the little girl in her arms and began walking through the crowd. How could she tell who the parents were? People would turn and look at Eva, seeing the Park Service emblem on her shirt, but then they would look away. She circled in wider reaches around the area where she had first found the child. Surely, her mother could not be too far away. Finally, a woman came running with tears in her eyes. The little girl was jubilant. Eva was relieved.

Eva had no sooner solved this problem then she met some tourists who wanted to know how to get to the ferry to the Statue of Liberty. That was easy.

Then Eva stopped at the public restroom, only to discover it needed a cleaning. She reported it over the radio. That request gave her a sense of satisfaction because, if Curtis were in the park today, he would hear her voice. It was amazing how little things could give so much hope. It would be nice to talk to him again. In her mind, she heard Judi's voice taunting her about getting a boyfriend. Why was she thinking about this now? Why should she care what Judi thought?

On the last day of her workweek, while sitting under a tree sipping some water from her canteen, Eva heard a radio report from Curtis. He requested that all summer workers come to the office for a special project. Finally, she had the chance to meet up with him. She hurried back.

"You are going to learn plant identification," he announced to the crew. "Or, I should say, some of you already know, some of you will learn, and, if you don't learn, we have other projects for you. So climb in," he said.

They climbed into several trucks and headed to an overgrown area of the park. At that location, Curtis gave them gloves and hand tools. stood before them and looked around.

"Ok, here we go. Do you see this plant? This is red knot from Asia," he said holding the triangular leaf of a plant that grew in great quantities. "We are going to be weed-whacking this thing before it goes to seed. Once it goes to seed, those seeds blow everywhere. It is an invasive plant that chokes out other plants of greater value to the wildlife. Cut it down and put it into these bags."

"This is garlic mustard, from Asia. It, too, is a prolific breeder casting its seeds everywhere. Do you see the shape of the leaf and the stem? See the cluster of small white flowers? When you see these, pull them out and put them in these bags. Put on your gloves and let's get to work. As we go along, I'll show you some more weeds to pull. I may get the chance to show you some native American wild flowers too. But don't pull the natives or we'll send you out for garbage collection."

Eva was appalled. She had learned the names of all these plants, as if they were friends. Now, to earn a paycheck, she was obligated to pull them out. As the crew began pulling and whacking the weeds, insects filled the air with their fury. Eva wiped the sweat from her forehead and swished the insects away from her eyes. This was not what she wanted to do. She longed to be answering the questions of tourists and scolding dog owners.

Curtis showed them more plants to add to their task of annihilation. "This is called "butter and eggs." You can see the two shades of yellow in the flower. It's invasive from Europe. I don't care how pretty it looks, pull it out. This is a pretty one too, it's called yellow mustard, it's from Europe also. Pull it out. Oh, and look here, this is bindweed, another one from Europe. It has heart-shaped leaves and is from the morning glory family. See how it chokes everything? Pull it out."

The sun paused at its zenith and then rolled down the side of a solid blue sky. Tourists strolled along sidewalks and took pictures of park workers in wet, sweaty shirts working knee deep in weeds beyond the civilized areas of the park.

After clearing one section, Eva stopped and looked up. "Curtis, about these plants, they have been here for more years that I can remember. Why does the state want us to pull them out now? Haven't they evolved as part of the plant community here? Wouldn't the wildlife be adapted to them by now and need them?"

"Eva, you are starved for an education," Curtis said and laughed.

Eva stood up straight and rubbed her lower back. "Speaking of starved, I'm also starved for lunch. When do we get to eat?"

The other workers looked toward Curtis.

"Let's take lunch now," he said. The crew immediately put down their tools and gloves. They quickly climbed into the trucks and drove back to the park lunchroom.

Over lunch, Eva asked Curtis about the courses he took to qualify for the job he was doing in the park.

"Biology, of course," Curtis explained, "but I found chemistry is useful in understanding the molecular processes in plants and between plants and the soil."

"I see," Eva said. She wondered if she would do well enough in those subjects to earn a degree. As she munched her roast beef sandwich, she listened to Curtis go on about his favorite subject.

"Take, for instance, when the wind blows a tree to the ground, the wood fiber goes through a deterioration process. Cold temperatures shatter the wood, warm wet weather is conducive to molds that break down the fiber. As the wood crumbles into the ground, the soil is full of microbes that help to break it down further. Over time, this process produces the best top soil."

In her mind, Eva envisioned some branches lying on the ground. She began to think of some other branches she had seen somewhere recently. Then she remembered.

"Oh Curtis, I have something I've been meaning to tell you.

"What is it?"

"Let me explain. I was looking for an endangered heron and I saw some guys climb out of a B & L Foundation truck. They dumped a full load of tree branches on the ground. They aren't allowed to do that in the park, are they?"

"What part of the park were they in?" Curtis asked.

Eva did not really want to tell him, but she felt she had to give him the exact location.

"In that new parkland over by the train tracks."

Eva saw a look of doubt on Curtis' face.

"You weren't inside that area, were you, Eva?"

"No," she said, "I was just near-by."

Curtis looked puzzled. "Why would they be dumping branches there?" he asked. He took a bite of his sandwich. He looked thoughtful as he chewed his food. "I suppose they are just using it for a temporary dump site," he continued. "They must be trimming the trees at their office complex. It's just down the street from the park. They have a lot of trees and shrubs. It looks better, in many ways, than the park does."

"It does?" Eva asked.

"Well, of course, they have the money to fertilize the land. They hire an arborist to inspect the trees for disease. They can afford chemical sprays to kill infestations."

"The pine branches looked kind of sickly to me. They looked like they had some sort of fungus or mold on them."

"Oh, of course, molds and fungus help to break down the wood fibers. They can also help break down toxic chemicals in the soil— that's the point I was getting to."

Eva interrupted him. "But could the mold contaminate other trees in the park?"

"I suppose they could," he responded.

"So it could be a problem for the park if the Foundation is dumping those contaminated pine branches in the park?" Eva asked, frowning.

"It could be. We should have a look over there. You never know what those clowns are up to. Eva, maybe later, you and I can go look at their dump and take a sample. I'll show you the types of molds and fungus that exist on the old wood and in the leaf matter and soil. It'll be an educational opportunity."

"Oh great, I'm looking forward to it," she said. Finally, her work in the park was focusing on nature and environmental studies. She might get to have more time with Curtis and get to know him better.

When she looked up, she saw a look of approval in Curtis's eyes. She felt a special excitement that went beyond the mundane work of the park. She was happy now. Her life was taking on some greater meaning and direction.

The work of invasive weed removal sent Eva to the library the next day to look for more books on plants. She was astonished to find that so much of what she saw growing everywhere around her was actually not from the Americas, but from every other part of the world. Clearly, immigration and global trade had brought a diversity of people and plants together on the land that made up this park. Why were they now removing the "invasive" plants?" Were the native flora so helpless against the intruders? Eva began to think it might just take a college degree to figure this all out.

Tuesday, when Eva was again back at work on foot patrol, she saw Curtis driving down Freedom Way.

He yelled at her from the window of the truck, "Eva, I just got the official assignment from the state. We're going to do a thorough study of the plant life on the new land. Come with me now. I have all the equipment we need in the back of the truck."

Eva let out a cheer and ran to the truck.

"This is great. This will be fun." She yelled as she climbed into the cab of the truck. "Maybe we can find rare plants or even new species. It will be like a treasure hunt."

They headed off down Freedom Way and soon arrived at the entrance of the newly acquired land. They slipped through the gap in the fence, bringing with them notepads, magnifying glasses and several books to aide them in plant identification. Curtis also brought a small case in which to put samples of plants to take back for further research.

"I want to be sure to get a sampling of the pine needles with the mold on them," he said.

"Oh yes," Eva replied, "Let me show you where they were."

Eva led the way and soon Curtis was snipping some of the pine needles from the branches and putting them into small glass jars. He labeled them and put them into a bigger plastic case. He looked over at Eva, "Now, we need to work up a procedure so that we don't miss anything on this land."

Curtis explained the method they would use in assessing the area. Then he took twine and stakes along with hammers and measuring tapes out of the truck and put them on the ground.

"We're going to mark this as our first study area," he said.

Soon they were walking back and forth, making a grid with the twine and stakes. After they built the grid, they bent down to look with their magnifying glasses at each plant, from stem to leaf. They marked any plant of interest in their notes.

Eva paused from time to time to look around at the birds. She was delighted that she was now authorized to come into this area to work. This would give her a daily opportunity to watch for the yellow-crowned night heron. She decided she would keep her small camera on her at all times on the chance she would get an opportunity to photograph the endangered bird.

They worked diligently for several hours. When the sun reached the treetops on the other side of the field, they decided they needed to end their work for the day.

"This is going to be a long-term project," Curtis said, wiping the sweat from his forehead.

Eva nodded and smiled.

They gathered their tools and kits and climbed back into the truck. The truck rolled along fast and strong, like a motorized Clydesdale horse, trudging through potholes and climbing over mounds of gravel until they reached the maintenance garage.

"You can sign out here," Curtis said, handing her the time sheet. "From now on, when you start in the morning, come here, get these tools and head out for the grid. I'm going to bring a few other summer helpers in so that we can get the grids done quickly. Then we can concentrate on the plant survey."

"Ok, great, working in the morning on this will be interesting," Eva said. It couldn't have worked out better. Now assigned to be there every morning, she could watch for the endangered bird.

"In the afternoon, you can go back to helping the tourists," Curtis advised her.

Eva laughed, at least part of her day she would be learning more about nature.

Chapter Twelve

Survival Strategies

The Saturday afternoon meeting of the Friends of Nature was again held at the Hungry Fish Restaurant. As loyal residents of the state of New Jersey, the group decided to support their local agriculture by eating blueberry pie.

Amanda watched patiently as Eva's sister Judi moved back and forth between the tables, taking orders from the restaurant's other patrons. Soon she came to the big round table where the Friends were seated.

"So you guys want the blueberry pie today? Let me bring a couple of pies to your table."

"That sounds great," Amanda said.

The Friends watched as Judi placed the pies, pie plates and utensils on the table.

Amanda stood over one of the pies with a knife in her hand. "How big should I make the slices?"

"Big," Colleen said.

"Is this a good size slice?" Amanda asked as she began carving out slices and putting them on the plates.

"Just right," Curtis said. He had come to the meeting with a preliminary report on the plant survey.

Colleen handed the plates of pie around the table.

Once all the pie was distributed, Amanda sat down to eat her own slice. She marveled at the deep blue color of the berries. She had read just recently that blueberries were good for improving your memory. It was nice that something as fun as blueberry pie could also be healthy.

Gary Russo left his pie waiting on his plate while he lifted up the agenda. He looked at it then looked around the room. "Now, I'll give my report."

"Please do," Amanda said, as she dunked her tea bag in her cup.

"What we have to understand is: this land is not pristine. It is not in a truly natural condition. This land was ravaged by industry. The fact that nature has tried to retake it is only what nature does in the environment every day after natural storms, fires and floods. We can undo the damage done by industry. We can turn this land into the wonderful things that human and wildlife communities need."

"So, Gary, are you saying that a lot of the land is going to be removed? Are you saying that we will see a lot of destruction before it is restored?" Amanda paused for only a second, "I found out that plants can decontaminate the soil. If that is the case, it wouldn't be necessary to destroy so much, would it?"

"That's only a possibility. They haven't used plants on a large scale to prove that it really works that well. Besides, some of the toxins are so great in some areas that it would take plants too long to detoxify the soil. We need to give nature a little help in processing these heavy metals. What I'm doing is preparing you for the changes that may occur. Even with our plan, there will be some destruction. Curtis has given us a preliminary report." Gary nodded toward Curtis who nodded back. Then Gary continued, "There are no endangered plants on the land. Truthfully, I didn't expect any."

Amanda looked at Gary and then around the room to see Eva's response. Eva looked up at Amanda with big sad eyes that showed her disappointment.

Amanda did not like what Gary was saying. Was he slowly bringing them to accept digging up most of the land and hauling it away?

Gary continued, "We can work on the land, section by section, year by year. This will allow the wild birds and animals to have enough time to move into the improved sections while we work on the contaminated areas."

Again Amanda looked over at Eva, hoping that Eva was not losing faith in their plans to protect the land.

"But Gary, can't we do more research?" Amanda pleaded. "We need to find which plants are detoxifying the soil. It may already be happening so we won't need to remediate to that extreme."

Ed Wilson, the unemployed steelworker, raised his hand and Gary called on him to speak.

"I'm a new member of the Friends of Nature and I'll tell you why I'm here. I know that land was soaked in poison. I'm here to make sure no one glosses over that fact." He looked hard at Amanda and she felt him accuse her of weakening on the issue of remediation. He leaned forward in his chair and began hammering her with his words.

"Serious work needs to be done to clean up the mess. No offense, madam, but it's ridiculous to think that weeds will do the best job. Just the same, I'm not here to fight with you. I'm here because I know that the Foundation will try very hard to convince everyone that the toxins aren't really so bad. They will do this so they can move forward with their plans. Corporations are powerful and they use the media to manipulate people's thoughts."

Amanda laid her fork down. She felt like she was being overruled. Was she sitting in a meeting that was going to favor total excavation of the new land? Could this be happening? She was in no mood now to eat, not even blueberry pie.

Ed Wilson shuffled his feet and leaned back in his chair. "In the labor movement, we've been fighting these dogs for a long time. I'll tell you what they'll do. They pit different factions of your community against each other: young against old, one nationality against another. Like here, you've got a potential split. The real sports enthusiasts are going to want the whole thing turned into ball fields while the nature buffs, as you know from Mr. Murphy's opposition, are going to resist all change. The company will work that split every which way to make a mess of you and cause all of you to fail."

The members listened and looked at each other. Ed lifted his fork, finished off his blueberry pie and then sipped some coffee.

"Ok, so we have to face the fact that some of the land may need to be thoroughly remediated," Amanda conceded, wondering what Murphy would be saying now. She could hear his doubts about the reliability of the Friends of Nature. In her mind, he was screaming, "The Friends will let the state dig the whole place up and destroy it."

Luckily, Murphy was not in the room. Again, he was refusing to come to the meetings.

Amanda needed time. She could not let them sit here and vote to excavate the park. Besides, there was a more pressing problem.

"Now, Friends, we have many issues to contend with" Amanda said to the group. "It worries me that we aren't doing enough to secure our right to carry out our plan. Were you there on Earth Day? I watched the program of the B & L Foundation. It looked like the audience loved what the Foundation was promising. They were promising a hotel, a sports complex, and a big glass box which they called a botanical garden."

"Ah see, your sports people will move right over to B & L's side," Ed warned.

Amanda looked around the room before continuing. "We need stronger tactics, I don't think the Friends of Nature are fighting back hard enough." She dropped her shoulders in apology. "I don't mean to be critical, but . . ."

She heard her own voice sounding whiny and depressed. It wasn't the sound she wanted to have. She wanted to come to this meeting with conviction and hope to move them to do the best they could. She looked down at the draft of a petition she held in her hands. She sat up in her chair, pulled her shoulders back and looked around at the faces circling the table.

"Colleen and I have a petition we created. We think it is important to show that the majority of the people are really in favor of some simple recreation, like a ball field and nature trails in a restored wildlife habitat." She handed the petition to Gary.

Gary took it and looked it over. "Yeah, this is good. There's another public meeting coming up at the end of the summer and we can present the government with hundreds of signed petitions." Gary passed the petition around for everyone to see. "But it's a lot of work," he added, "and I hope you are ready for it. Do you all agree that this is the next tactic we should use?"

Ed Wilson nodded in support, "This should help unify people without going to extremes." He looked at the others, "We can use the petition campaign to find out what people really do want. We can educate them about the issues. We can get their support for this up-coming meeting with the government."

The Friends of Nature took a quick vote and the petition campaign was approved.

"Good work," Gary said. "Amanda, you are in charge of coordinating our efforts on this. I will be busy working on our vision of what can be done and getting our experts lined up to speak at the government hearing. Curtis Elliot will continue to work on the biological assessments."

Curtis nodded and Eva smiled.

Gary ticked off several other items on his list before continuing. "We need to get a financial advisor. I believe that our plan is the most economical way to go with this project. The state is a little short of funds right now. That might make it easier for our view to win. Wildlife areas don't take a lot of expensive building and management. The park already has the equipment to maintain a couple of ball fields."

Everyone nodded in agreement—except Amanda. She had doubts. She spoke up, "But Gary, wouldn't the state be persuaded by the extra tax dollars coming from B & L Foundation's plan?"

"Amanda, I'm glad you see the problem clearly. Can you research and find us an economic expert of some kind? I'll be at an environmental conference next week and won't be able to make the phone calls."

"Yes, of course." Amanda said. First, she was drafted into coordinating the petition campaign and now she had to find a financial expert. She thought of the stipend they were paying her. Since they needed her so much, maybe this was the time to ask for a raise.

"So, we've reached the end of our agenda. Any new business?" Gary asked and looked around the room. "Ok, so we have a new petition campaign. I expect our campaign committee will meet after this meeting, yes?"

Amanda and Colleen nodded in agreement. Eva winked at Judi who was now seated across the room filling saltshakers.

Some of the Friends got up from the table and left the restaurant while a few stayed for further discussion. Among those who stayed was Ed Wilson.

"I've worked on a lot of petition campaigns for the union," he explained, "so I'm staying to give my effort and advice."

Amanda smiled politely. "We're glad to have you on the committee, Ed. And don't worry; I'm for whatever it takes to make the land safe for humans and wildlife."

"I'm sure you are," Ed responded. "It's just that I know it's going to take a lot of work. That land is a mess."

"Don't worry about it too much, Amanda," Colleen said, "I grew up on a farm and I know the trees and shrubs will grow back in a short time. Besides, after they dig up the toxic soil, they can put in a pond. That will draw all kinds of wildlife."

Amanda knew what Colleen was saying was true. Nature re-grows. She still didn't want to see so much destruction of the sanctuary they had just toured. She decided she would resist the remediation plan Gary offered to them. But, for now, she pushed her doubts aside and focused on the petition campaign agenda.

The most dedicated among them sat down again at the table to begin the petition campaign meeting. They discussed in detail where to print the petitions and where to go to gather the signatures. At last, they were ready to meet the people.

On Tuesday morning, Amanda was just finishing breakfast when the phone rang.

"Gary, what's happening?"

"Amanda, I need your help again. We just heard that the Foundation is holding a luncheon at Barnaby's on the Waterfront. They're inviting big heads of industry and many politicians to wine and dine. We've got to get noisy to get our message into the press. Can you come to a press conference and speak as the Friends of Nature? You can announce that you are the coordinator of our petition campaign."

Amanda had done press conferences in the past—back when she was wrapping herself around a big sycamore tree to keep the city from cutting them down—but she had never played the role of spokesperson for a campaign. She thought of her promise to Stephanie to do whatever she could.

"Sure, I'll do it," she told Gary.

"I knew I could count on you," he said. His voice rolled on with the details. "The press conference is going to be next week on the plaza next to Barnaby's on the Waterfront. I'm applying for a permit to hold a rally. Colleen will put out an email encouraging every member of the Friends who could possibly be there to attend."

When Gary finished the call, Amanda felt overwhelmed. She went to her daughter's room.

"On my dear, you see what I'm doing now? Where does it stop? Oh goodness, I've got to figure out what to wear. What does a radical activist look like anyway? I guess I'll just go looking like myself. I'll put on that same old gray suit that I always wear."

Two days before the press conference, Colleen and Amanda decided it would be a good idea to get out and begin the petition campaign. Having some signed petitions in hand, to wave around before the cameras, would give them confidence. They met in the park to gather signatures.

It was difficult work. First, they had to overcome their own inertia—that desire not to move out of your normal range of everyday activities. Then they had to overcome a sense of shyness about walking up to strangers. Repeatedly, they veered away, worried that a certain person may be hostile to their efforts. A few people would sign without enthusiasm, and some signed because they made it a practice to sign petitions. Others listened to the explanation and walked away disinterested.

Getting signatures on petitions was tiresome work. Amanda began to look forward to the excitement that would occur on the day of the press conference.

When that day came, Gary Russo gave her a ride in his economy-car to the plaza where the press conference was being held. They met Raj and Nikunj who had set up the sound equipment and podium for the event. Television cameras were poised across from the podium ready to broadcast Amanda's comments around the world.

A crowd of supporters gathered around them.

Gary gave the explanations and introductions. Then Amanda was on her own.

"We are here today to represent the people of our community. We know that many wish they had a nature area where they could take their children to study and enjoy nature. We also know that there is a desire for ball fields and flower gardens. This is what we are fighting for."

A strong wind blew in from the harbor forcing Amanda to grab her long brown neck scarf to keep it out of her face.

"Why should we have to fight so hard for what the community needs? It just goes to show you how unfair this struggle is. This parkland should belong to the common people for us to enjoy. But inside, at Barnaby's Restaurant, the big corporations are scheming to take our new park land away . . . ."

Words poured out of her and continued to pour. For a moment, she felt as if she could not find her way to the end of her own speech. She needed to round it up nicely. Was that the governor over there? Was that the mayor?

"That is why we are doing a petition campaign. So please sign our petition and show that you want a park for the people not for corporate profit-taking and greed." Finally, the words stopped pouring out of her.

Colleen pushed through the crowd handing out pens and petitions. "Be sure to take some extra copies of the petition. Get your friends to sign," she advised.

A small crowd, made up mostly of the Friends of Nature, cheered at Amanda's speech. The television cameras zoomed in and then backed away, as if driven back by her powerful pronouncements. Reporters pushed forward with microphones in their hands as if to attack her. "Can you just step over here for a minute; we'd like a quick interview with you."

One interview after another, Amanda blabbered away, wondering sometimes what she was saying. Were her words really helping the campaign? The media was so tricky with their questions. After several interviews, she resorted to just repeating herself. Finally, Gary grabbed her by the arm and led her back to his car.

"You did a great job, Amanda, now let's go home and watch the television and see what happened."

That night, Amanda was so exhausted; she didn't even look at the television. She sat silently in her daughter's room and looked out the window at the blooming purple iris and lavender phlox in the backyard.

The next day she woke up feeling surprisingly like the person she had always been. She fixed two scrambled eggs with some breakfast sausage and two slices of whole-wheat toast. Her mind drifted out to distant farms in the Midwest where chickens were clucking over lost eggs and pigs were giving birth to new piglets that would soon become sausage. Amanda laughed at herself. That crazy farm girl, Colleen, was certainly an influence.

Amanda drank her usual cup of tea—wondering about the tea-pickers in India, and then she headed out to the backyard to survey what she would plant and where she would plant it in the space that had been Stephanie's flower garden. On the borders of the flowerbed were tulips blooming bright red and yellow. She had planted them last fall. The special bulbs were shipped to her directly from Holland.

She could hear her phone ringing in her pocket. She answered it.

"Did you see the news last night?" Colleen asked.

"No dear, I was so exhausted from the stress of it. What are they saying?"

"They had a headline that said, "Local Environmentalist Opposes Fun in the Park""

"What?"

"They are telling the story as if you were a crabby old lady who opposes all the wonderful things that the Foundation is promising to put on that parkland."

Amanda was shocked. She wanted to hide. How was she going to survive this distortion of her words and her dreams for the park? How could they take her honest message and twist it so much that it looked like she was opposed to what the people really wanted?

After she finished the call with Colleen, Amanda no longer felt like working in the garden. She needed to think and she always did this best in her daughter's room.

She put away the gardening tools and washed her hands. Up the stairs she went with another cup of tea.

"My dear, you see where I'm at now? The entire town knows me and they know me as a crazy old woman who wants to stop them from having fun. I have always cared about children and nature. I have always done what I could do to carry out your dreams, my dear. You see what kind of trouble it gets me into? But I made a promise to you. I will take all risks."

She looked around at the pictures in the room.

"Why do we always feel so helpless in this society? I feel like I've just been knocked down again. I need to stand up. I need to push forward. But what can I do? That media is twisting my words. I hate that. They are deliberately twisting my words—just so the Foundation will get what it wants."

She moved to the window and looked down at the garden where she had been hoping to plant that morning. This life as a rebel was now disrupting her normal life.

"I should just call them up and insist on an interview. I wonder if I talked more, if I could explain to them what we of the Friends of Nature are really trying to do here." She sat quietly and thought.

The house was still. Then a wind came and she could hear the eaves creak. Outside the window, she saw the weeping willow trees swaying in the breeze.

"I'll call them up now and tell them I'm coming in to their office for an interview. I'm not afraid of them." She called and got an appointment.

The next day, she put on her gray suit, only this time she decided to give it some flare. She'd wear that bright pink flower-print scarf. As she browsed her closet, she thought back to her more radical days. She and Murphy were tying themselves to a tree on Main Street. Somewhere high up on the trunk of the tree, a heart had been carved into the tree's bark with the initials of two young lovers, D.M. + A.W. Their relationship had never formed a marriage, but they were partners in protest. And how did it all end? Amanda remembered. The Judge ruled in their favor. The trees continued to grace the avenue. The issue faded away.

Now dressed in her gray suit with a bright pink neck scarf, and her black purse on her arm, Amanda left home and soon arrived in the lobby of Media America, Inc. The marquee indicated on which floor the office was located. She entered the elevator. On the ride up, she prepared herself for the explanations she would give them. Then the elevator doors opened.

She introduced herself. The receptionist looked to see which reporter was assigned to follow that story.

"Mirabelle is the reporter on that. Let me see if she is in."

Within minutes, Mirabelle came out to greet Amanda. She was a small woman with possibly a Philippine background.

"Hello Amanda, I'm so glad you decided to stop in. Can we have a little talk? I'd like to do an interview."

Amanda was pleased. They went to a conference room and Mirabelle prepared to record the conversation while a man named Paul moved about Amanda taking pictures of her.

"I came here to let you know I did not like the headlines in your media coverage. I am not opposed to people having fun in the park."

Mirabelle laughed, "Oh well, we just do that to catch people's attention. Don't worry about that. Now, tell me, why are you involved in this issue? What are you most concerned about?"

"I'm concerned about the children in our community. They need to experience nature or they will grow up not knowing how to value our Mother Earth. We must take care of the park; in a small way, it is like taking care of the whole earth. You know how it is, if you give a child a puppy, they will learn how to be responsible. Well, as I see it, if we teach the children of this community to take care of nature in the park, they will learn to care for the planet they live on."

"Oh I see, well, that's an interesting angle. And you don't believe that a sports complex or a botanical garden will educate children?"

"I, well, I think we have enough of that sort of thing in our area. We need nature, open space, time to drift and think in the natural world. Our community is deficient. We are so built up that we need green places for children to play and for old people, too. Older people need the parks as a place to go to enjoy nature, go fishing, take walks and appreciate the gardens."

"So you think this is more of an asset to the community than corporate development?" Mirabelle asked, but before Amanda could answer, Mirabelle continued, "Now, as I understand it, the B & L Foundation gave the land to the Park Service. Don't you think they should have a voice in how the land should be handled?"

"If they owned the land, they could have developed it in whatever way they wanted. Instead, they gave the land to the park. The park is the people's land."

"Oh I see, the Commons, like in ancient Europe, the land given to the poor commoners."

Amanda stopped and looked at Mirabelle. How could a young working woman be so unsympathetic toward the restoration of nature in her community? It seemed Mirabelle's thinking was exactly like Barbara Harrison's.

"Look, all I know is that we need nature and parks for a happy community."

"Well, of course," Mirabelle said.

Amanda realized this was the time to discuss the petition campaign.

"That's why we are circulating a petition."

Mirabelle looked at the petition and then made some notes. Suddenly she stood and extended her hand. "I wish I could spend more time with you, Mrs. Walters. Let me thank you for coming in today."

The interview was over. Just like that.

Amanda was standing on the street again. Automobiles whizzed past her. Busses roared by and spewed fumes into the air. Amanda did not have a sense of victory or accomplishment. All she could do was wonder how the media would twist her words this time.

When evening came, she tuned on the news. The local media quoted her, especially the words about saving the park and how it was like saving the earth. There was a picture, too, of Amanda looking anxious but sincere.

Unfortunately, the next story was on the B & L Foundation's response. There was Barbara Harrison, looking sophisticated and professional. Her highly polished comments in defense of what the Foundation planned to do for the park made Amanda's words look emotional and silly.

Still, the effect the interview had on the people was incredible. The professional images of the Foundation did not persuade very many. When Amanda, Colleen and her daughters went petitioning in the park, people came forward on their own to sign the petitions. They laid down their spatulas in the middle of grilling their meat to put their names on the simple sheet of paper that they hoped would mean so much more. They stopped their cars and climbed out to sign. They quieted babies in carriages long enough to put their signatures on the line.

Amanda felt rewarded for her trip to the media office. Whether the petitions would really be accepted by the state or heralded by the media, it didn't matter. The response from the people was giving the Friends of Nature the hope and strength to continue their battle.

Chapter Thirteen

Bluebird Trail

Outside the rain was coming down hard. Eva was glad that today she had been assigned to work in the park office. She was sitting at the computer now entering data that they had collected from the plant identification project. While she was there, Curtis came in. He leaned against the doorpost and, for a moment, watched her nimble fingers typing the names of plants and their GPS location into the database.

"Eva, we have a big event coming up at the park this Saturday."

Eva stopped typing and looked up at Curtis, "What's the big event?"

"The Scouts are coming to hang their bird houses. It's an annual event. Every winter the Boy Scouts make about fifty birdhouses. In summer, both Boy and Girl Scouts come to the park to hang them up. This year they want to create a bluebird trail. They'll be putting up special bird houses designed especially for bluebirds. The tree swallows like to use the boxes too."

"Oh that's great," Eva said. "I love scouts and bluebirds."

Curtis smiled at Eva and added, "I have the Hungry Fish donating some snacks and beverages at a hospitality table for the parents and scouts when they arrive at the nature center."

Eva looked up at Curtis. Would her sister be there this Saturday? Eva suddenly felt uncomfortable. Working at the park was Eva's special world away from her family where she could demonstrate her skills and talents. She did not want Judi around passing judgment on everything she did and said. Eva loved her sister, but, at times, she hated her too.

Judi was opinionated at home, but once in the public eye, she had a bubbly personality with the social grace that Eva lacked.

When Eva got home that evening, the talk at the Kaufman supper table confirmed that Judi would be in the park Saturday staffing a table.

"Eva, why are you looking so glum," Colleen asked after dinner.

Eva just shrugged. She did not want to admit that this would be one day on her dream job that she dreaded.

Saturday morning, Eva and Judi took the train together. Eva looked out the window as Judi chattered.

"I don't usually work this early," Judi said. "How do you get up so early? I like my late hours. I get there at mid-morning and start serving lunch."

"I like the early morning; that's when the birds sing," Eva said. How had Judi not realized that after all this time? When the train arrived at their stop, Judi walked to the Hungry Fish Restaurant. Eva walked to the nature center.

As Eva approached, she saw Curtis talking to some of the scout leaders. An army of boys and girls dressed in uniforms were running around, full of excitement about the project and the wonderful things they were about to achieve. It brought back fond memories to Eva of her days in scouting. She wrapped herself up in this good feeling and jumped into her day.

Today, they would do their best to prevent the extinction of another of the earth's treasures. The bluebirds had been having a rough time finding nesting places. Unfortunately, during the 1900s, the old forests with their hollow tree branches had been cut down to clear the land for farming. The use of agricultural pesticides poisoned the bird's food. The bluebirds needed positive human intervention to restore them. The scouts had done their part by building the boxes. Now it was time to place the nest boxes in the wild.

Eva watched from inside the nature center as a truck from the Hungry Fish dropped off a table, supplies, coffee canteens and her sister, Judi. Some park employees helped Judi set up the table near the door of the nature center. Eva continued to watch as Judi began putting out the snack packs, jugs of juice and packets of tea bags. Park workers put the large coffee canteens on the table. Judi placed several stacks of paper cups with the logo of the Hungry Fish next to the coffee. Eva was amazed to see Judi so engrossed in her task. All this dedication to the Hungry Fish Restaurant. Eva laughed. They really needed to do something about that restaurant's name.

No longer busy, Judi looked up. Eva waved at her from the window. Then Eva saw Curtis come down the path behind Judi. Eva left the window and went out of the nature center. Outside the door, Eva glanced cautiously over at her supervisor, Curtis, to see if he might need her for any immediate assignment. Fortunately, he was sidetracked by a troop leader, so Eva joined her sister.

"I met Curtis when he came to the restaurant asking for a donation," Judi whispered into Eva's ear. "I introduced myself as your sister. He's your boss, right? Isn't he the one at the meeting who made the plant report?"

"Oh, yes, you've seen him at the meetings," Eva said. She looked over the table to see what kinds of treats were offered.

"He's nice. He's a supervisor. I rate him as a good catch, especially for a young woman hoping to get into the Park Service."

Eva grimaced. "Don't start, sister, please."

It was unfortunate, but Eva knew the contest had already started. She was standing there in her staid park uniform looking rather plain. Not even a ribbon in her hair. In contrast, Judi had her blonde hair up in braids that wrapped around her head like a golden crown. A touch of eye make-up and lipstick displayed her feminine ways. Eva felt a rush of jealousy that Curtis might find Judi appealing.

"The Hungry Fish has certainly given you a nice supply of snacks and drinks," Eva said. She quickly reached for a cup and made herself some tea.

"Oh, there you are, Eva," said Curtis. He had left the troop leader and was now standing at the table. "I met your sister here. She's very nice." Curtis turned to Judi, "Thank you for coming to staff the table. I'm glad that the Hungry Fish was willing to donate the goodies. We really appreciate it. Now, the scout moms don't have to do it."

Eva smiled at Curtis and Judi, but her nerves were tingling. Was she imagining it or was Curtis practically drooling over Judi? Eva took a deep breath.

Curtis turned now to the crowd and raised his hands into the air. "Scouts, volunteers, help yourselves to the refreshments here.

Meantime, I'm going to give you an education about the park and this project."

Curtis walked away from the table and jumped up on the steps that led into the nature center, giving himself greater height over the small crowd.

"It's projects like this that bring our community together to share . . . ." on he went. Eva stepped behind the table to assist Judi as more and more scouts and parents came to the table to gather their packet of treats.

"He's really nice, you should consider him," Judi whispered into Eva's ear.

"Not now," Eva whispered back.

"It looks like he's the head man in this project, he'd be a good catch," Judi whispered again. "I'm impressed."

Eva was glad that Judi was impressed, but she still did not feel like there was any substance to Judi's suggestions. Eva did not want to make a fool of herself. Curtis had not shown any special interest in her. Sure, they had been working together on the plant project for several weeks, but that was just part of the job.

"Curtis is my supervisor," Eva said, "I wouldn't dare do . . . ."

"He's cute enough, seems to have a very friendly disposition," Judi said smiling at her sister. "And you wouldn't need to spend money on beauty supplies."

"Oh, now you're being sarcastic," Eva said. She opened up another box of coffee cups.

Why had Curtis turned to the Hungry Fish for the hospitality table? Eva was beginning to feel like there were types of people in everyone's life that just did not mix well and should never be brought together.

"Ok, everyone," Curtis announced, "we're going to head out now and take these bird nest boxes to the location. Sam? You push the wheelbarrow with the tools and birdhouses. Sally, you bring that bag of plastic straps."

"Troops lineup," a scout leader called. Unruly children and teens scurried to place themselves into a line. They marched out with six seasonal park workers behind them.

Eva walked along looking ahead at the wheelbarrow full of finely constructed boxes. They had the proper sized, oval-shaped holes to keep other more aggressive birds out. Since bluebirds stayed all winter in New Jersey, they might also use the nest boxes to hide from severe winter winds. Focusing on the task gave Eva some relief. She looked back down the trail at her sister who stayed to restock the table.

When the volunteers arrived at the trail where they had planned to post the boxes, everyone cheered.

A scout leader stood at attention, saluted the troops, and then gave them his assessment.

"See this habitat. It's perfect. Bluebirds like meadows with some trees. Look over there, plenty of berry bushes. Bluebirds time their nest building so that the berries are ripe just as the chicks are hatching. Did you know that?" he asked the scouts and then looked over at Eva.

"Did you know that tree swallows also use bluebird nest boxes? As a matter of fact, the two birds are compatible. The tree swallows will act to protect the bluebirds from predators."

Eva smiled at him. "I know that. I learned about birds when I was a scout."

The troop leader looked at Eva and smiled. His eyes looked deep into hers and she laughed.

"And now, look where she's at: working here in the park." He lifted his hand and pointed Eva out to the scouts. They looked at Eva with pride.

Eva smiled and watched the troop leader continue his lecture. As he spoke, he looked to the scouts and then he looked at her. He looked her up and down, smiling at the crisp park uniform that she wore. He nodded in approval.

Being so noticed by him, Eva found herself assessing him. He, too, looked neat in his scout uniform. She thought his age to be about twenty-one.

As he spoke, he turned and looked over his shoulder where he saw a young scout climbing a tree. "William, oh no, Teddy, get William, tell him he'll miss the bird project if he climbs into that tree."

The troop leader turned back to Eva and said, "These scouts, I try to use persuasion rather than yelling at them all the time. It really keeps me alert trying to out-think them."

Eva laughed and nodded in agreement. He did not show anger or bark orders, but coaxed the child out of the tree. He had just the right attitude, Eva thought. It was clear he liked working with the young scouts. Eva watched him with growing curiosity.

"Eva, bring those bird boxes over here. Clarisse and Marta are going to take a group of girls and go down that way," Curtis commanded.

Eva looked up and blinked. She had forgotten about Curtis. She quickly loosened the boxes and handed them out to the Girls Scouts. The Boy Scouts grabbed hammers and started mending the fences and posts where the bird boxes would be attached. Eva watched as the boys and girls dashed about lifting, fitting, strapping and nailing the nest boxes into place.

It was a beautiful day, sunny and clear. The temperature was perfect. Eva looked around. There were some girls standing to the side, completely uninvolved.

"I guess you aren't interested in the bird box project," Eva asked.

"I'm just here 'cause my mom said I have to be," one girl declared. The others remained silent.

Eva thought of all the activities the park offered. She wanted to see what would spark an interest in them. They were quite a bit like her sister Judi. What would Judi like?

"Do you like flowers?" Eva asked.

The girls hesitantly nodded.

"Good, we have a Saturday morning gardening project. Would you like to sign up for that?"

The girls nodded again, but still not with as much enthusiasm as Eva hoped to see. She got a clipboard and handed it to them to sign.

"I don't like bugs," one girl stated.

"Oh, you don't have to worry, the bugs are not dangerous," Eva reassured her. After each girl had signed, Eva took the board and submitted the names to Curtis. "I have some potential gardening volunteer," she said.

"Good job, Eva," Curtis said. He tucked the information into his duffle bag.

After all the bird boxes were placed on the wooden park fence posts along the trail, the scouts stood back and admired their work. The troop leader called them to attention.

"Good work, scouts. You can be proud of yourselves. You did a great job."

The scouts cheered.

"Now, in case you don't know it," he looked at Eva, "my name is Matt Merriweather. You won't forget that name, will you?" He laughed. The scouts all laughed. "I have to say, we've done a fine job here today. Look what we've accomplished. These bluebirds will get years of use out of these bird nest boxes. As scouts, we can now begin our nature-science study. We will be monitoring the nest boxes next spring to see how many are used and if nesting was successful."

Eva saw the happy scouts looking up at their leader. He swayed back and forth, lifting his hands in the air, making jokes and showering the scouts with compliments. They loved him for it. Eva could see their shoulders and heads lift in confidence. This, she told herself, is how a teacher ought to relate to students. She made a note of it and decided that she needed to learn how to do this so that she, too, could inspire students and scouts with nature study.

Tired now, the group gathered their tools and tossed them into the wheelbarrows and headed back to the nature center.

Judi was still there ready to hand out more cups of coffee, juice and snacks. Parents arrived and were greeted by their happy children.

Eva felt relieved. So far, the day had gone well. Maybe that was because she had left Judi behind at the table.

"Let me help you clean up, Sis," Eva said.

Judi's attention was distracted. "Well, well, look at this," Judi said and nodded toward Curtis.

Curtis was having a very energetic conversation with a woman who was about his own age. She had a pretty face, with bright eyes. She fluttered her extra-long eyelashes. Her lips and fingernails were bright pink. She wore a pretty, clingy dress that accented her shape.

Eva looked at her, but quickly turned away. It didn't really matter. She felt Judi's finger poke her in the ribs.

"Don't worry about it," Eva said, "It's nothing. He's friendly to everyone. This woman may have donated money to the park, or her children may come often to park events. Please, let's just get the table cleaned."

"Don't worry about it? Aren't you crazy, you have competition big time here and you're just going to turn your back?" Judi asked.

"I didn't say I was interested in Curtis. You were assuming," Eva whispered. "He and I are just fellow employees at the park. Quit making it into something else."

"My sister is being made a fool of and she's not going to do anything about it. Amazing," Judi responded.

"It's not amazing," Eva said. "It's nothing. Just stay out of this."

Eva gave Judi a stern look. Why had fate put the two of them together on this day? Thankfully, the event was almost over. Maybe they could end the day successfully.

"I'm going to find out who that woman is," Judi said. "We need to know, so you can be sure what you are up against."

"Forget it," Eva said firmly. She turned and looked up. She saw Matt Merriweather standing nearby. When he smiled at Eva, she felt like a balloon lifting in the air. She turned and looked at Judi. Judi was glancing back and forth between Curtis and Matt. Confusion filled her face. Eva laughed.

"What? Oh, maybe it's not Curtis," Judi whispered.

Eva felt triumphant; she had her sister caught in a dilemma.

Judi looked at Eva and then boldly walked up to Matt. Without hesitation, she turned on her charm.

Panic swelled up in Eva. What was Judi up to now? Would she try to steal Matt away? Eva trembled; she felt she was in serious trouble. Here was a brief acquaintance, one she hoped she might meet again. But now, Eva's chances could be ruined **by her own sister**. Judi had done it before, swept boyfriends and even girlfriends away from Eva, leaving her floundering in a windless sea of shyness.

Eva fumed. When would she ever make friends without the intervention and destruction brought by Judi and her fast-talking charm?

"Well, a man in uniform. You are certainly likely to impress any woman," Judi said. She was now wiggling, all sexy-like, and it was making Eva sick. Eva watched to see how this dance was affecting her troop leader. He stepped forward and engaged in the conversation. Eva knew she was losing her chance. It was happening again. She walked over and stood next to Judi.

"We did some good work countering the destruction humanity has done to bluebird habitat. Why didn't you come out with us?" Matt asked.

"Me, ah, well, someone had to stay here and maintain the provisions," Judi replied.

"My sister was never one for scouting or appreciating nature," Eva injected. She looked at her sister with disdain. Her expression carried the message to her new scout friend and he laughed.

"Oh, she's your sister? That explains a lot," Matt said.

"Would you like a cup of coffee?" Judi asked.

Eva's mind raced, she had to come up with something better than coffee that would steer Matt in her direction. What could it be? Oh, a park event, but which event?

"Have you heard of the Friends of Nature?" Eva asked Matt.

He held his coffee cup with the Hungry Fish logo on the side and looked at Eva.

"We're trying to save the new land that was donated to the park. We want to preserve it as a bird sanctuary."

"You're involved in that? Great. I've been looking for a way to get the scouts involved on issues rather than just projects. But I've been wondering, this land donation seems to be getting very political."

Eva read caution in the tone of his voice. It worried her that he might not want to associate with her. Maybe the conflict over the parkland's future was too controversial for scouts.

"I've helped with the research. We're documenting the plants in that area. I'm also watching to see if there are any endangered birds nesting there too."

"Really? That sounds like an interesting project to be involved in."

"Yes, I really love the work I do in the park."

"Oh, the park's politics are so confusing," Judi whined. "As a troop leader, you might want to stay out of it." She looked at Eva and laughed. Then she turned to Matt, "How would you like to have a parent-child awards dinner?"

Eva huffed. Now it was clear. Judi was using her charm to drum up business for the Hungry Fish. Eva saw Matt look at Judi with interest.

"At the Hungry Fish Restaurant, we could set up a buffet with your choice of entrees and dessert. The price would be reasonable and it would give scout families an opportunity to share their experiences. You could do it as a fund-raiser as well."

Judi paused and waited for Matt's answer.

Eva still could not believe it. Judi was always hustling. If she wasn't looking for love, she was looking for loot. Eva turned to see what Matt's response would be.

"We already have a good location for our dinners," Matt explained. "But I want to know more about this parkland. I heard there could be a sports complex put there. Now, that's something the scouts would like. Scouting isn't just about nature."

Eva wondered why a scout leader would prefer a sports complex to a wildlife preserve. His interest in a sports complex was destined to put him in the enemy camp. Eva had to think quickly. What could she say? She had to pull him back toward nature. She didn't want to look negative by attacking sports. She decided to just drop it and begin talking about nature projects.

"We want to create more nature trails on that new land. They'll be great for bird watching," Eva said. "We'll need a steady supply of bird nest boxes for years to come."

Matt laughed. Eva felt better now.

Judi offered him another cup of coffee.

"Besides," Eva continued, "wouldn't a sports complex be expensive? How will scouts be able to afford to go there?"

"That's true," Matt responded. "I prefer the park as a sanctuary for birds, but I get a lot of pressure from the parents. I secretly think they hope their kids will become rich and famous sports stars. There's no big money to be made in scouting . . . or bird watching, for that matter."

"But there is plenty of money to be made in the catering business," Judi stated. "That's why I'm into it."

Her statement seemed disconnected from the issue they were discussing, but it was typical Judi.

Matt laughed at her but then looked over at Eva. They smiled at each other realizing that once again their interests were in harmony.

"I like kids, so I decided to become a teacher." Matt told Eva. "I'm doing this scouting thing, well, like you, I was a scout growing up, and now I get some credit for doing it. I put this toward my teaching experience."

Matt's explanation of himself had been so personally directed toward Eva that it gave her a sense that, maybe this time, Judi and her charm had just lost the contest.

"I'm going to college in the fall, first year." Eva said, "I just started working here in the park this summer. I want to become a naturalist. I could teach students about nature, take them on field trips. I'd like to do that."

Eva looked up at Matt. He smiled. It was a warm personal smile; again, his eyes looked deep into hers.

"Ok, it's time to wrap-up this event," Curtis said, shaking them out of their gaze. "I want to thank all of you for coming."

Eva looked around for Curtis's new woman friend, but she was gone.

A parent with two boys came up to Matt and began asking questions.

"Here comes the truck," Judi said. "Sis, help me finish cleaning up this table."

Eva went over to her and began boxing the remaining snacks.

"So it's not Curtis?" Judi whispered as she put the remaining napkins into a bag.

"No, of course not," Eva responded. She now grabbed a garbage bag out of a box and began filling it with dirty paper plates.

"You like the scout master?" Judi laughed. "Oh sister, you are getting so fast! You are really growing up."

"Fast?" Eva said. She wanted to think over the actions of the afternoon, but there was no time now. "Let's just get this place cleaned up," Eva growled.

"Help me with these empty coffee canteens," Judi commanded. "The other park workers are gone."

Eva tried to lift the canteens, but they were too awkward to grab or lift.

Matt came running up. "Here, I'll help you with those," he said and quickly lifted them into the small truck. "You're all loaded up now," Matt announced.

Judi thanked him and then climbed into the restaurant's van. "Later, Sis," she yelled, "Nice meeting you, troop leader."

Eva waved good-bye.

Eva and Matt were now standing alone together outside the nature center.

"It was a successful event," Eva said.

"It certainly was," Matt said, "Here's my phone number."

Eva nearly fainted. What a summer this was. She had once again surpassed her sister, and on her own merits.

"Yeah, here's my phone number," she said. "I'm off work in the evenings."

"I'll be sure to give you a call. Maybe we could go out to dinner."

Eva nearly lost her breath. "Oh, yes. Nice idea, as long as it's not at the Hungry Fish."

"Oh, no, we won't go there," he said. "We'll go someplace better."

Eva was delighted.

Chapter Fourteen

An Invitation to Trouble

"Did you get your invitation?"

Murphy's loud voice rang in Amanda's ears. "It seems B & L Foundation has decided to be kind to us. They are having a luncheon and I was invited."

"**You** were invited?" Amada asked. "Why would you, of all people, be invited to go to a luncheon held by the B & L Foundation? Why didn't they invite **me**?"

"I happen to be aware that others were invited too. Gary Russo, President of the Friends of Nature, was invited," Murphy stated. "Don't you ever look at your "snail mail" these days?"

Amanda began poking through the mail in the box near her kitchen door.

"Murphy, it's usually junk or advertisements. You know I can't spend a lot of money."

Amanda continued sorting until she found something that looked like a formal invitation, an envelope made of fancy paper. She tore it open. A small tissue paper fell to the floor.

"Ok, I was invited too. Obviously, they're inviting everyone. It's at the Riviera Restaurant. Oh, I see, we get a choice of entrees: fish, chicken, beef . . . . or vegan! How nice! Dessert, coffee and a glass of wine or beer. Oh, this is fancy. Where did they get the money for such an event?"

"I'll tell you what, I'm not going. I don't care how fancy. I won't sit there and listen to that Barbara Harrison blah, blah, blah with her big mouth going on for hours."

"Well, I know what you mean, Murphy, but when you're in a battle, you have to keep track of what your enemy is doing and saying. Well, I am torn. I don't want to look like I have any hope that Barbara and the Foundation will do good things for the park. But, I won't be able to just sit there and be polite."

Murphy sputtered and coughed. "Amanda, you will be on your feet telling them a thing or two. Trust me, I know you and I know you will be having your say."

"Then I should go. I need to know what they are doing. I need to respond."

"Well, then you've decided to go. As for me, I've decided to stay home and watch the ball game. But please, give me a call as soon as you can and let me know how it went."

Having discussed and decided what to do in regard to the invitation, they bid each other a good night.

Amanda began preparing her dinner. With a sharp knife in her hand, she needed to focus on slicing the tomatoes, but her mind drifted away again and again to ponder what to say or do at the Foundation event. Her experience with the media so far made her aware that she would need to be clear about what she was there for and how she would answer the multitude of questions that could come at her.

She suspected the reporters would ask if she were endorsing the event. She thought about what exact words she should say. She would tell them that she was always happy to attend a party and was willing to work with the Foundation, but the community's needs were her deepest concern. This way she would look like she was flexible and cooperative, but still holding out to a different plan of action. The Friends had always said they represented the real needs of the community. Then she worried she might look too flexible. Some might think she was going along completely with the Foundation's goals. What would she tell them? She thought for a little while. The tomatoes were sliced. She put them in a bowl. She would reassure them, "We need to keep to our own plan and not be swayed by what the Foundation wants to impose on us."

It would be the same; she would tell them "We want a nature area where the community can experience the passing seasons. We want a few ball fields for the youth and we want gardens for the beauty they give." She listened to her own words and felt impressed. Yes, that is what she would tell them.

It was all so simple. Why had this turned into such a battle? Why did the community have to fight so strenuously, for what it needed and wanted?

Amanda knew also that her image was important. After all, Barbara Harrison would be there dressed in her corporate best. Americans were so image conscious. If you didn't look like you had money, you had no right to an opinion. Amanda knew she needed to wear something that gave her a look of sophistication, without looking like she was too much under the corporate influence. After all, she was a tree-hugging environmentalist. What should she wear?

She went upstairs to look into her closet and assess her wardrobe. There were suits that looked too professional, from the days when she worked as a legal secretary years ago. She worried that her suits may be outdated, but then again, suits were suits, they were always plain and business-like.

Last year, she had tried to get into the new fashions with the sweaters, blouses and scarves. She could match these with some comfortable pants. After an hour of trying to decide, she sat on the bed and wondered why women spent so much time worrying about clothes. Would a man be sitting here about to cry over this? She couldn't wear the same clothes she had worn at the press conference or the media interview. She had to have something nice, the kind of thing you would wear to a luncheon, but something that would make her stand above the crowd. She also had to worry if the clothes in her closet would still fit her. She began trying on various outfits and looking at herself in the mirror.

A few hours later, after trying on six suits with a variety of scarves and blouses, she settled on the olive green suit. The jacket for this suit was not as formal, but had a scalloped collar and cuffs. She selected a print blouse decorated with the images of green leaves and yellow roses. When she stood before the mirror, she felt like she was close to a final decision, but then realized that the jacket needed some accessory, some small item to distinguish her. She remembered the broche. It was a gift from her daughter on Mother's Day. It was shaped to look like a golden leaf. That particular Mother's Day, Amanda and Stephanie had argued with each other over whether Stephanie should be allowed to take the field trip to Pennsylvania.

"But Mom, I want to see what the real forest looks like. I want to see the Appalachian Mountains. I've never seen them except in pictures. I want to know what the Hickory trees in a northern rain forest smell like. I want to see black bear, elk and eagles. I don't want to live without knowing what they are like."

Stephanie was only seventeen years old and was already considering studying biology in college. Amanda had opposed her trip.

"Why not go to north Jersey, dear? Its closer and there are the same types of black bears and Appalachian forest."

There were no alternatives. The trip that the school was offering was a take-it-or-leave it chance to go on a certain day of departure to one location. The students would be staying a week in a campground.

What an irony that Stephanie died there, one of three to die in the accident. It was as if the forest had claimed her. Amanda tallied up the time since she had lost her daughter. It was ten years ago that Stephanie was taken like a leaf in the wind.

Amanda found the broche and pinned it on her suit.

"I will wear this in honor of you, my dear. I'm going there to fight on your behalf."

Now Amanda was ready.

The day of the luncheon was actually quite exciting. Everyone was there (except Murphy). Gary Russo greeted Amanda when she entered and led her to the table. The centerpiece was made of pine cones and acorns with a small sign that indicated "The Friends of Nature" were to sit here. Colleen, Eva and Judi were already sitting there next to Sally.

Amanda could see that the young women were enjoying this special event. Judi wore a sunshine yellow party dress with a print of tulips. Sally was dressed in pink with a print of roses. The two looked like nymphs from a garden. Eva looked stunning, if not floral, in a shiny acrylic dress in dark blue that made her stand out among the pastel colors worn by the other young women at the event. Amanda looked to Colleen. She was wearing a light green suit that Amanda had seen before. Colleen had only a few dress suits, since she worked primarily in nurses' uniforms.

When they were all seated, they looked around the room and began marveling at the grandeur of the B & L Foundation's event. Amanda worried that this might lure some of the young people to shift their support to the Foundation.

The hotel had given them a large room with a chandelier overhead and thick burgundy-colored carpet at their feet. Fancy sparkling lamps brightened the walls. The tables and chairs were draped with white linens. Each table had a green glass vase with a huge flower arrangement done in orange, yellow and red. The plates on the tables were a soft green with heavy silver cutlery that had floral designs on the handles. Green bottles of red and white wine stood next to pitchers of golden beer. Waiters, dressed in tuxedos, strolled through the crowd offering hors d'oeuvres and sushi.

Amanda and Colleen put their heads together and began to whisper.

"Well, this is a nice spread. I don't get out much so this is fun," Colleen said.

"But we can't let something like this change our minds," Amanda reminded her. Over the years, Amanda had seen how easily people can turn. At a meeting, they would say one thing and at a public event, they would spin around like tops, saying exactly the opposite just because that is what they were hearing around them. Amanda hoped that Colleen was not this spineless.

As the guests chatted with each other at the tables, the restaurant staff set out bowls and began serving the salads. Several fancy baskets of small breads were handed around. A pianist played classical music that splashed droplets of sound over the rushing waters of conversation.

Amanda looked up at a banner hanging from a balcony that proclaimed the Foundation's goals for nature and the community. In strong green letters, it said: GROWING A NEW TOMORROW WITH NATURE. What were they up to now?

Amanda knew young people always enjoy a party the most. Amanda sat at the table, watching and listening. The excitement of this luncheon had swept over both Judi and Sally who were sitting next to her. Amanda heard them whisper names as they shifted their eyes from one person to another.

"He's cute, look at that suit."

"I wonder what brings him here."

When Eva sat down with them, Judi and Sally bubbled over with giggles. Amanda watched Eva's reaction. She seemed less interested in the people and looked around at the decorations that seemed to bewilder her. Amanda knew what she was thinking. She leaned forward and called out. "All these decorations are just going to become trash, aren't they?" she said to Eva.

"Yes, I assume so. Such a waste of the earth's resources," Eva said shaking her head.

"Oh, look over there," Judi said, pointing carefully so as not to look impolite. "Look at the guy standing next to that huge fruit basket. Let's go look at it and find out who that guy is. I'll bet he has a lot of friends, too."

Sally placed her napkin on her chair and went with Judi. Eva looked at her mother and shrugged.

"Oh, go ahead," Colleen said.

"I'll go with you," Amanda said. "I'd like to see that fruit basket myself. Come on, Colleen, come with us."

They soon joined Judi and Sally.

Judi and Sally quickly glanced at the fruit basket and then they introduced themselves to the young man standing next to it. He smiled at them and waved to his friends.

Colleen and Amanda scrutinized the basket and made note of how it was constructed.

"Do you think we could make one of these," Amanda asked Eva.

"Oh, you and Mom could try, and it might not look bad, but I would bet Judi could really do it."

Amanda turned to find Judi but saw, standing next to her, a well-dressed man with a glass of wine in his hand.

He spoke, "So you got an invitation to this event as well?"

It was Curtis.

"We certainly did," Amanda responded. Then she realized he had directed his question at Eva who was also standing next to her. Amanda felt embarrassed. She should have been used to it by now, the way young people would address each other and totally overlook older folks in the crowd.

Eva looked up at Curtis. He smiled down at her.

Amanda watched the two young people. It occurred to her that they would make a nice couple.

Curtis looked down into the glass of red wine in his hand. He looked so sophisticated. Amanda saw Eva blush then look down at the floor.

"I never thought you would be here," Eva stuttered.

"You look beautiful in that satin dress," Curtis said.

Amanda struggled to suppress a giggle of surprise and delight. Was a romance about to bloom? Did Colleen know? Then Amanda had another realization: the young people were using the occasion to pursue each other. They really didn't care about the politics of the B & L Foundation.

"Where are you all sitting?" Curtis asked.

This time Amanda realized he was talking to all of them.

"We're at the Friends of Nature table over there," Amanda said and nodded. "Where are you?"

"I'm supposed to be with the park administration." He nodded in the direction of his table.

Amanda noted that his table was all the way across the room. She felt disappointed that he would be sitting so far away from them.

"This restaurant has nice furnishings. I hope the food is as good," Amanda stated.

"Oh, Amanda, yes, they have good food here. I was here for an award ceremony last winter," Curtis stated.

"Attention, attention everyone," a man called. The crowd quieted and turned toward him.

"I'm Andrew Spencer, and I'm your host, along with Barbara Harrison, today at this luncheon. We want you to all have a seat and we will begin our special program."

The B & L Foundation turned down the lights and turned on their propaganda.

"We invited you here today to see our *Dreams for the Park*. This will give you an opportunity to see what potential exists for the land that was donated by the B & F Foundation. This is our opportunity to show you what can be done to make these newly acquired acres a sparkling gem in our community."

Seated now, Amanda turned to view the screen. She saw the digital version of Barbara Harrison above the podium. The music played and the icon of the B & L Foundation floated around on the screen as ribbons of color formed rainbows. Silhouettes of birds flew through fluffy white clouds.

"Gary, this is the same program they showed at the Earth Day event," Amanda said. He was sitting right next to her at the table. On his other side was Colleen.

Gary lifted his cup of coffee and nodded.

The voice of the program vibrated through the room. "The B & L Foundries has donated the land to Liberty Park."

"They sure are making a big deal out of that," Eva grumbled to Curtis, who was sitting next to her.

Amanda looked at Curtis in surprise. She had assumed he would be sitting at the parks administration table. Instead, he was sitting next to Eva.

Now Amanda noticed there were two empty chairs. Judi and Sally had disappeared into the crowd. Amanda looked around. Where were they? She nodded to Eva and pointed to the empty chairs.

"Should I go look for Judi?" Eva turned and asked her mother.

"No, forget it," Colleen responded.

"But where is she?" Eva persisted.

"I know where she is."

"But where?"

Colleen sighed, "Well, if you must know, Judi and Sally are sitting at the front table with the real Barbara Harrison."

"What?" Eva lifted herself from her chair to see this strange occurrence.

Amanda leaned forward also to see where they were. She saw Judi's braided blonde hair piled high on her head. They were now far away at the front.

Amanda watched Eva sit back down and give them a look of incredulity.

Colleen laughed, "Who knows what will come of this?"

The program voice announced, ". . . we are ready to contribute funding for the development of our dreams. Our dreams will bring to the community all the liberty that we seek here in Liberty Park."

Again, the iridescent pictures appeared on a silver screen. Beautiful, brightly colored flowers appeared in deep purples against soft lavender. Suddenly the image of a sparkling glass and steel castle appeared. The audience gasped at this vision.

The Friends of Nature looked around the room at the bedazzled guests.

"Yes, ladies and gentlemen, we could have a botanical garden here just like the famous New York Botanical Garden."

A swirl of green leaves, trees and blue sky led them to the next scene: a garden bursting with color. The audience gasped again. Amanda made gagging sounds to indicate her disgust. Gary laughed.

"An international hotel," the screen version of Barbara Harrison exclaimed. Colleen held her nose as if she smelled something stinky.

"And now for some fun . . ."

Amanda grimaced and looked at Colleen.

Pictures of laughing children appeared.

"A Sports Complex," the video image of Barbara announced.

The crowd at this luncheon also roared with approval as they had done on Earth Day. Then the floating icon of the B & L Foundation reappeared and the program was over.

Barbara Harrison stepped up to the podium as if to be recognized as the star of the video.

"It is just so thrilling, isn't it?" she asked the audience.

"Disgusting," said Eva, turning to Curtis. He laughed.

"What are we going to do?" Amanda asked, leaning toward Gary. "She's brought us into the midst of her followers. Now, she is swaying our followers as well."

Colleen and Eva looked at each other.

"Are Judi and Sally turning their backs on the Friends of Nature?" Eva asked.

They cast a look in the direction of the distant table where Judi and Sally were sitting.

Amanda saw Judi lift a glass of wine and salute her mother with a smile. Sally gave them a cute little wave of her hand. Eva waved back in similar fashion, but gave Judi a sarcastic smirk. Judi frowned and waved her sister off.

Amanda looked at Curtis, who was busy loading his plate with more sushi and filling his glass with more wine. She pointed this out to Eva.

"Oh, don't tell me you're going to let them buy you out with a little wine and sushi?" Eva asked Curtis.

Amanda laughed.

"Don't worry about it. I know how to bite the hand that feeds me," Curtis replied. "I just want to take advantage of the feast before the war begins."

"There may not be a war if that Barbara Harrison steals our supporters," Amanda said, now feeling doubtful.

"Judi and Sally are just having fun with this event," Colleen assured her. "Well, I hope that's all they are doing." She laughed and put her hand over her heart.

Barbara Harrison was conducting a survey now and people were raising their hands.

"How many people want a botanical garden?"

Hundreds of hands around the room lifted into the air.

"How many people want an international hotel?"

Only a few hands went up. Barbara looked amazed.

"This is a great hotel here," said Andrew Spencer, the co-chair. "But come now, doesn't our community deserve even more of the best?"

Hands rose again, more this time.

"How many people want a sports complex?" Barbara Harrison questioned.

Hands were raised in greater numbers; some were raising both their hands. A man skipped through the crowd whispering, "Get them up, get them up, stop talking and raise your hands."

"Did you hear that?" Amanda said to Gary. "This event is just to make it look like they have support for their plans. They are trying to demoralize us. They are trying to buy us off."

"We just have to keep going with the petition campaign," Colleen reassured Amanda. "We can come up with more signatures than they have supporters in this room right now. I'm sure of it."

The restaurant staff began entering the room with covered plates loaded with hot food. The aroma of gravies and sauces filled the air. Entrees were set before each attendee. After the entrees were distributed, just enough time passed before the staff appeared again to deliver the desserts. Soon the tables were covered with dishes of sweet tarts, smooth, creamy cheesecakes, cookies burdened with chocolate and nuts. In addition, the side tables held pies and plates of flakey scones with fruit fillings. The waiters brought more coffee pots and made the rounds. The guests lazily sat and complained about how uncomfortable it was to be so full of food.

"We've got to do something," Amanda said when she realized that even the coffee was delicious.

Gary looked around at everyone seated at the Friends' table.

"We need to hurry up and get that financial advisor and have him crunch the numbers. Obviously, we have more hotels in this community than we need. I don't think local people will visit a botanical garden more than just a few times a year. The sports complex will likely be too expensive for most to use. These things sound good, but I doubt they will thrive without bringing in people from outside the area to keep them financially viable."

Amanda did not hear Gary's words. For her, now was the time and place to take action. She stood up and went to the middle of the room.

"You needn't think, Ms. Barbara Harrison, that this community will be swayed by your fancy luncheon. Just outside this hotel are thousands of hard-working people who can't afford a lot of luxuries. They need a place to go to have fun that will not cost them a fortune. That is why we have parks. We need them for the community. You should listen to us. We're telling you what the community needs. We don't need profitable corporations that brag excessively about the very few jobs they do create."

Heads turned and looked back at Amanda. Someone complained, "Oh, she would just try to ruin this lovely event."

Barbara Harrison stepped beyond the podium.

"Now, dear Ms. Amanda, don't you worry, we are deeply concerned about the needs of the community," Barbara said. She stepped off the stage and came down the aisle. When she arrived next to Amanda, she rested her hand on Amanda's arm as if they were old friends. Amanda wanted to pull away but didn't want to look so hostile. She dropped her head, feeling embarrassed and weak; disappointed in herself that she was not stronger in these situations. Amanda knew Ms. Harrison was using friendly tactics to confuse the people, but what could she do right now to change the situation? When Amanda's head lowered, she saw the golden leaf on her lapel and remembered her promise to Stephanie. She needed to be strong. She lifted her head and spoke.

"I am from this community and I know what this community needs." Amanda pulled away from Barbara's hand.

"We appreciate the food and drink, but we are still insisting that the land be used to preserve nature for the people," Amanda announced. She stood up tall and looked out at the audience. "We don't need more hotels and more development."

The audience clapped, roared and cheered. Amanda felt stunned. She watched as a few members of the audience stood to yelp and whistle. Some of the guests began leaving their tables, satisfied that they had taken what they could get and seen the best of the confrontation. Others stood and continued clapping. Several came to Amanda and commended her for her words. Amanda felt relieved to have some support. The crowd began to disperse. Unfortunately, Barbara Harrison was still standing next to her, unwilling to give up. "I'm sure you are respected in this community, Amanda, for your demand that the land be preserved for the people. I just want you to understand," Barbara said, as she again slipped her arm over Amanda's shoulder, "that Andrew and I, on behalf of the Foundation, are always willing to meet with the Friends to discuss the development of this land that the Foundation donated to the park."

Amanda hated the way Barbara was holding her in the grip of the Foundation. She needed some way to break out, but she saw no escape.

"Ta daaaaah!" came a yell from across the room.

In the doorway was a man dressed in a cape and mask. He flourished a child's toy sword in the air.

"I am the Toxic Revenger! I am here to get revenge for all the wrong that was done to man and land," he announced. He leaped into the room and held the plastic sword over Barbara's head.

"Are you the representative of the B & L Foundry that disguises itself as the B & L Foundation? And is that the company that contaminated the land, poured smoke into the air, and poisoned the workers in your foundry?" His voice grew louder. "Are you the company that is sending all your industry and jobs overseas where you are now polluting and poisoning people there, just like you did here? Are you not the same evil force in the universe?"

The Toxic Revenger lifted his sword and twirled around in his black tights and flowing cape.

"I am here to bring the truth to this community. We can no longer let these companies rule our lives. We must take command of them, for the good of the community."

People laughed and cheered.

Barbara's face was filling with rage. She looked at her assistant, Andrew.

"Who is this?"

Andrew shrugged and turned to the Toxic Revenger.

"Look pal, you have no right to come in here disrupting this luncheon. I can have the police throw you out of here."

The Toxic Revenger pulled down his mask. "I'm an old employee of the Foundry who is dying of cancer, you fool. I have nothing to lose, so go ahead, throw me out. I came here to bring enlightenment and understanding to these people."

The man was Ed Wilson, the steel worker, who had just joined the Friends of Nature.

Amanda smiled when she saw his face, but the news of his illness hit her hard.

"Ed, I'm so glad to see you. You've saved the day. This is just what we needed, someone to make it clear just what is going on with the B & L Foundation."

"At your service," Ed said as he bowed.

By now, the crowd had thinned to only a small group. Gary stepped forward.

"Barbara, Andrew, we'll meet again to discuss what will be done. The Friends of Nature is willing to work with you, but we will not be bullied."

"That's right," said Amanda.

Barbara and Andrew repeated their promise to work with the community. They then stepped away from the small gathering that came to see Ed Wilson's costume.

"They tried to do so much damage today," Amanda said to Ed. "They have fattened us for the slaughter. But Ed, you have saved us."

"In the end, we will win, **they** will be slaughter, not us," said the Revenger, lifting his plastic sword.

By now, the guests were gone. The food servers were quickly moving about clearing the plates.

Amanda saw Eva walk toward Curtis. He was at the dessert wagon finishing off the last of the scones and tarts. Amanda laughed, "Now there's a man with the right attitude." She went to the dessert table and grabbed a cookie before sitting down at their table again. Colleen came and sat down beside her.

Amanda looked at Colleen, "Are you aware that your daughter, Eva, may be interested in Curtis?"

Colleen looked at Amanda, "Are you serious?"

"That's the feeling I'm getting."

Colleen looked at the two young people. "I don't know what to say. He is her supervisor on the job, but really, I haven't heard her say anything about him."

"Well, keep your eyes open for more signs," Amanda said and giggled.

Suddenly, Judi and Sally came skipping across the room.

"Now don't ruin everything. I just acted as a good reference for Sally," said Judi.

Sally smiled at her friends, "I was just offered a job with the Foundation. I start to work next week. It's a really good paying job and I will get to work for a good cause in a nice clean office."

Amanda listened in shock. Colleen frowned. Eva made a face at her older sister.

"I knew it, you two have no sense," said Eva. "Sally, you will be working for the enemy now."

"Oh, go kiss a worm, Eva" Sally sneered. "It's a great job. I won't have to pull weeds or empty garbage cans in the park any more. You are just jealous. The Foundation's mission is about providing good jobs for the community. And I got the first one."

Chapter Fifteen

Daddy's Girls

"Well, it's a good thing we decided to get our picture taken that day at the mall," Eva said. They walked quickly from the train into the mall and across the mall to the photo studio where their picture package awaited them. Four weeks had passed since their last shopping trip. Eva was excited about getting the wall portrait. It would forever display them in their youthful years. The digital version was the one she knew Dad would like best. He was always on his device doing business. He could easily click and see his girls.

"I suppose you're right, but I'm very upset," Judi responded, "I wanted to look my very best. But in the picture we chose for printing, I just do not look right."

"We posed for twenty pictures. You were dressed in all the new clothes you bought that day. I even put on some of the sweaters you bought. Remember? We looked fantastic. I'm not going through that again," Eva protested. "We picked out the best pictures and they are fine. The one we had printed and framed is great." Eva said. She was amazed at herself. Usually she just tolerated Judi's tantrums, but this time, Judi had pushed it too far. What was wrong with the picture? Nothing. What was really wrong? Judi didn't look like the fashion models in the magazines she always read. That's what was wrong. Eva felt frustrated.

"You remember why we are doing this?" Eva continued, "To remind Dad that he has two daughters. We don't want him to forget us when he's traveling far from home and family and gone for so long."

"Well, he emails us and sends pictures," Judi said. She paid the clerk for the pictures. "But it's not like having him here to do things together. That's what a relationship is, it's about being together." Eva explained.

Judi took the package in her arms and looked around. Seeing a sofa and small table, Judi went to them and opened the package. Eva followed her. Inside was a card with the link for the e-photo for his device. They had also purchased a large print with a nice frame for his office wall. Judi held it up and looked at it again.

Eva looked at Judi and then turned to the picture and smiled. "I like the expressions on our faces. We are both looking into the camera at Dad, making him look at us, face to face. We want him to remember us, to come back to us." Eva looked back at her sister for agreement.

"I wanted it to be a group shot. Our whole family. Remember?" Judi pouted.

"And as usual, scheduling problems kept that from happening. Mom was working the night shift at the hospital. She told us to go ahead. Now, typically, Dad's not coming until next month," Eva reminded Judi.

They placed the wall photo back into box and strolled out of the studio.

Eva felt as if, in these days, the world had turned into water. Nothing was solid anymore. Everything was free floating. She and Judi were growing up and about to leave home. Mom would be alone and Dad? He had been drifting away from them for years. Someone had to do something to save the situation. If nothing else, at least acknowledge that this was a family and it always would be—somehow.

"We should have seen this coming," Eva said as she and Judi marched across the mall.

"Seen what coming, dear sister? You seem to be convinced that our parents are about to divorce. What proof do you have?"

"Think back on it; I always felt like Dad was just a visitor in our lives, even though he was the one who made our daily lives possible— all the clothes we have, our nice home, my chance to go to college . . ." Eva said. She went from a walk to a skip. "When he was away from us, think of it, he must have had a life of his own somewhere else—maybe even **with** someone else."

Judi gasped and ran to catch up. "Eva, what are you saying? Do you think Dad was having an affair all those years? You have no proof. You are out of your mind."

"Sometimes parents just stay together because of their children. If you think about it, our parents only have a few years until we both leave home. Because of the nature of Dad's job, they only had to spend a few months of each year together. So, I think they have been waiting it out, just to make it look good for us, their children."

They both suddenly stopped.

"Eva, don't you understand, Mom and Dad are just busy with their separate lives right now. They will retire together. What else could they do? It's too late in their lives to find someone else. You know what their plans are. Why do you doubt it? They are going to Arizona to that nice retirement community they showed us. I don't want to hear anything more."

"Believe what you want. Someone has to be at Mom's side. I will do it, but I can't do it forever."

"No, no Eva, you are just trying to justify staying home with Mom. You don't really want to get married. Grow up!"

They took off running again.

"Why are you walking so fast?" Judi asked.

"I want to catch the next train back." Eva said.

"Back? We're at the mall. I want to relax and look around. I might do some more shopping." Judi looked up at all the brightly lit store signs and took in the hum of the crowd.

"You and your shopping!" Eva protested.

"Oh look! Who is that?" Judi pointed toward a young woman standing in front of a store window.

"It's Sally." Eva declared. "And thanks to you, sister, she has money to spend from that new job at the Foundation." Eva waved at Sally. "We should go over and talk to her."

"Yes, I coached her on what to say in the interview and who to use for references," Judi said proudly. "I even gave her a good reference, myself. I wonder how she's doing."

They walked toward her before she had time to move on.

"Are you spending all that money you're making at that high paying job?" Judi yelled.

Eva laughed. Sally turned toward them.

"Oh, yes, what a job. I certainly like it better than that job at the park. All they ever let me do there was pick up trash and clean toilets."

"Disgusting," Judi said and curled her lip. "Hey, have you had any lunch yet? Let's go someplace and eat. You can tell us more about your new job."

Sally smiled, "Ok, I'm up for that, but it has to be vegan."

They picked a Chinese restaurant that was compatible with Sally's meat-free diet. She had Vegetable Delight. Judi got Chicken Fried Rice and Eva ordered Moo Goo Gai Pan.

"So how is the job?" Judi asked. Eva looked on.

"I love it. The job is great. I have my own office. People come through the door and I'm the first person they see. Barbara Harrison says I have to look nice all the time. So, I'm always in here shopping for clothes. It is so nice to be able to afford good clothes. I never could do that ever before in my life."

Eva saw the look of delight in Sally's eyes.

"I know," Judi said. "Clothes are important. I'm always telling my sister that, but she doesn't care that much for clothes."

"Are you still feeding the kitties?" Eva asked.

"Yes, I'm still feeding them. With this job, I can buy them more and better food."

"Oh, of course," Eva replied.

"I'll bet you have a nice apartment now, too," Judi commented.

"Oh, I'm living in Amanda's house."

"You live with Amanda Walters?" Eva asked in surprise.

Sally closed her eye and smiled, then she explained, "Amanda's a very nice lady, but you know, she's really poor. She has to rent out rooms to keep her taxes paid. So get this, she rents a room out to her nephew. His name is Peter. He's a vegan just like me. I've been cooking meals for all three of us. It's so much fun."

"Peter?" Judi turned and looked at Eva.

"Yes, he's so nice. He's so dreamy. I think he's cute. Wish me luck with him."

Eva picked up a piece of chicken with her chopsticks. "Well, Sally, your life has certainly improved. I knew you didn't like the job at the park. I'm glad you're doing better. What's that woman, Barbara, like to work with?"

"It must be great to work for a professional like Barbara," Judi injected.

As Sally began to describe her day with Barbara Harrison, Eva wondered what her mom and Amanda thought of Sally now.

"Oh, yes, it's great. Barbara's fun to work for," Sally replied.

Eva watched her face for hints of exaggeration, but Sally seemed sincere.

"How is Amanda taking it?" Eva asked. "You're working for the Foundation that wants to take the park away from the people and destroy the nature sanctuary."

"Oh, no, the Foundation isn't for that. They just want to make the site more welcoming to the community," Sally explained.

"More welcoming to the community?" Eva raised an eyebrow and looked at her sister.

Judi smirked at Eva, and then she explained to Sally, "People like my sister don't understand that it's the corporations in this country that have the money and the workforce that can really get stuff done in our modern society. I wish I could someday own my own business. I want to be a corporate executive."

Eva rolled her eyes, "Oh my sister. What incredible aspirations you have."

Suddenly Eva's cell phone rang. It was the unique ring that she had assigned to Matt Merriweather's phone number.

Eva gasped. What a time for him to call.

"Who is calling you?" Judi asked.

Eva looked at her companions and announced, "It's Matt. Sis, you remember, the troop leader who brought the scouts to the park to hang the bird boxes?"

"Oh, my, do you mean to tell me he actually called you? Just now?"

"I'll return his call later today," Eva said. "I'm busy now." Eva's nerves were jangling.

"You're what?" Judi sputtered. She turned to Sally, "My sister just has these men climbing all over her. Who knew?"

Sally laughed, "Good for her."

"Are we done with this?" Eva asked, lifting the sauce-covered trays. She knew she could not deal with Matt's phone call with her sister so close by.

"Yeah, I'm done," Judi sighed. "Let's go shopping."

"Where should we go?" Eva asked. She was contemplating leaving Judi and going home on the train alone.

"I'm here today to go to this new boutique," Sally told them. "It sells organic and natural beauty supplies. It's at the other end of the mall."

"Good idea, let's all go there," Judi said, her eyes sparkling.

"Organic and natural?" Eva asked. "Ok, let's have a look." She tossed their trash into a bin, and followed them out the door.

The boutique was set in one of the many passageways of the mall. Its window appeared to be like an old time Victorian shop window, displaying utensils that were once used to make soap in the days of old.

The young women stepped through the door. Sally led the way to the counter.

Eva looked around the room. Harpsichord music filled the room with bright and cheerful tunes. The décor was in soft blues and greens. The scent of sweet flowers filled the air. The little stuffed chairs in the corner looked inviting.

"You've got to try these. No animal products were used in making these crèmes and lotions. They are all organic and safe for your skin," Sally explained. "And look, the bottles are recyclable. Isn't that great, Eva?"

Eva nodded. Maybe she had misjudged Sally. Maybe Sally was a good person and only needed a chance in life. Eva picked up a test bottle and read the description. She poured some of the lotion into her hands and sniffed it. It smelled nice. It felt nice, too.

In the end, all three bought several products before leaving the store.

"That was a really nice store," Eva said. "I'll have to come back."

"My sister just needed to be told it was natural," Judi said to Sally. They were walking next to each other like old friends.

Eva smiled and looked at the white paper bag with the pink ribbon. It had been a fun time, sharing the scent of the soaps and lotions as they considered what to buy.

"So listen, gals," Sally said, turning toward them, "it was nice to hang out with you, but I've got to get going."

"Ok, thanks for showing us the shop. See you another time, Sally," Judi responded.

"Later," Eva said and waved her hand.

They stood and watched as Sally turned and wandered into the crowd.

"She seems like someone who's had a rough life," Judi said.

"She does. I'm glad that she likes the job," Eva said.

Judi nodded, "I commend Barbara Harrison for bringing a poor woman like Sally out of poverty."

"She probably only did it to spite the Friends of Nature." Eva reminded Judi.

"Don't be so critical. I'm happy for Sally."

"Oh, I'm glad that Sally got the job. She needed it. And her attitude has improved," Eva said. She felt better now thinking of Sally as a friend rather than a co-worker.

They walked along in silence looking into the store windows. Then Judi pointed to some benches and they sat down. Eva watched as Judi pulled the portrait of the two of them out of the package and look at herself again.

"You look great in that photo," Eva cooed. "Oh, please, Judi don't start."

"Ok, ok, I guess I do," Judi said. "It's nice. Yeah, this will do. So next month when Dad gets back into the country, we'll give him his birthday present."

"Let's try to get Mom and Dad to talk about their plans for retirement," Eva suggested. "I just want them to confirm for us that they intend to stay together." She looked to her sister for a mature response.

Judi looked back at her. Then she quickly looked away. "Let's just see what happens."

Eva shrugged. She was going to make it a point to see what her parents were planning to do with the rest of their lives.

Chapter Sixteen

The Value of Forgiveness

Amanda felt dazed by the outcome of the luncheon. She had expected Barbara Harrison to use the event to persuade the community to endorse the Foundation's plans, but she had never dreamed that Barbara would hire the young supporters of the Friends just to get them on her team. Worst of all—hiring Sally, the very one that was living in Amanda's own home. It was, as the old saying goes, a "bitter pill to swallow." Amanda could not throw Sally out on principle. She needed the additional rental income that Sally provided.

Sally and Peter were growing closer to each other. This had made Amanda happy. She remembered how the two women had joked once about Sally's becoming Amanda's daughter. Now, when Sally might actually become a part of Amanda's family through marriage, there was this dilemma with Sally working for the Foundation, or as Amanda saw it, the Enemy.

Over the next few weeks, Amanda quietly observed Sally's confidence growing with her experience at the new job. She stood taller and smiled when she showed Amanda her first big paycheck. Sally was moving away from her identity with the pitiful and the weak. Amanda noticed that feeding stray cats was starting to go out of focus in her life. Going on day trips to museums in the city with Peter was consuming her free time.

This was all good for Sally. Amanda liked to support girls that were pushing aside the identity of always being the victim. So, in spite of the politics of the park, Amanda tried to appreciate Sally's effort to make the most of her opportunity at the Foundation.

The Friends of Nature had plenty of work to do. Amanda and Gary were back and forth on the phones.

"Amanda, I just remembered, from now on when I call you, I should make sure you can talk. You have a spy in the house," Gary said and laughed.

"If you are referring to Sally, don't worry, she's at her wonderful job most of the day."

"Good for her. Listen, stay close to Sally and Judi," he said. "Sally can tell us what's going on in the Foundation. Don't let her know we are using her as a spy for our purpose. I'm sure she'll want to talk about what she hears. This is great, Amanda, it could prove to be very useful."

The thought had never occurred to Amanda. Usually when someone seemed to be a traitor, you just pushed the traitor away from you. Now, she realized that having Sally around was still an asset to her cause.

"How's the petition campaign going?" Gary asked.

Amanda gave a brief report, hoping to satisfy his request. But the truth was they had fallen behind. She needed to call Colleen and get out there again to gather signatures on the petitions. After speaking with Gary, she made another call and the two women arranged a time and place to continue their work.

The next day, they went back out to gather more signatures. This time they went to a grocery store. After setting up their signs and a table with extra petitions, Amanda began calling aloud: "Show your support for a people's park with nature and recreation that our community can afford."

Colleen beckoned people to her as they walked by on their way to the store, "Sign a petition. Let your opinion be counted."

It was going to be a long slow day. Amanda thought about how to make it better. During one of those times when no one was coming down the street, Amanda decided she would talk to Colleen about what had happened at the luncheon.

"Listen, Colleen, I just wanted to let you know, I've been doing some thinking."

"Oh Amy, you must be really mad that Sally took that job offer and is working for the Foundation. I would be upset if I were you.

After all the favors you've done for her. She's right there under your own roof."

"I know," Amanda admitted. "I was sickened at first, but Gary called me to discuss it and everything will be all right. I just have to take some precautions." Amanda stuck her pen behind her ear and continued, "You know, with that job, Sally could be very helpful to our cause. She may hear things we need to know. So, I'm **not** going to get upset with her. I'm going to keep in contact with her. She may open up to me about what's happening there."

"Oh, of course," Colleen responded, "and I'm sure Judi will tell me anything she hears either from Sally or from conversations at the Hungry Fish. Everyone drops in there for coffee, so you never know what she may overhear while working there."

Amanda smiled. "Yes, this may work out to the best for our cause."

"And, to think, my Judi helped Sally get the job by giving her a good reference."

"It couldn't have happened better if we'd planned it."

Colleen and Amanda laughed.

"You know how aggravating a job can get sometimes. A person needs to talk," Amanda said.

"Yeah, and I'll bet Barbara is a tough demanding boss to work for." Colleen smiled as she turned to hand a petition to another supporter and waited until it was signed.

"You know what, Colleen, there's an old saying, "The young are strong, but the old are devious. We have to be a little devious just to survive.""

Amanda handed her petition board over to another supporter for signing.

"Oh, yes, you are right about that," Colleen responded.

"I'm glad it turned out this way," Amanda added. "I like Sally. Now I can stay friends with her. Did you know? She and Peter are hitting it off really well? I'd like to see them get married. Peter will be out of college soon and working. He could be the best thing that ever happened to Sally."

They called out to more of the grocery store's patrons. By the end of the day, they had a huge stack of petitions signed and ready to give to Gary for presentation. When Amanda stopped by the office the next day to drop off the petitions, Gary had another request.

"Amanda, please research this for us. Here is a list of three financial advisors. Call them and see which one likes our action plan and is supportive. We need to make sure that any professionals we hire are truly on our side. No more spies for us. The professionals could sabotage us and cause us to fail."

Amanda took the list as Gary continued, "I can't stress this enough, be sure whatever financial advisor you choose is truly on our side. Interrogate each one. Be vicious. Here's the list. Start making some calls soon."

Amanda took the list and headed home to begin her work.

Financing, money, this was the power and center of society. How could the Friends of Nature, a group financed by meager contributions, convince the government that a park for the people, the birds and animals was easier to create and maintain than a corporate development?

She sat at her desk with the phone in her hand. It was difficult to make the calls. Her mind kept bringing up arguments in opposition to her goal. In her heart, she still feared that the government would only see the tax dollars promised by the developer.

"Then after the government supports the development, the corporation will ask for a tax abatement," Amanda said aloud. "They always want favors for creating jobs for the community. Why am I so cynical?" Then she gave herself an answer, "I guess at this age, I know too much. I've been through it before."

She reconsidered the work she must do at this moment. "I need to believe in this. We need to convince the government that the corporate development would be a financial risk. We need a financial advisor that can crunch the numbers to support our stand. I must get these phone calls made."

She looked at the names and phone numbers and began to make the calls.

She listened to herself stumble along with an explanation to the first person who picked up the phone:

"I'm looking for a financial advisor that likes nature and cares about parks. Here's the deal; I need someone to prove that the proposals of the B & L Foundation are not viable. Or prove that the costs and benefits of a nature area and ball field—oh, yes, and some flower beds—are easier for the government to maintain and provide."

What did she just say? She listened intently for a positive response on the other end.

With that kind of introduction, she was not succeeding. These businesses were in favor of development. Where had Gary gotten their names?

Amanda reworked her introduction, making it slicker and more professional sounding.

"Have you seen the headlines about Liberty Park and the battle over the donated land?" Finally, one financial advisor had actually been following the story. He sympathized with the Friends of Nature.

Amanda was relieved to hear his response. She only had two more names on the list. She explained what they wanted. The financial advisor took her home phone number and said he couldn't talk now, but he promised he would get back to her in the evening. He ended the call quickly, leaving Amanda disappointed.

Well, at least she had one positive response—even if it was weak. By now, Amanda was tired. The stress of making the calls had dimmed her fragile enthusiasm before she had even finished the list. What were the chances of the last two being any better?

The doorbell rang. It was her neighbor, Murphy.

"I ran out of coffee and thought I'd stop by and see if you have any," he explained. "So what are you up to today? What kind of trouble have you gotten into?"

"Coffee? You know I hate coffee. I've been making calls to find a financial advisor for the Friends. We need to prove our point in terms that the government might understand."

"Lots of luck with our government. And as for the professionals, they're trying to make a living. To do that they have to kiss the cheek of the corporate gods."

"Is there no one willing to help on the peoples' side?" Amanda asked.

"You and I have been in these battles over the years, have we ever met anyone who was really willing to challenge the powers above—I'm not talking about God, you know, I'm talking about those little gods called politicians and corporate Chief Executive Officers."

"Murphy, I'm a foolish old woman with a young girl's heart. I need to believe there are good people out there somewhere that can help us."

"So tell me the truth, do you have any coffee in this house?"

"Well, yes, Peter drinks it."

She got up from her chair and made a cup of coffee in Peter's one-cup percolator. "Here's the sugar and cream, if you like."

"Sorry, my doctor says no sugar and no fats. Actually, the doc said no caffeine either, but when have I ever completely obeyed doctors? Bunch of greedy professionals. You know what they do? They withhold information from the public so they can sell it to you in the form of pills. I read an article that said you can reduce your blood pressure through exercise. So why do I need to take pills?"

"Murphy, is bird watching a sufficient exercise to lower your blood pressure?"

"I doubt it, but it does calm my nerves. Revenge calms my nerves too. That's why I'd like to do something cantankerous like set fire to the B & L Foundation office."

"Murphy, please, don't do anything like that."

She wanted to invite him for dinner, but his remark set her against him.

"Well, Murphy, I have to make two more calls. I hope you enjoyed your coffee."

He finished his cup then winked at her. "Don't forget, when you need the "big guns" you always have me. I'm ready to do the job."

That evening after dinner, the phone rang. Surprisingly, it was the financial expert who said he would call her later. He actually did.

"Hi, listen, I can't help you through my job. They wouldn't approve of this, but I'm a financial advisor and I think I can crunch the numbers for you. Tell Gary Russo I'm on the case and here's the information that I need. I can make a report that the state will listen to and take seriously. I'm on your side. Anyone with any sense can see the development cannot be sustained in the present economy. Everything is over-built, paved to the walls and other projects are losing money right now before they are even completed. I'd love to help put an end to this kind of excess development; it only serves to ruin the development that already exists."

Amanda felt she had the right person to do the job. She promised him secrecy in exchange for his help. She called Gary and let him know she had found a trustworthy financial advisor. Gary was glad and rewarded her with yet another task.

"You've got to get Sally to go through their files and make copies of pertinent documents. We need to have some idea what their figures are so that we can argue against them," he explained.

Amanda was dumbfounded. How was she going to get Sally to do this? The poor young girl was just starting to succeed at a new job. She would not want to take the risk.

Amanda washed the coffee cup that Murphy had left as she pondered what Gary expected her to do next for the cause.

Chapter Seventeen

Big Plans for the Hungry Fish

"Get up, sister. You've got to go to work today." It was late morning. Eva had been up with the birds, but Judi slept in late every day. She now worked the afternoon shift at the restaurant, covering the lunch hour and, later, the dinner slot. Eva knew the real reason Judi liked her late schedule. They paid her more money for working later in the day. "You'll miss that big paycheck if you get fired for being late," Eva called.

"I'm getting up," Judi responded from under the flower print sheets that were twisted in a huge knot on the bed.

Eva stood in the bedroom doorway sipping a glass of cranberry juice. Schedule changes had given her the day off from her job at the park. Now, she was looking forward to some entertainment watching Judi dash about getting ready.

"Hey, Sis," Eva called, "did Charlie's son, James, come back from Spain yet? Is he working at the restaurant these days?"

"Oh, yes, dear sister, and he's handsome." Judi leaped out of bed wide-eyed and gushing. "Oh, he's so handsome and smart."

"Oh dear, poor man. I'm sure you are in hot pursuit."

"I'm not stupid, Sis, I'm playing my cards carefully. There's serious competition among the other women who work there. But I intend to win. I'll show you how to catch the man of your dreams."

Eva watched as Judi stood before the mirror in the hall and admired her half-dressed body and facial features.

Eva laughed and then sat on the small chair in the bedroom. "Tell me, oh wise one, how does the temptress work her magic?"

"You know what my plan is, Sis. I've already followed through on Stage One. After some serious flirtation with James, I was able to show him how he could expand the business of the Hungry Fish." Judi pulled her white uniform out of the closet and over her head. "Eva, tell me, seriously, don't you think that if the 'Fish' held a fund-raiser party for the Friends, it would bring in some money for both the restaurant and the nature group?"

"I'd like to think so," Eva responded.

"If I could impress Charlie and James on the financial level, how could they not fall in love with the gorgeous Judi Kaufman?"

"Oh dear, my sweet sister has love and money confused already," Eva murmured.

"Think of it, Sis. If I were to marry into the family, I would become co-owner of this restaurant. I would soon turn it into a delightful little café. But I will admit something to you."

"That you are dreaming, if not totally crazy?" Eva asked.

"You doubt me," Judi whined. "No, you watch, it's going to happen. I'm making this happen. I will find my way to the heart of James Vern."

"To the heart of James Vern?" Eva asked.

"You'll see, but here's what I will admit."

"Oh, do tell me."

"That restaurant needs a new name. It will never make big money with that silly name. Hungry Fish? What was that? Sounds like one of those strange names the hippies used to give places back in the 1970s. You know how you can tell? Mom thinks it's great."

Judi explained to Eva, in intervals as she dashed about grabbing necessities for her purse, all the other ideas she had for re-designing the restaurant. After the name change, they would get rid of the fishing bait refrigerators in the corner. Her compromise position would be to put them behind the restaurant. She tugged on her stockings and continued, "I would redecorate the place to look like a quaint country café with wreaths of vines and straw flowers. I'd call it Café Liberté. What do you think? Everyone will come. I don't need a college degree for this kind of work, I'm a natural. They will be impressed with my ideas."

"So tell me more about my future brother-in-law."

"Oh, please, he has such intelligent hazel eyes and his tall thin body is sleek and strong. He's a little quieter than his father, but not actually shy. Several times I've seen him solve problems with customers in a better way than his father did."

"What did James study in school? Business administration?"

"No," Judi said as she combed her hair out and tied it into a bun on her head. "He studied math. If the business fails, he can teach college math. He's so smart."

Eva choked on her last drop of cranberry juice. "Well, if the business fails, you've thought of everything, Sis, it's good to have a Plan B."

Judi nodded gratefully.

It was another one of those days when Judi was acting like she had the answers for every question. These days, Eva felt less annoyed by it. Now, she knew her sister was only bragging.

"I get to have a lazy day today," Eva announced. She yawned and stretched her legs and arms.

"Oh, yeah, well it's your day off," Judi said, racing around the living room in search of her keys and train pass.

"I have a big date tonight, you know."

"With your boy scout, Mattie?"

"Why do you always ridicule my accomplishments? For all you know, I may get married before you do," Eva said, but then she frowned. She had never really considered getting married and she would certainly not presume that she would marry Matt. She didn't really know him. It was just such a treat to see her sister light up with surprise.

"I won't be home to help you select what to wear," Judi cautioned.

"Oh, please! I don't need you to help me decide what to wear."

"Ok, I'm just letting you know," Judi stated.

"Besides, Matt will appreciate a natural woman—that's me."

"My sister Eva, the Mother Earth Goddess," Judi sighed.

"Go now, Sis, you'll be late for work."

Eva spent most of the day reading more about plants, similarities in subspecies, why various plants received the Latin name that they had and what kind of climate different species favored for the best growth. Much of this information was just like what she had read about the different species of birds, how they had adapted to the various environments. Plants and birds, they swirled around in her mind. Migratory birds relied on a variety of plants all over the world. Was it possible that invasive species of plants were not the threat that scientists were saying? After all, birds fly and live in different habitats across the world. Or, was a thousand acres planted in broccoli in Mexico a habitat denying threat to the survival of migrating birds?

By early afternoon, she had to stop reading or go crazy. She decided to check her closet and figure out what to wear. Keep it simple. That was her motto. Just put on slacks with that nice blouse her mom gave her for her birthday. It had a print of "Bluettes". She had some Cloisonné earrings with small blue blossoms that matched nicely.

She and Matt had planned to go to a neighborhood restaurant that offered outdoor dining. At the dinner hour, they both arrived at the same time and saw each other as they approached the door.

"Oh, let's sit here," said Matt. Eva nodded in agreement.

They sat down, reviewed the menu and placed their orders.

Then a heavy silence wedged itself between them. Matt stared out across the street.

Eva wondered how Matt had frozen silent when he had been so charming at the park with his scout troop in tow.

"Well, it's a beautiful evening," Eva said.

"Yes it is."

"Maybe we could take a walk after we eat," Eva suggested.

"I suppose so."

"How are the scouts?"

"Fine, oh, they're fine. We're getting ready for our tournament next month. It's a bow and arrow contest. Have you ever used a bow or shot arrows?"

"No," Eva responded. Bows and arrows had never entered her lifestyle before. She thought for a moment. "Do you use them for hunting wild animals?"

"No, just for competition," Matt replied.

They sat silently awaiting their meal. Eva felt like failure was creeping like a poisonous spider into their evening.

"I hate this silly dating routine. Why are people supposed to get together and feed their faces in front of each other?" Matt asked. "What does this accomplish?"

"I know, I'm sitting here worried I'll drop my spoon or knife and you'll hold it against me forever," Eva replied.

Matt reached over and knocked her spoon to the floor. "Oh, look I've ruined everything. Now, you don't have to worry."

Eva looked at the spoon on the carpet and laughed. "I guess you did."

A waiter came and placed their food on the table. He gathered the fallen spoon and replaced it with a clean one.

"Have you ever been owl watching?"

"What?"

"Would you like to go with me to the park? There's a gathering tonight to watch owls."

"Interesting," Eva said, but then doubt and mistrust overwhelmed her. Was this a trick? She couldn't remember seeing such an event listed on the park calendar. Was it right to have a first date take you into the dark woods in search of owls. That didn't seem safe. "Let me think about it," she said. Did the women's magazines that Judi read ever warn against dates in the park?

They ate their meal in continued silence. Occasionally, they would look up to see waiters seating other guests at other tables.

"Ok, we've finished with that. Do you want to see if there are any owls? It's not a gimmick; there really is an owl prowl tonight at Liberty Park."

"I spend so much time at the park," Eva said.

"But this will be different," Matt said. He laughed, "You're looking at me as if I were going to take you into the bushes. Eva, really, there's a full moon tonight and it should be good for viewing owls."

Eva blushed in embarrassment. The lack of dinner conversation made her feel the need for adventure. She looked at Matt, assessing him closely. Matt looked sincere; he really wanted to go to an owl watch.

"Well, if you don't want to go, let's call it a night. I'm heading over there," Matt stated. He waved to the waiter to get the check. "I'm sorry this has not been the best date. I'm not much good at this formal dating stuff."

"I'll go," Eva heard herself saying. "Yes, I'll go with you." After all, Matt was a scout, he could be trusted. Couldn't he?

Matt smiled. He quickly paid for their meal. "Great, I've been hoping to see the barn owl. I'm glad you want to go. You do really want to go?"

"Oh, yes, I do want to go. I've never seen many owls."

They rode the train together without much discussion. Eva took quick glances at Matt—this stranger who seemed so inviting just a few days back.

They got off the train with several other people.

"Are you going to the owl watch tonight?" one man asked Matt.

"Sure, follow us, this way."

Eva felt relieved. Now she had proof that there was, in fact, an event.

They strolled along the paths toward the interior meadow. There on benches were several other bird watchers. One was that old guy, Murphy. Eva waved and said hello.

"Welcome to the County Bird Watchers Association," Murphy called to her.

"Oh, this is amazing. You're all out here to see owls?" Eva said looking around.

"What else would be out here at this time of night? Rodents?" Murphy asked.

"Well, of course, rodents. What else would an owl want?" Eva replied.

"I told her about this," Matt said laughing, "but she couldn't believe me, now you see Eva. I'm surprised you didn't know about this event."

"I guess I'm out of contact. Maybe I've spend too much time working in the park and not enough enjoying it."

"And how is it, working in the park?" Murphy asked. "Do you know any secrets you can tell us? Do they really recycle all those bottles in the picnic garbage? Do they use any pesticides in the park? Herbicides, maybe? The County Bird Watchers Association is keeping an eye on them. They try to pretend they are such environmentalists, what a bunch of phooey. We've seen dead birds and animals and we're suspicious."

Eva kept silent and looked around for Matt. He stepped up next to her, "Don't let that old goat make you crazy. Come this way, we'll get the best seat for owl watching."

"Ahh, don't go over there," Murphy called. "My girlfriend's over there and she'll talk your leg off."

They went to the picnic tables near the edge of the meadow. To Eva's surprise she saw Amanda sitting on a bench talking to one of the other bird watchers.

"Amanda, hello!" Eva said, and saw a genuine look of surprise on Amanda's face.

"Oh, hello, Eva. So you are here to see the owls."

"We're on a date," said Matt. "How do you like this? I bring a gal to an owl prowl and call it a date."

"Very good, and you picked just the right gal. Eva knows a lot about birds," Amanda said and winked at Eva.

It was easy from here on in. They sat at Amanda's table and talked like real adults. Matt occasionally slipped his hand around Eva's shoulder. At first, she felt strange, but in time it seemed so comfortable.

"Eva, let me ask you something," Amanda said. "You know we're trying to protect the new land, you know where it is, Murphy took us for a walk there—it's his favorite bird sanctuary. We need to raise money. It's unfortunate that all of this rests on money, but we need to think up ways to raise money. Do you have any ideas?"

It didn't take Eva any time to respond. "My sister may have an idea. You know she works at the Hungry Fish."

"Ah, yes, she tried to get me to hold a scout fund-raiser there," Matt said. "She's a real go-getter."

"Yes, she is," Eva said. "She was just talking to me today about fund-raising. The Hungry Fish donated snacks and refreshments when the scouts put up the bird boxes on the Bluebird Trail."

"Oh, that's excellent. Has she discussed it with your mom, Colleen?"

"I don't think so, not yet."

"I'll call Colleen tomorrow and see what we can do."

"Good idea," Eva said.

Matt looked at her, "You're quite involved, aren't you?"

Eva smiled. "Do you still want to get your scouts to help save the park's bird habitat?"

"I'll give it serious consideration," Matt said. He took her hand. "Come with me, I think they've spotted an owl over there."

They walked quietly over to a crowd of bird watchers gazing through night scopes.

"What kind of owl do you have?" Matt asked.

"A barn owl," one man explained.

"That's great," Eva whispered, "I've never seen an owl in the wild. I could never be in the park after sunset and that's when most owls come out."

The moon rose in the sky like a big silver disk. Its light shined down on the grass that glowed eerily around them. Nothing could be seen clearly, their faces were hidden in darkness, but Eva could feel Matt holding her hand, his voice inviting the crowd to join them. "There it goes, everyone, it's the barn owl." They watched as the large, lightly-colored owl drifted down Freedom Way on its wide opened wings.

Eva knew she too was drifting down a new path in life. Already she felt the complications. How would her life be different if she and Matt formed a relationship? She stared up at the moon. Not far away, her sister was busy working at the Hungry Fish. Eva wondered how Judi was doing in her pursuit of James.

The next morning, both young Kaufmans were sleeping late. Neither had to go to work that day and neither saw any reason to get out of bed until suddenly . . . Judi sat up in bed, "I can't believe what a night I had."

"What a night you had? I had an incredible night too," Eva replied.

"Oh, you don't mean it? What happened? No, let me go first. I had the most incredible night. I talked to James about the idea of a fundraiser. He liked the idea. He and his dad agreed they could do it. All I have to do now is come up with a plan and a budget."

"What? That's great." Eva gasped, excited about what she wanted to tell, but Judi continued.

"James and I are on the same wave-length. I just know this is going to happen."

"Well, let me tell you about my night."

"Yes, how was the dinner date with Mattie?"

"Please, stop saying "Mattie." The dinner date was, well, in a word, horrible. But after we ate, Matt invited me to the owl watch. There, we had plenty to talk about. And guess what?"

"Oh what? Would you please get on with the story."

"I saw Amanda there and she told me they needed a fund-raiser. So, guess what, Sis, I told her that you had the same idea. Amanda is eager to talk to you and Mom and get this thing going."

"Oh, this is wonderful. I've got to get up now and work on my plan and budget. I can't believe I slept in so late."

All day, Eva and Judi discussed the fund-raiser party and laid out their plans. Colleen explained that the Friends had numerous expenses: the cost of experts and soil tests, the cost of mailings and advertising and the need to give Gary and Amanda some sort of stipend for their work.

Judi called James and gave him the good news. He provided her with the restaurant's expenses and set the profit he would want to make from the event. They finished with a budget that fulfilled the restaurant's expectations and offered a nice gain for the Friends of Nature as well. Colleen put together a proposal and called Amanda. They decided to vote on the proposal and budget at the next Friends' meeting.

Eva watched as Judi's whole plan was coming into being. It was happening with such accuracy and perfection that she felt a shiver go down her spine. Her sister was amazing. If she were successful with this, would she someday succeed at marrying James and becoming the co-owner of the Hungry Fish? (And would Judi succeed at getting the name changed? That could be even more difficult.)

A week later, the Friends meeting, was held, of course, at the Fish. Amanda stood to speak.

"We need an event that will surpass what Barbara Harrison of the Foundation did with her luncheon."

The members roared with approval.

"That will take some doing," said Curtis. "Are you serving sushi?" He laughed and looked over at Eva.

"All you want is more sushi." Eva teased him. "Wait, aren't the oceans being fished empty?"

"A good point, we need to avoid foods that are politically incorrect," Judi responded and laughed.

"My sister is now concerned with being politically correct," Eva gasped. "I can't believe this, but whatever it takes."

"Yes, whatever it takes," Curtis agreed. James looked at him and smiled.

They considered the possible choices for the menu.

"We should include vegetarian and vegan dishes as well," Eva suggested. She would never have said such a thing if she hadn't grown to accept Sally. Eva was surprised when Judi and James agreed. Eva felt bold now. She decided to make more suggestions.

"Let's not decorate with stuff that's going to create more garbage," she suggested.

Curtis made a note. "We could use wild vines from the park. There are plenty of them. We could make wreaths to hang on the walls."

Gary voiced his major concern: "What will we do for a program?"

This led to more discussion. The meeting went on into the late evening and ended on a high note with a sense of satisfaction.

On the way home, the Kaufmans could not stop discussing the details.

"Well, Judi," Eva confided, "I have to hand it to you. It looks like James is very impressed with you. You now have your winning ticket: a fund-raiser that will bring in a big crowd."

"I made plans, I followed through on them and now we are going to do it," Judi said. Their mother looked at her with pride.

"You've done a great job of organizing this," Colleen responded. "But good luck, my dear, keep in mind, life can play tricks on you."

Eva laughed. "My sister the entrepreneur. Profiting from being politically correct. Now there's something I did not have the nerve to imagine."

Eva soon realized she also had not imagined the quantity of work it took to put on this event. After weeks of announcements, mailings, phone calls and decisions about the food and how to arrange and decorate the restaurant, the day of the event arrived.

As the guests walked through the door, they saw in the Hungry Fish Restaurant a spectacular mix of creativity and environmentalism. Eva and Curtis had made several large wreaths from grass reeds, pinecones and vines from the park. Amanda had persuaded Sally and Peter to get involved. They prepared four entrees of beans, grains and squash. Bowls of nuts and berries were served as appetizers. Six different herbal teas were offered along with juice and seltzer. The napkins, paper plates and paper cups were made from recycled paper. The utensils were stainless steel and washed after use. A florist donated bouquets of Sunflowers and Black-eyed Susans to top each table. For dessert, they had blueberry pie and an incredible fruit salad basket just like the one they had seen at Barbara Harrison's party—re-created by Colleen and Amanda, in an attempt to save on the cost of the original fruit basket.

For music, they hired a local band that played mandolins before and after the program. A lone harpist played music as they ate. Gary Russo invited a poet friend to give a reading of several poems about nature before Gary stood and explained the purpose of the fund-raiser.

"The money we make tonight will be used to finance our top weapon against the Foundation's risky development schemes. I can't tell you what that weapon is exactly, but we feel it's the best we can do. The hearing is coming up in just one month. At that time, we will be making our best presentation. Then, the state will deliberate. We won't get an answer until maybe early next summer."

The audience groaned.

"Why does government always take so long?" someone yelled from the back of the room.

To lift their spirits and direct them away from further complaints, Amanda stood up and explained the rules for the fund-raising auction that was to happen next.

The audience focused on the prizes that Eva held up to display. James gave each item the marketing pitch it needed to entice the audience. There were Friends of Nature tee shirts, new rain gear, and modern camping equipment donated by local stores. Some of the gifts were discounts on dinner at the Hungry Fish and binoculars from the County Bird Watching Association, (CBWA). Bids went up and soon a feverish battle was being fought over the prizes.

Amanda was impressed with what the young people had done with the event. "This was such a lovely party. I'm sure we'll make lots of money for our cause."

Curtis walked around the room acting the part of the auctioneer. Sally and Peter quickly placed dishes of fruit dessert on the tables.

"A little more meat with this meal wouldn't have hurt," Murphy grumbled. "Now I have to go home and see if there is any liverwurst in the fridge."

Ed Wilson, Steelworkers Union Local 583, went up to the podium. Everyone began to cheer.

"Here he is, the Toxic Revenger," someone called.

"Good work, Ed You told that Foundation. You looked them in the eye, brother, and let them have it."

"Yeah, you spoke the truth."

Cheers erupted and then slowly quieted.

"It's great to see everyone here tonight. It helps . . . it helps a guy like me. As you know, I have cancer. I believe it was caused by the chemicals I was exposed to all those years. I thought I was working and had a good job, but every day I was killing myself and polluting the earth. But it feels good to know that I finally got to take a stand against the things the bosses made me do." He fought back a sob.

"You're a good man, union brother,"

Ed looked up at the audience again. "If I die, it feels good to know that there is a community here that will keep on fighting. Get this land cleaned up and give it back to the community in the form of a wildlife area for people and animals. I hope to see this thing through to our victory, but if I don't, I know that you won't give up the fight. Don't ever give up the fight!" he yelled.

The audience roared back, "Don't ever give up the fight. Don't give up the fight."

When the crowd had finished its chant, one man went up to Ed, "You, don't give up the fight either, Ed. Keep fighting for your health. We're with you."

Some of the guests were in tears of sadness and some were in tears of joy.

Eva looked around the room from her position next to the cash register. She watched as Charlie and James counted the funds. James turned and whispered into Judi's ear.

Eva saw Judi turn pale. Disappointment drew her youthful pretty face down to a frown. Eva's heart was sinking. Judi turned and whispered to Eva. "We only made two-thousand dollars over our expenses. I was sure that, with all the effort we made, the return would be in the tens of thousands."

Eva looked around. Yes, the restaurant was full of supporters, even the media had come, but the people were just not donating in the way they had expected. Gary came to the two sisters and asked if he could announce the results. Judi looked up at him in panic.

Gary turned and looked at the audience.

"We're trying to get an exact number on it," he said.

Eva knew he was stalling. Judi's great plan was failing. Eva felt sad. She looked over at Charlie and James and saw them put their heads together. They looked down at the money in their hands. Eva looked at them and wondered what would happen.

"What do you say, Dad?" James asked.

"Ahh, I guess,"

James turned to Judi.

"Tell Gary we made twelve-thousand dollars tonight. Tell him that."

Judi looked faint, but then turned to Gary and quoted the number. Gary smiled.

"Folks, we just want to announce that—even though this has been a modest party compared to what we all experienced at the Foundation luncheon, we have been able to raise twelve-thousand dollars."

The crowd cheered, impressed with itself and the work they had been able to do.

Eva and Judi looked first at each other and then out at the audience where Colleen and Amanda were leaping from their chairs and cheering. The young women stood and watched then turned back to look at each other.

"Congratulations, Sis, on your persuasive efforts," Eva said.

Judi leaned forward and gave her a hug.

Chapter Eighteen

Conflicts of Heart and Mind

Amanda breathed a sigh of relief. The Friends of Nature now had the funding they needed to continue their campaign. She marveled at how, year after year, in various ways, they had been able to do this. This year, they had to thank the Kaufmans who organized the luncheon at the Hungry Fish Restaurant. Even though the Foundation could get thousands of dollars from its corporate sponsors, Amanda felt assured that the Friends of Nature still had the potential to score some victories.

What the Friends needed now was some kind of strong proof that could support their plan against the Foundation's. Amanda had hoped that someone would find that endangered yellow heron's bird nest. She hated having to ask Sally for something that might risk her job. Unfortunately, persuading Sally to get them the Foundation's financial records was the only hope.

Sally would not be home until late in the afternoon. Amanda paced back and forth in the living room. It was late morning. She looked out the front window. After the storm yesterday, the wind had scattered tree limbs around the front yard. She grabbed her gardening gloves, a trash bag and her pruning shears. Focusing on yard work would help her pass the time.

It was a beautiful day. The sun was up, the sky was clear. Amanda bent to gather the sticks and litter. Several neighbors stopped by for a chat. After rather lengthy conversations, Amanda went to the backyard and trimmed the Lilac and the Butterfly bushes to make them more compact and balanced. She took a few segments of roots and moved them to other areas of the garden. She surveyed her work. It gave a sense of satisfaction. In this backyard-world of hers, she had total control—well, as long as the rain cooperated.

As Amanda was putting away the gardening tools, she heard Sally enter the house. Sally's footsteps came closer, until finally the door on the enclosed back porch came open.

"Oh, Sally, you're home. How was your day?"

"Fine, fine, it was ok, what can I say? It was a day. It's over now. I'm so tired. I don't know how I can be so tired. I sit at a desk all day working at the computer. But that Barbara Harrison, she is so demanding."

Amanda sensed Sally's need to blow off steam.

"Well, let's go have dinner together and you can tell me all about it."

"No, no I can't. I've neglected the kitties too long. I need to get their food and get out there."

Amanda felt discouraged, but then she had an idea.

"Let me help you with them, can I? Then you can get it done quicker."

"Oh, Amanda, would you?"

Soon they were busy loading bags of cat food into Sally's old used car.

They climbed in and Sally drove off.

Amanda listened as Sally chattered on and on about how she felt ashamed. Her new job with the Foundation was taking up so much of her time and energy. Amanda looked at Sally and nodded sympathetically. Sally continued to explain how it had been three weeks since she had fed the kitties in the park. "I felt so ashamed, I stopped going to the animal protection meetings. They didn't get any reports from me for nearly a month. I'm a horrible person."

When Sally arrived at the first site, she looked around then wailed, "How could I have neglected my little friends?"

The two women lifted the big bags of dry cat food from the trunk of the car. Amanda looked around and saw aluminum trays. Sally picked them up and filled them with dry cat food.

"Come eat," Sally called. "Come on guys, come eat. Here I am again. I apologize for not feeding you more often. I hope you are well."

The two women stood together waiting and looking around. Finally, a calico kitten stepped out of the tall grass and meowed.

"Frisco, it's you! Look, I have canned kitty food for you," Sally called. She reached in her pocket and pulled out a can of cat food. She scooped out the soft meal with a small plastic spoon. "It's fish flavor, not chicken. It's better for you. Now that I'm working I can afford it—if only I could get here. I'm so sorry, kitties. Please come out."

More kittens and cats crept out of the tall grass. A black cat appeared, and then a brown tiger showed up. Eventually, seven cats were eating off aluminum pie pans at a feast of dry and wet cat food.

Amanda saw how the stress of the day dropped from Sally's shoulders. Sally greeted each cat with smiles that showed her heart was full of joy and hope.

Satisfied that these cats were doing well, Sally indicated to Amanda that it was time to move on to the other two sites. At the second site, Sally waited for two cats that never appeared. She looked at Amanda. "I wonder what might have happened to them." She called again and waited.

Amanda looked up and down the street. "Maybe someone came by and adopted them."

"I don't know if it's possible. Stray cats like these can't be made into house pets. They have been hurt too badly to recover their trust," Sally explained. "I have to get to the last site and feed those cats. And I'm getting very hungry, too."

They turned and climbed into the car. After a short drive, Sally parked near a field under a mulberry tree where several small weathered cardboard boxes remained. Out came some kittens that looked like they might have been born just a month ago. The mother cat seemed to be nowhere near.

Amanda watched as Sally inspected the kittens for worms or infections. They were in good health. She dished out some canned cat food and attempted to get the little ones to eat. She pushed their little mouths into the soft food and watched as they sneezed and shook bits of food out of their nostrils and then licked their lips. "Once the flavor makes it onto their tongues," Sally explained, "I know they'll eat." She laughed, "I'm their foster mother. I'm teaching them." Soon she had all of them eating ferociously.

Amanda leaned against the mulberry tree and watched the sun go down behind Caven Point Cove. She wanted to forget the real reason she was standing there with Sally.

"Amy, you sure have been a good friend to me," Sally said. "I just want you to know that."

Amanda smiled and looked down. She stirred her toe in the dust.

"If it wasn't for you, I don't know where I'd be right now," Sally continued.

"You'd be fine," Amanda said. "You're the one that got that good job. They wouldn't have hired you if they didn't think you could do it."

Amanda watched a smile appear on Sally's face. Then Amanda added, "I know a job can be difficult, but a good paying job makes life better for everyone."

"It's great when I get my pay, but it's not just the job. It's so nice to come home to you and Peter. I feel like I belong now. I have some kind of family. People I can really count on."

Amanda remembered her own struggle to survive as a young woman. She put her arm around Sally's shoulders. "We're glad to have you in our home, Sally."

Sally looked down at the kittens and sighed, "In spite of it all, I now have a lot to be thankful for. But still, I wish for more."

"We all do," Amanda said and laughed.

"Sometimes, the job at the Foundation is so boring. It leaves me feeling disappointed. Then there's Barbara Harrison, it seems all she wants to do is use me. She barks orders at me, but never talks to me like a fellow human being. It just isn't fair. Sometimes, I feel like all my energy is sucked out of me for the benefit of Barbara Harrison. I work all day answering phones, creating displays and processing updates to the web site, all done to make the Foundation and Barbara Harrison seem so impressive to the community."

Amanda nodded sympathetically. "I know what you mean dear, I used to have jobs like that. There's not much you can do about it. Be thankful you have a job. I must say, I've appreciated the rent you've paid, but I have also enjoyed your friendship. You are family. I'm so glad that you and Peter get along so well."

They looked down at the empty pie pans. With full round bellies, the kitties climbed into the weathered cardboard boxes. Some had already curled up on old rags to take a nap.

"We better get this mess cleaned up," Sally said. She bent to pick up the empty cans and trays. There at the edge of a path, she saw the mother cat step through the tall grass.

"Oh look, it's Ginger."

Amanda turned and saw a big orange cat.

Sally frowned, "Ginny, what do you have there in your mouth?"

The cat stood and stared up at Sally. In her mouth was a squealing baby bunny.

Sally gasped and watched as the mother cat ran quickly to the box where the kittens were now sleeping.

Amanda leaned forward to see inside the box. The mother cat was calling to the kittens to come eat. They only raised their heads a little and meowed. The mother cat then bit firmly into the bunny's neck. She laid its limp body down for their consumption. When the kittens failed to respond, the mother cat began to devour the feet from the silent soft body. The blood oozed across the ground.

Amanda heard Sally choke.

"Amanda, oh, let's go," Sally said as she turned her head away. "Why did she kill the bunny?"

Sally ran back to her car. Amanda followed.

"That was a mother cat taking care of her kittens," Amanda explained as she climbed in. "She brought them food."

Sally wiped back her tears and started the car. "It's all my fault. If I had fed them, she would not have killed the bunny."

"Don't blame yourself," Amanda pleaded. "She's a good mother cat. That's what cats do. Wouldn't you want her to be a good mother?"

Sally bowed her head and sat quietly in the driver's seat.

Amanda looked at her, "Let's go home now and feed ourselves."

After a moment, Sally laughed. Then she quietly drove the car home.

Once they were back in the house, in the kitchen, Amanda felt it was safe to continue the discussion about Sally's job at the Foundation.

"So let's think, maybe I can help you. I had to face a lot of problems on my jobs. Maybe I can give you some tips on how to cope," Amanda suggested.

Sally grabbed a skillet, poured in some oil, and a sprinkle of oregano. Soon, she added chopped onions, sweet red peppers, broccoli florets and some tofu.

"Barbara Harrison treats me like I'm trash. I'm already sick of the job. I go to help the kitties 'cause usually it makes me feel good, but today, it has turned out terrible. I didn't really think that they killed baby bunnies." She looked up at Amanda, her eyes dripping with tears. She wiped them away with her apron. "I hate Barbara Harrison."

Amanda held back a laugh. Kittens and Barbara Harrison, what did one have to do with the other?

"That's how nature operates," Amanda said.

Sally turned the heat down on the burner. "So tell me this. Why is Barbara so mean? Why can't she be my friend, like you are, Amanda?"

Amanda began setting the table. "My dear, be strong. You have to understand. Jobs are stressful. Bosses sometimes make extreme demands. But another thing to consider about any job is that it's not like every-day life. You are playing a role, so don't take Ms. Harrison's arrogance to heart." Amanda laughed at herself. Such good advice she was giving! She should remind herself of this when dealing with Ms. Harrison.

The task of persuading Sally stood like a goal post in Amanda's mind. She took a deep breath and thought harder. Sally seemed to be calming down now. Perhaps she was considering Amanda's explanations or she was just busy with the cooking. What approach would make Sally willing to help the Friends of Nature obtain the crucial information from the Foundation's files? One word popped into Amanda's head.

Revenge.

Amanda remembered some of the little pranks she had done in years gone by to get revenge on bosses she hated. Well, not extreme revenge, just a little. It made the job easier to cope with. Like the time she reported to the manager about finding the pornography magazine. This got the attorney she worked for in trouble. That was sheer delight.

"Ah, Sally, let me tell you what I did once to get revenge on one of my bosses."

Sally looked at Amanda with admiration. Amanda began the story as she continued setting the table.

"So I went into the office and started looking for that file he lost. That's back when we did everything on paper. He was always losing his documents. I pulled open every drawer, every cabinet door, and what did I find? A porn magazine."

Sally laughed.

When the story ended, Amanda smiled and looked at Sally. "Sally, in regard to your job, there is something you can do. You would get a laugh out of it, and just a little revenge, too. Most of all, it would benefit the park."

Amanda looked at Sally to see if she was curious.

"What do you have in mind, Amanda?"

Amanda turned away, almost afraid to ask. But what was there to lose? Sally might get angry and say "No." Amanda felt she had to sweeten the deal a little more. "You could be one of our park heroes. You are in a good position to do so."

Amanda could see that Sally was waiting.

"The Friends of Nature need the financial statements of the B & L Foundation. We need copies of their plans for the development of the new land. We need to know how they think they can succeed with this development."

Sally looked at Amanda and smiled. "Yes, I know what you're talking about," Sally said. "I know where those documents are."

"You know?" Amanda gasped.

"Yeah, and Barbara will be in a meeting all afternoon tomorrow. Those documents would be easy to get. I cannot email them. The Foundation looks at our outgoing emails, but I could make paper copies and put them in my purse."

Amanda smiled. "You have to be a little sneaky to survive in this society, especially if you want to do good deeds."

Sally laughed. "Amanda, you have such weird notions. I like having you for a friend."

A thumping sound came at the door. Sally looked out the kitchen window.

"It's Peter."

"Well, you know what we need, Sally, so I hope you can give it some thought." Amanda said, quickly wrapping up their discussion.

Peter came through the doorway. He sniffed the air. "Ah, another great vegan meal."

"Yes, join us, Peter, we were just talking about the kitties."

"Ah, Sally, you worry too much about those kitties," Peter said.

"I guess I do. I'm tired of getting depressed over what silly animals do."

Peter sat down at the table.

"Now take me, I have a degree in psychology. I'm interested in what silly humans do. That's quite a preoccupation."

"That's some preoccupation all right," said Amanda. "We humans need to get our priorities in order. Nature has to keep a balance and if we don't understand that we're in for trouble."

"That's what we need in human society. A balance," said Peter. "But it is disrupted all the time by the lopsided structure of present day economics." He tossed his bag in the corner and turned toward the table.

"Lopsided? You mean rich and poor?" Amanda asked.

"Please, enough of this discussion. Our next priority is dinner," Sally said. "I'll be serving it in just a minute."

Chapter Nineteen

A Time of Discovery

Eva heard Curtis on the park radio. "Eva, go to Curtis. Do you copy? We got the report back from the lab. It's not looking good. Come to the garage as soon as you can."

"Copy. I'm coming right now." Eva clipped the radio on her belt. She picked up her hat and started walking. She knew it meant they had proof that the pine branches they had collected were contaminated. The Foundation workers who dumped the waste on the new parkland had put every tree in the park at risk. Eve entered the gardening shed where Curtis worked.

"Yes, Eva, we have a problem on our hands."

Curtis was sitting at his desk looking at the report. He began reading the report aloud.

"The pine needles were infected with Diplodia Tip Blight. The needles had pycnidia that causes fungal spores. All our park pine trees are now vulnerable. Spores will be blowing in the wind and will soon contaminate all the other conifers."

"So Curtis, why did this happen? Were the horticultural workers doing a sloppy job?"

Eva followed Curtis around the shop. He began pulling together the tools they needed.

"Do you think they did it deliberately? Or accidentally?" Eva grabbed several pairs of gloves and put them in with the tools.

"Well, it's possible that the tree trimmers saw the contamination among the lawn trees and, instead of burning it as they should have, they just decided to cut off contaminated branches and throw them away. Pure convenience for them."

"Simple enough," Eva replied. "But then, they do work for the Foundation and you know the Foundation wants that land for other uses."

"Yes, I realized there's a motive for dumping the fungus in that part of the park," Curtis continued. "Maybe the B & L Foundation is using the fungus to justify cutting down the trees. They would need to clear the land anyway for sewer and water lines to put up their hotel and sports complex."

Eva looked up at Curtis. "Of course, but what can we do to stop them? We have no absolute proof that they did it deliberately."

"No, we can't prove they were being malicious," Curtis said, "but they certainly have a motive. I think I'll go over there sometime today, meet up with some of the guys and just see what's happening. You know, just get some shop talk going with them about what tree diseases they may have seen in the area."

"Oh, that would be a good thing to do."

They loaded the gloves, chain saws, barrels and shovels into the back of the truck and climbed into the cab.

Eva pushed a small camera and laptop computer out of the seat and placed them into the storage chest between them. "Why do you have these here?"

"We're always taking pictures of damaged property. You wouldn't believe the vandalism in the park and the erosion due to weather. We have to document it for the state so we can get money in the budget for repairs," Curtis said as he started the engine. "Hey, I have a large jug of water in the refrigerator and we need some cups. Can you run back and get them?"

Eva jumped out of the cab and ran to get these supplies.

Behind her, she heard Curtis say, "Grab that box of peanuts and cookies, too."

Eva returned with a basket of supplies and placed it behind the seat. She then climbed into the truck.

Curtis began calling on the radio to the other park workers.

Soon the work crew joined them near the new land. They all picked up tools from the truck and made their way through the hole in the fence. Down the narrow path, they went to the location of the contaminated pine branches. Curtis began shouting directions.

"We're going to cut this stuff up, put it in garbage bags and haul it out of here. It's got to be burnt in the state incinerators. Here, wear these safety goggles," Curtis said, holding out a bag of goggles. "I don't want any injuries. Be aware, this stuff is contaminated. After you work here, go to the clean-up room and wash your clothes. We don't want to spread the fungus ourselves."

The work crew put on their gloves and goggles and began breaking down the branches.

"So this is what a fungus infestation looks like," Eva said, looking around. The fungus had spread to more tree branches.

"Yeah, make note of that for your future biology class and hope you never see so much of this again in your life. This is a real mess." Curtis got the camera out of the truck and began documenting the dumpsite with photos. "Eva, set up our canteen base here. Then follow through on your other assignments for today."

"Ok," Eva replied. She watched the park workers begin swinging axes and shoving the broken limbs into bags. She brought the basket of food and water from the truck, set up the table and placed the supplies out for everyone's use.

"What else were you assigned to do today?" Curtis asked, looking at her with curiosity.

"I was assigned to go to the Nature center and help with an environmental education workshop that is being held there."

"You do that," Curtis said. "I'll talk to you later. After we remove this debris, I'm going to have a talk with the Foundation horticulture crew."

"Good luck, see you later." Eva said. She lifted her radio and called for a ride, but no one responded. "I'll just walk," she said and headed down the trail.

It was a beautiful afternoon. The sky was clear blue. The noisy birds, such as the Brown Thrashers and Mockingbirds, were singing from the tops of the big Cottonwood trees. Eva walked out to Zapp Drive, a cobblestone road, one of the oldest in the country. She soon realized that getting to the nature center would involve a long hot walk. When she saw a white car with the park emblem on its door, she decided it was best to flag down the driver. The car stopped. Eva waved and ran toward it. The driver was one of the regular park office workers.

"Can you drop me off at the nature center?"

"Sure, what's happening at the center?"

"They're having a guest speaker, some famous environmentalist."

When Eva arrived, she saw a crowd, including the media with their cameras and microphones. A sign posted in the entrance explained the talk was about the horrors of mountain top removal.

Eva went into the center and began setting up the chairs in the auditorium. After that, she sat down in the back row to relax in the darkness. Her relaxation soon turned to anxiety. On the screen, she watched explosions. First, there were mountains and then there were none.

Mining companies were hauling away entire mountains to obtain coal, or whatever mineral they wanted, so they could sell it on the market and make huge profits. While Eva had always doubted how deep mining could be good for the earth, she sympathized with the coal miners who had lost their jobs. The program explained that mountain top removal was the fastest way to reach the minerals with few workers employed to do the work.

As she sat in the cool air conditioning of the auditorium, Eva's mood turned for the worse. How could the corporations destroy the land the people lived on? Then it occurred to her that these same earthmovers could easily haul away much of the soil in the new section of the park. They could carry it all away in just a few days.

As the program went on, she began to feel like the battle to save that little patch of land in the park was so trivial compared to the need to save the earth's mountains. She had spent many days trying to keep dogs out of the nature area so they wouldn't disturb nesting birds. How many nesting birds died when whole mountains were blown up? How much difference did it make if she dashed into playgrounds to scold children about releasing their balloons. A fallen balloon in the harbor's water would strangle a turtle, but how many streams and rivers were ruined by the wash of so much loose soil after the mountain's disappearance?

The guest speaker took questions after the program. He talked about the need to take action. Eva felt the tug of his request. Her concern for the environment was strong, but as he spoke, he enumerated a list of issues that overwhelmed Eva's weary heart. The constantly increasing need to protect the earth made her feel as though she were carrying it on her shoulders. The environmentalist pleaded for people to send letters, make calls, attend protests. Saving the planet seemed to rely on doubtful politicians and careerists that left her feeling frustrated and hopeless. She slouched down in her seat.

Finally, the program was finished. Eva watched as the crowd meandered out of the auditorium. In the alcove, the news media began interviewing local celebrities and organizers.

Eva joined the other park staff in putting everything back in place. When she had finished folding the chairs, she looked at the clock. It was time to go home. The air conditioning sent a chill up her back. She wanted to get out of it.

"See you tomorrow," Eva called. She grabbed her small backpack. "Thanks for helping."

Eva pulled open the front door. Outside, the day had turner hotter and more humid. She compared her situation to that of Curtis and the maintenance crew. She had been lucky to get an indoor assignment this afternoon.

Eva started walking down Freedom Way toward the train station. The program she had just seen was still playing in her head. As she walked along, she felt her cold body warm to the true temperature of the day. That air conditioning was excessive. She began to wonder if the electricity to cool the auditorium had been generated by burning coal. What an irony, burning something to stay cool. Just then, she thought she smelled smoke. She laughed. Was she just imagining that? It could not be smoke from burning coal.

Then she realized that she, in fact, smelled real smoke. Where could it be coming from? There was often a lot of smoke in the park. Park patrons enjoyed barbeques where charcoal fires spewed embers from hickory trees long dead. Ships on the New York harbor occasionally sent heavy diesel smoke billowing out of their smoke stacks. There was no need to be concerned; smoke was normal here.

Eva thought about the long walk ahead of her and then the long train ride home. Fortunately, she had brought something to read—a book on the basics of cross-pollination. She felt for her book in her bag—but it was not there.

"My book," she yelled. Then she remembered that she had been showing it that morning to the park superintendent. She realized she had left it on one of the desks in the park office. She took off on a run back across the park. The office would be closing soon.

She ran as fast as she could, past the now-closed nature center, up the trail past the muskrat nests and then down through the parking lot. She saw the superintendent coming out.

"Hey, hey, I forgot my book."

He did not hear her. He got into his car and drove away.

Now, Eva was faced with making the trip without anything to read. To top it off, she now had to walk all the way back through the park to get to the train station.

The heat of the day was beginning to get to her.

She started down the trail. She needed to refill her water bottle. If she took Freedom Way, it would take longer to get to the train station, but there was a water fountain at the picnic site. It would be safer to go that way, rather than take the short cut near the highway that offered no chance of getting water. No matter what, it was going to be a long walk. The summer heat was burning the back of her neck. She pulled her collar up to block it. As she walked, she continued to smell the smoke.

Finally, she arrived at the picnic site. She went to the fountain and filled her bottle. She used her hat to soak her head. This should keep her cool enough to get to the train.

The air here smelled even heavier with smoke. Charcoal mixed with the smell of diesel fumes and a hint of burning pine. Burning pine? She remember that Curtis had said the contaminated pine would be burnt in the state incinerator. Could that be the cause of the smoke?

Eva continued to walk down the trail. Here, the smoke lost its bitterness. It mingled with the sweet smell of honey suckle and the earthy musk-like fragrance of the sycamore trees.

As she approached the edge of the park, near the train station, she saw a column of smoke. It appeared to be rising from the new land—the very area where she had left Curtis and his work crew. She walked up a side trail hoping to see more clearly just what was happening.

Something was on fire. But what?

She wanted to go home. She was feeling hungry. The column of smoke was getting wider and darker now. For a moment, she stood and looked first toward the path that led to the train station and then to the land grown over with weeds and brush. She did not feel like trekking into that thorny mess on a hot day. The insects would be capable of committing murder.

The smoke reached into the sky before it flattened and rolled downward. It was white, but more like dust than steam. Something was burning deep in the interior of the new land. There was no way she could let this mystery go. She knew she had to find out what was happening to her beloved park.

She took a sip of water from her bottle and then ran toward the opening in the fence.

Here, no birds were singing. The crickets had stopped calling. The summer song of the cicada was silent. She saw the smoke wafting through the cottonwoods. As she moved over the land, she realized that the smoke was coming from the area of the dumped pine branches. It was hard to believe. Curtis would never set them on fire right there in the park. He would never do something so dangerous or stupid.

Could it have been a spontaneous fire? Caused by lightening? There had been no rain or lightening. Eva approached the area and saw the burning heap of branches. They were on fire and smoke was rising. The grass was catching on fire too, but the green leaves of the trees were only being singed and adding to the smoke.

Suddenly Eva tripped. She stumbled forward then caught herself and stood up.

Her toe had hit something hard. Probably just a rock or a turtle.

She looked around. Smoke was consuming what little fresh air she had available to breathe. She needed to get out of there and report the fire to the fire department.

She looked down again at her feet.

She had not hit a rock or turtle . . . . it was a boot.

She looked into the tall grass. The boot was connected to a leg. She had tripped over someone in the tall grass.

She bent down to examine it.

It was Curtis.

"Curtis!" she screamed.

His eyes opened and he began to look around.

Eva panicked, "We've got to get out of here. The field is on fire."

She tried to lift him up. He was a tall man and heavier than she could carry.

He fell back down. She tried again. He leaned against her, but the two of them fell back to the ground again.

"Come on, get up, Curtis, you have to help me. Let's go."

She felt him make an effort to lift himself.

"Eva, Eva, what happened?"

"I don't know. I just saw the smoke and came in here to see why."

"It's those guys from the Foundation. They punched me out. I saw them dumping more branches and setting more fires. Where's my camera?"

Eva looked around on the ground. She saw no camera.

"Curtis, we have to leave."

"No, where's my camera? I have pictures of them setting the fire."

They lingered for a minute. Curtis crawled across the ground, raking his fingers through the grass.

Eva stood and assessed the damage the fire was causing. More and more of the field was burning and the fire was quickly spreading.

"They must have taken it. Damn it!" Curtis screamed.

"Let's go!"

"No, I want my camera."

Just then, Eva saw an object that she could not clearly identify at the edge of the flames. She reached over. It was his camera.

"Here it is."

"My camera? I hope the fire didn't damage it."

"Let's go."

They stumbled through the trees into the distant fields and through the opening in the fence. As they pressed themselves through the narrow passage, fire trucks came racing up to the edge of the road. Park and city police cars followed. The entire roadway began to fill with curious park patrons who wanted to know what had happened.

"What were you doing in there?" a city police officer yelled.

Curtis and Eva stood together looking confused.

"We can explain," said Curtis. "See," he pointed to the park emblem on his uniform. "I work for the park, I'm a botanist. We were removing debris."

Eva nodded and pointed to her emblem as well, and then she saw the dry blood on Curtis' chin. "Curtis, you've been hurt." She turned to the police, "He needs medical care."

"Great," said the police officer. "All I know is I saw you two running out of the fire. You'll get your chance to explain."

The city police officer looked toward his team, "Give this guy some first aid. Take them in for questioning," the officer commanded. Two other officers came quickly to their sides and led them to the police car.

As they were led away, Eva saw Judi coming down the path on her way to work at the Hungry Fish. Eva called to her.

"Tell Mom, we need help."

"What's going on here?" Judi yelled.

"Tell Mom, get us help," Eva begged.

Instead, Judi screamed at the officer. "You can't do this to my sister."

He turned his back, leaving her to face the broad black wall of his leather vest.

"I'm going to get help, Eva," Judi yelled. "I'm going right now."

Eva sighed and watched Judi run off toward the restaurant.

Eva and Curtis sat in the back seat of the city police car, staring out the windows, feeling embarrassed as they rode through the crowd. Among the spectators, they saw Amanda and Murphy, binoculars hanging from their necks, their mouths dropped open in surprise.

Chapter Twenty

Blamed for the Death of Trees

"Can you believe it?" Murphy asked.

Amanda was bewildered. She had just seen two park employees escorted out of the park and put into a police car. They were Eva and Curtis. Meanwhile, a fire billowed out of control over the treetops.

"Why would the police take Eva and Curtis away?" Amanda asked. Around her, people were gathering on the road to watch. Firefighters unloaded heavy hoses. They tore open a hole in the fence and began dragging the hoses into the fields.

"There's a house on fire in there," someone yelled.

Firefighters turned and looked.

"Keep going Henry, never mind that kid. There's no house in there."

"There were some old cars in the back field. I'll bet that's what caught fire," another voice explained to the spectators.

Murphy and Amanda continued to watch. More firefighters ran into the park with shovels. Sparks flew into the air.

"What's going to happen to all the birds?" a gray-haired woman asked. She peered into the treetops with a look of horror.

"They'll fly away," Murphy snarled. "Why do you think they have wings? Birds can fly away from trouble."

"You don't need to be so hostile," Amanda pleaded. She knew from his gruffness that he was upset that his favorite bird sanctuary was aflame.

"That's why I've always liked birds, they are free. They can leave a bad situation at any time," Murphy said. Amanda took his words as a consolation for herself as well.

"Such a pretty park to be having a fire," a tourist mused.

"Pretty?" Murphy huffed. "That was my special place, my sanctuary. I knew it couldn't last forever."

The smoke rose up into a cloud that looked like a mushroom, and then fell back down into a smoldering heap of soot.

"Stand back, stand back everyone," the park police warned.

Murphy nudged Amanda, "I think I know that guy, that firefighter over there." He stepped forward, "Hey, Chuck, Chuck Standowski, hey, what's going on in there? What's on fire?"

"Looks like it's nothing but wood. Maybe someone's campfire got loose."

"Nah, campfires aren't allowed in that part of the park," Murphy said.

Chuck shrugged, "Don't matter to me, I just go in and put the fire out. Hey, maybe some Mexicans were in there camping. There is a construction site not too far from here. They sleep under the trees sometimes, ya know."

"That ain't it," Murphy growled. He looked around at the spectators. "I'll bet it has something to do with that Barbara Harrison and her gang," he yelled. "They want that land destroyed so they can develop the property." Amanda watched as people turned to look at Murphy. She knew what he was doing and she felt she had to counter it.

"It looks like the fire is under control now," Amanda said. She watched as the media cameras came to interview the fire captain. Amanda went to stand near them to listen. Yes, the fire was almost out. It was a relief to know.

"Let's go Murphy, we need to get out of the way and contact Gary about this. I'm sure he'll want an investigation. We need to know the real reason that fire started."

She grabbed his shirtsleeve and nudged him away from the crowds.

"You know, I really can't tolerate what is happening these days to the few natural areas we have," Murphy complained as he walked. "Maybe I should just pack up my stuff and move as far from the city as I can get. It depresses me so much. Here in Liberty Park, I had a little place all to myself and now that's burned down. I'm sick of it."

"Come on Murphy, let's get your bike and I'll give you a ride home in my car."

"I'll tell you what. I'll stay until we get this park issue settled, but then I'm leaving for good. Amanda, you might want to think about joining me. We'll sell our houses and head for the deep woods. We'll have our very own mountain. Out there, no one can bother us. We'll be far away from these ruthless greedy corporations."

As she drove home, Amanda thought about Murphy's invitation. It was not that she would ever take him seriously. Moving out to the countryside would leave her feeling isolated. What would they do? Sit in the woods and look at each other all day? Murphy was ranting on and on about how crazy most people are, consequently proving his own membership in the human race.

Amanda tried to think of something to distract him.

"Do you need to stop by any store for something?" she asked as she drove.

He paused. His silence was golden.

Finally, he responded. "Yeah, I do need something. Take me over to the hardware store. They're having a sale on bird feeders. I want to see if they have the type that keep squirrels away."

Amanda looked at him and smiled. "Ok, I'll take you over there."

She turned the car down the next street and they headed for the hardware store. It was amazing how a little shopping could make a grumpy person so happy.

Soon, they were walking between the shelves scrutinizing the different types of bird feeders that were available.

"Feeding the birds is so expensive," Murphy complained. "They **can** find enough food in the wild, but I put seed out so I can take their pictures. Did I tell you? I made a good piece of money last year with my bird photos."

"But how much did you spend on birdseed?" Amanda asked.

"I buy the cheap stuff. See, here are the feeders that are on sale."

He picked up one and examined it. Happy with its design, he went to the cashier and paid. They climbed back into the car.

When they arrived at their homes, Amanda waited as Murphy retrieved his feeder from the car.

"Good bye, Amy, I know you'll be on that phone making more trouble." He laughed delighted that he could count on her to do so.

"Murphy, do try to have a quiet afternoon. Don't work yourself into a rage," Amanda advised, "You need to take care of your health."

"Oh sure. My sanctuary was set on fire today and I'm supposed to stay calm. Yes, I'll stay calm." He slammed the car door and carried the feeder up to his porch.

Amanda parked the car in the garage. She was glad she had succeeded in pacifying him with the bird feeder. He was right about one thing; she had a lot of work to do now that the park was damaged by fire.

Amanda walked through her backdoor, feeling like a little wren going into its birdhouse. She felt tired and glad to be home. She had been up early again in hopes of seeing the bald eagle. What they actually saw were red-tailed hawks. In late morning, they had twisted their heads around in the bramble trying to identify warblers that flitted in circles at top speed. Now she had to get to work on park issues.

She went to the living room, sat down with the phone, and called Gary Russo.

"The Friends of Nature are going to need another meeting. Something crazy happened in the park today," Amanda began.

Gary laughed. "I already heard from the park superintendent. A park employee took pictures of the men who set the fire. We've got proof now to hold against the Foundry and their Foundation. They have not been playing by the rules."

"Pictures? Who took them?"

"Yes, Curtis took pictures. He was in the area trying to stop the arsonists." Gary said, sounding triumphant. That was reassuring to Amanda.

"But the Foundation gang punched Curtis out cold. He would have died in the fire if Eva hadn't rescued him."

"Oh, no," Amanda gasped. Had this battle between the Foundation and the Friends actually turned violent? Would a court battle result from the pictures that Curtis took?

"So, Eva rescued Curtis? I'm so glad," Amanda said, trying to imagine how it happened. Her favorite park employees had been in danger, but they had caught the bad guys. They were truly park heroes.

The park needed heroes to protect it. Someone was always trying to do something that would turn the soothing sanctuary of green leaves and bird song into the maddening circus of a city street.

Thinking of park heroes, Amanda now thought of Sally and the mission she hoped Sally would perform.

What kind of a day was Sally having? Amanda tried to envision it. The Foundation would have received a phone call from the park police. What did the park police see in the pictures that Curtis took? Sally would have answered the phone. She would have been told that the Foundation yard workers had set fire to the park's trees. The police had proof. Sally would refer them to Barbara Harrison. Barbara Harrison would go crazy. That would put pressure on Sally.

Amanda wished she were a fly on the wall. To see Ms. Harrison so perturbed would make her laugh.

Then Amanda began to worry. Would all this commotion block Sally's chances of getting to the financial records and making copies?

Amanda was glad that Gary had learned right away of the details of the day's events. What a day! Eva and Curtis had been chasing down arsonists. That was exciting news. Amanda went to her computer to see what the local media was saying.

A big picture flashed before her showing two park employees being led away by the city police. The headlines blared: "Hired to Protect Parks, Are Park Employees Doing Their Job?"

Amanda was horrified. The local media was at it again—distorting the news to catch more readers and sell more advertising copy. Amanda grabbed her phone and called Colleen Kaufman.

"Colleen, what's going on?" Amanda screeched.

"Yes, yes we know. Eva's picture is in the news. That headline makes it look so bad, but read the article. It's not what you think."

Amanda could hear Eva scream in the background. Then Colleen was gone from the phone and Eva was speaking.

"We are not to blame. The attorney has the pictures that Curtis took. Besides, I saved someone's life. I should be a hero. Look at that picture. I look like a criminal."

"I knew you couldn't have done anything bad, Eva," Amanda reassured her.

"But the picture makes it look like park employees were to blame," Eva raged. "We'll have to put up with this nonsense for weeks."

Amanda looked again at the article and quickly read it.

"I see what they are up to. The media is deflecting the blame onto the Park Service because they need to cover for the Foundation. The

Foundation is the one with the tarnished image in this case," Amanda said, gloating over the Foundation's difficulty.

"What's important is that I rescued Curtis," Eva wailed, "and I found his camera. So, we have pictures of the Foundation workers setting the fires. See at the end, it finally explains this in the article."

"You are our hero, Eva," Amanda declared. "Now listen, we are planning an emergency meeting of the Friends to discuss what to do next. I'm sure you'll all be there."

"We'll be there. Just let us know when," Eva assured Amanda.

"Great, I have to go now. There's much to be done."

Instead, Amanda went to the kitchen to make a cup of tea. She needed more time to think. When the tea was ready, she went to Stephanie's room and sat down on the bed.

"My dear daughter, Eva is our hero. You would be proud of her. She's a kindred spirit. I feel that she is an angel that you sent to save the park. I must dedicate my energy to helping her. I will do what I can to help Eva."

Amanda took a sip of tea, looked out the window at the garden below and then continued her conversation with Stephanie.

"My dear, as you know, I'm still having financial problems. I cannot keep this house much longer. It needs repairs. I should sell it before it completely falls apart. I must sell it. But, rest assured, I will use the money for saving the environment and helping girls."

She thought of the campaign against the Foundation. With the money from the sale of the house, she could pay off the taxes, have more money to live on and help finance the Friends of Nature, rather than be dependent on the stipend they paid her. But could she give up this house?

Amanda looked at the dolls sitting next to her on the bed. Their sparkling glass eyes seemed to plead with her. She turned and looked at the china tea set on the small table in the corner, the cups and saucers with their pink rose buds and silver trim still waiting for that special tea party. From the tops of the lavender curtains, Amanda regarded again the paper fuchsia blossoms that draped down over the windows, always in bloom as if time had stood still.

Outside was Stephanie's flower garden in mid-summer bloom. Brown-eyed Susans and Purple Cone Flowers lifted their petals to the bright sunlight. It was so hard to part with this house and its garden.

But what else could she do?

Suddenly Amanda heard a thumping noise. It was the door downstairs. She heard Sally scream, "Amanda, Amanda, I'm home. What a terrible day I had."

Amanda smiled and hurried down the stairs to greet Sally.

"Tell me all about your day!" Amanda said.

"I will tell you everything," Sally said and let out a big sigh.

A week later, at the Hungry Fish Restaurant, Amanda sat down at the big table in the back where the meeting was going to be held. She thought of what Sally had said and done. It was incredible. As she thought, she watched Judi, dressed in her crisp white uniform, guide each member of the Friends of Nature into the room for the meeting.

"We have delicious salads today. Fruit or vegetable," Judi said, smiling at her guests. "So look over our new menu and let me know what you want."

"Oh, wonderful. Is this the new menu you helped to create? Harvest Fruit Salad?" Colleen asked.

Amanda turned to Colleen and smiled. She wanted the blueberry pie again, but decided it was best to try the new item that Judi had created. It had apples, blueberries, peaches and pecans. "I'll have the Harvest Fruit Salad," Amanda said.

"I'll have that too," said Colleen.

"Let's order a big bowl of it and each give it a try," Gary Russo suggested.

Soon Judi was handing out small bowls into which they ladled what they wanted of her new menu item.

"Here's what I found out from the authorities," Gary began.

Amanda watched as Murphy sat down and looked up at Gary. She had promised him an interesting meeting. Murphy seemed eager to hear some real dirt about the Foundation. Amanda had invited him to the meeting, hoping that if he were not so isolated, he might join in their more sensible activities.

"It's good news—bad news time," Gary said looking around the room. "The bad news, in case you haven't heard, is that a part of the park was on fire. The good news is that we now have something else to use in our fight against the Foundation. Neither the Foundry nor the Foundation had a burning permit to dispose of those pine branches," Gary announced. "They will have to pay large fines for this."

"Good!" Murphy called out and looked around the table at the other members.

"That's ok, but look at this press release that the Foundation put out," Ed Wilson said. They laid down their spoons and reviewed the press release.

Barbara Harrison was the Foundation's contact person, as everyone expected. The media quoted her saying that damage from the fire was of no consequence. She stated that it was contaminated land scheduled for removal.

"Is this true?" Amanda asked. "Are they going to dig up all that land and haul it away?"

"Not so, based on the park maps that I have access to," Curtis explained.

"Harrison is just trying to get the heat off the Foundation," Gary continued. "We don't know yet how the state wants to handle this land. There's going to be another public hearing. We need to be there with our testimony. We have an expert now. He's coming tonight. He'll be at this meeting in just a little while. We need to take care of all our other business before he comes."

The Friends of Nature stirred in their seats and looked around at each other. This lull gave Amanda the perfect opportunity.

"I'm sure you all read the article about the fire. My goodness, when I saw that picture, it worried me, but then I knew our dear Eva Kaufman and our friend from the park, Curtis Elliot, would never do anything wrong. They love the park and it is an important part of their lives."

The audience cheered and then broke into individual comments and witticisms. Gary pulled the groups' attention together again before looking over at Amanda.

"So Amanda, what is it you mean to say?"

"I just want us to honor someone who risked her life to save her co-worker and defend our park." Amanda stood up and pointed to Eva, "Eva Kaufman rushed into that fire and rescued Curtis. She is our hero and we must always honor our heroes. If we do not honor our own great works, who will? Eva, we are proud of you." Amanda sat down as the Friends of Nature clapped their hands and cheered.

Eva blushed and looked over at Curtis. He smiled and laughed.

"Yes, Eva is our special hero," he said. "If she hadn't come in there, I might have been burned to death. She also helped me find my camera and that is how we were able to identify the scoundrels that set the fire."

"She's our park hero!" Amanda proclaimed again with her arms in the air.

Soon everyone in the restaurant was standing and clapping their hands.

Amanda watched as Eva blushed and turned to see her sister Judi across the room lifting a coffee pot in salute.

"Now, back to our action plan," Gary insisted. "I think we need to do another press conference." He looked around the room. "Let's tell the media about the Foundation's failure to have a burn permit. And we'll show them the boxes of signed petitions that we have." He pointed to three boxes filled with signed petitions.

Everyone cheered again.

Amanda was happy. A sense of fulfillment had come over her. Her community was unified and ready. Surely, they would win their fight.

Murphy nudged her elbow.

"This is a good meeting. I'm looking forward to that actuary's report."

"But first we have to follow up on our decision." Amanda explained. She raised her hand and pushed for support of Gary's suggestion of the press conference. Murphy attempted to say something, but Amanda cut him off. She saw a critical look in his eye and whispered in his ear. "Let's get this vote finished." He laughed. Then Amanda announced, "Very good, we all agree."

Judi came to the end of the table with a stranger standing next to her. He was a middle-aged businessman wearing a gray suit but no tie.

"Mr. Martinez says he's to speak at your meeting," Judi said looking at Gary.

"Oh, yes," Gary responded and stood to shake the man's hand. He then introduced him to the Friends as the expert that would save the day.

The Friends began moving their chairs around to create a space to seat the expert. Judi brought him a chair, and then she gathered the empty bowls.

"My name is Burt Martinez. I must tell you, I'm not an actuary, but I can assure you that the records still point to a great risk for the B & L Foundation. I'm sure the government's actuarial agent will see it clearly." He looked at them to judge their reaction before he continued.

"After doing the necessary research, I can say, without doubt, that too much development of this sort has already occurred. This means that the Foundation would have to persuade people from outside the local community to come here. The likelihood of their persuading enough people to come is very slim."

Amanda looked at Gary. He nodded back at her with confidence.

"Profit taking on this kind of industry, in this current economic climate, is generally weak," Mr. Martinez explained, "because this type of industry depends on expendable income, which few people have these days."

"Very true, my friend," Murphy agreed and thumped the table.

The Friends looked at each other and smiled. Not so much because they understood what was reported, but the tone seemed to indicate that the Foundation's scheme was not feasible. The financial advisor went on.

"We also have some "insider information" that indicates that the Foundation is not getting the donations that it has gotten in the past."

Amanda looked around at all the thoughtful expressions on the faces of those who were attending the meeting. Only she knew that the advisor was referring to Sally as the "insider." Sally was an invisible park hero. They couldn't let Ms. Harrison know that the truth was escaping right under her nose.

The financial advisor continued, "Again, the bad economy is playing a role here. The income to the Foundation does not meet their budget expectations. They may actually need to reduce their staff."

Amanda jolted. What did he just say? *They may need to reduce their staff?* That meant Sally could lose her job at the Foundation. If Sally lost her job, Amanda would lose the rental income that she got from Sally. Every struggle included some sacrifice. But why this now?

The advisor showed some graphs, reports and calculations that impressed those who could understand them. This, in turn, impressed the others.

When the expert finished, Gary stood to speak. "We want to thank you for doing such a great job on this report. It is just what we need when we go to the government hearing." He looked around the room. "Any questions?"

There were none.

"So we have our petitions and our expert financial assessment," Gary continued. "At the press conference, we will need to make it clear that nothing is to happen to the land until the state makes a determination. It is not up to the Foundation to decide and move forward as they please."

Curtis sat up in his chair. "As you may know, we're doing a study showing the biological resources we have to protect. Our reports are based on pure science, not on someone's desire to turn a profit."

"That's right," said Ed Wilson. "We have the truth. The state has to listen to us."

"But, I want everyone here to keep this financial report a secret," Gary said looking around the room. His face was grim and serious. "We don't want the Foundation's people to know that we have a financial expert and financial reports. We want to catch them off guard. So keep quiet about all that we discussed here today."

Each individual nodded in agreement. Gary went to pay the bill. Judi accepted the money. The bird clock above the cash register tweeted the late hour of the evening. The Friends of Nature departed the restaurant with an air of confidence.

Amanda left with a heart full of joy. The pieces were coming together. They now had the ammunition to fight the Foundation and win. Yet the biggest steps were still ahead. They still had to get through the press conference, the government hearing and the long wait for the state's decision.

When she got home, Amanda felt too tired to climb the stairs to tell her daughter what had happened at the meeting. She began to wonder why she bothered to do such a thing. Stephanie had died years ago. But why give up on her ritual now? Up the stairs she went.

"Stephanie, I feel like we're going to win. I should have known. I've been through it before. If the Friends of Nature stick together and get the community's support, we will prove that we are right. With these happy thoughts, she lifted her arms and let Stephanie go.

Chapter Twenty One

Dinner with Dad and Mom

"Ok, remember, tonight we're trying to get them to confirm what they're doing in their retirement." Eva said before letting out a sigh and looking at her hair in the mirror.

The large mirror's ornate gold frame captured the expressions of Eva and Judi as they primped and fussed with themselves. Their young faces frowned with anxiety about tonight's dinner with their parents. They were about to celebrate their father's birthday. No, it wasn't actually his birthday. That had occurred three weeks ago. It was customary with Dad to celebrate almost every holiday or event late, due to his work schedule.

"Remember the time we had our Thanksgiving dinner in December because Dad was out of the country on the actual holiday?" Eva said. She watched in the mirror as Judi pulled a strand of hair across her forehead.

"I remember that, so what's the big deal? Do you think he loved us less because he could rarely keep a date?" Judi said and looked at Eva in the mirror, "I think everything is fine. Our parents are not on the verge of divorce. They are going to retire to Arizona, like they said they would."

"They said that five years ago," Eva replied. She looked directly at Judi this time. "Things can happen in five years. If you noticed, if you weren't so caught up with yourself, you may have noticed that our parents have had little to do with each other over that five year stretch. I don't see how they can keep a relationship going like that, unless there is something about being an adult that I've missed," Eva said.

"Well, considering you are just now becoming an adult, you may be in for lots of surprises," Judi responded. "In my friendship with James, I can see how, if your love is strong, you could get through times apart—short times, but no longer times. That would be harder for me."

"Yeah, your love is strong, especially when there's a decent living to be made from it," Eva added with a sarcastic sneer. "But I do think Dad's absences have created a gap in their relationship."

"You can't complain, Eva. They did it to support us. Now, we have to become a success and stand on our own two feet, like I'm doing."

Eva turned to Judi but said nothing. How could Judi call it love if she seduced a young restaurant owner into marrying her? Eva picked up her purse. "Come on, Madam Success, if you don't stop fussing over your looks, Mom and Dad are going to abandon us."

"Don't worry. It's good we left them at the table alone together. It gave them time to think and talk to each other," Judi replied.

When the two young women returned to the dining room, they saw their parents sitting at the table near the window that they had selected. Dad was reading a newspaper he had picked up at the door and Mom was staring out the window at the sailboats on the harbor.

So much for intimate conversation, Eva thought. She shot a quick glance at Judi who tossed a fake smile back at her.

They ordered their meal. Their drinks arrived. Dad began with stories about life in Egypt, India and Saudi Arabia, all the places where he had done his work as a consultant to the chemical companies. Eva and Judi politely listened. Then their mother gave a report about her work with the Friends of Nature. Dad asked questions and listened politely to their mother. Then he turned to Judi and Eva.

"So what have my daughters been involved with?"

"I've been working at a restaurant in the park," Judi announced. "I met this really great guy there and he's the son of the restaurant owner," Judi folded her hands in front of her. "They are really impressed with my talents. I've introduced some new dishes to the menu, brought in more customers, and advised them on the décor of the restaurant."

Dad's eyes brightened with approval. Soon he and Judi were going back and forth, the doting parent and the successful child.

Eva watched how Judi talked up her ambitions to be the owner of the Hungry Fish, her apparent goal in life.

The conversation stopped when the food arrived. Eva didn't remember if she had ordered rice or potatoes, but it made no difference to her. The food was irrelevant. She was wondering if Dad had always liked Judi better and if that had ever really mattered. From time to time, Eva glanced over at her mom. Colleen was busy prying apart mussels and dipping them into marinara sauce. It seemed like she was just "one of the girls." She was here to have a good time. She looked relaxed and unconcerned. This made Eva feel better. Maybe Judi was right. Maybe everything was normal.

Next, it was Eva's turn to talk.

"I'm working at Liberty Park. I do all kinds of things there. Helping tourists find their way, explaining some history about the park, telling people to keep their dogs on the leash. Oh, I'm also working on the preservation and restoration of a new area in the park."

"Eva, you are so modest. Your mom tells me you rescued one of the park rangers."

"Oh, yeah, that. I did. Well, I saw the fire and ran into it and found Curtis." Eva was talking to her father now, so she was trying to be careful. The day of the fire, she remembered, she was more interested in getting home than in becoming a hero. Yet when everyone hailed her at the Friends meeting as a hero, it sure felt good.

"You ran into a fire?" Her father looked at her with concern.

"I was worried that Curtis might be there. I found him by accident. He was on the ground and I tripped over him. We managed to retrieve his camera and the pictures he took will help get those guys punished for destroying the park and risking his life." Eva shrugged. "So that's what I've been doing—heroic stuff." She smiled and looked at her family. They smiled back at her.

"Eva is our new park hero," Colleen announced.

"My sister did something great," Judi chirped.

Dad smiled at Eva, who blushed.

"And your mom told me you were accepted here at the college."

"Yes, I was. I want to study environmental science." Eva announced.

"You'll need to take chemistry classes. Let me know if you need a hand with them."

Eva smiled. It was good to know she could turn to her father for help.

Yet with all this recognition, she was wondering how she could get the conversation to move away from her and onto her parents. She was feeling queasy today, as if she could cry for no known reason. She looked down at her plate and then looked up again at her father. The only thing she could think right now was: How could he leave her mom? Her serious, loving, kind mother. A woman who had stayed with him through the birth and raising of two children. A woman who had stayed with him when he had lost his previous job? Colleen had put up with tight budgets and limited vacations while he re-established himself for the job he now held. How could he just leave her? How could she just accept that? What happened to people that caused their relationships to fall apart? How could they lose interest in each other? Now was the time they should really be enjoying life together. What went wrong? Eva looked over at Colleen.

"Any plans to become engaged with Curtis?" Eva heard her father ask her.

Judi laughed. "Eva's got guys chasing her all over the park. Who knows which one she'll marry, or maybe she won't get married. Why settle for just one?"

Eva glared at Judi, but then realized that it did enhance her image as a young woman in demand. Eva laughed at the thought, but then she saw her opportunity.

"Speaking of marriage," Eva said, "You guys have been married a long time. How long has it been?"

Her parents looked at each other.

"Twenty-eight years," Colleen said, "A nice even number."

"And what do you plan to do when you retire?" Eva asked.

"Arizona, right?" Judi suggested.

"Retire?" said Dad. "I like the work I'm doing and I like the travel. Now, your mother here, she hates to travel. She's making a great contribution to her community. Who needs to retire? Dear daughters, back in the days when people spent their lives working in factories, they were aching in their bones and needed retirement. But I'm a consultant. I ride around on planes, meet with people over dinner, talk, take pictures of the places I've been. Oh, here look, you can go on the internet and see my pictures. I started doing this so you could all share what I've been seeing in my travels. Look." He held up his device and gave them a show with explanations.

At first, Eva was bored. They were pictures of buildings and business buddies, but then he showed deserts and jungles. The world had so many different types of habitats. It impressed Eva that her father had been there.

After Eva and Judi looked at the pictures, they passed the device to their mother, but she nodded them away. "I've already seen the pictures. They're amazing."

"Speaking of pictures," Judi said. She reached into the bag next to her chair and pulled up their gift, delightfully decorated in shiny blue paper with a silver ribbon.

"Here, Dad, it's your birthday present from the two of us."

He opened it and held the wood framed picture that Eva and Judi had posed for at the shopping mall photo studio.

"Oh, very nice, my dears," Dad responded.

"And it comes in digital too, so you can load it into your device," Judi explained.

"Very nice." Dad looked at Mom. "Here, Colleen, you can have this one for the living room wall and I'll take the digital one. It's easier for me to carry."

Colleen quietly took the picture, looked at it, then handed it over to Judi for replacement back into her bag. "Very nice my darlings. It will look good in the living room."

Eva felt sad. It seemed like their father just dismissed their picture with so little praise. She tried to hide her disappointment, knowing that he would have the digital version with him always. Unfortunately, the disappointment grew, it now included the fact that she still did not get an answer from them about their plans for the future. They had avoided her question. She decided to try again, but this time she would rephrase it.

"So, you two are happy with life the way it is?" Eva asked.

Colleen and Bob looked at her. They looked calm, settled in their ways. It was obvious they had what they each wanted. Eva stared at them and realized they had moved to a new stage in life. They no longer needed the big Thanksgiving dinners, the family vacations, the educational trips to the museum or the zoo. Those activities had been done for their girls and the girls were about to leave the nest and make their own way in life. Eva had felt the desire to spread her wings and fly. Now she realized that her leaving was what they wished for the most.

"Listen, your mom and I have made some changes in our plans. What would we do in Arizona? Sit and look at each other? Retirement feels like you're just dropping out of life. Not being a part of anything anymore. I don't want to let go. I want to keep being a part of society. I don't want to sit on the roadside. Your mom agrees with me on that. So, we may not "retire." We'll just keep going the way we are for a while longer. But we sure are interested in what our little darlings do with the life that we gave them. What are you going to be and do with your life, Eva?"

"My dear sister has no clue," Judi barked. "I'm on a path toward becoming a successful businesswoman and I'm going to do whatever it takes to get there."

"What do you plan to do with an environmental science degree, Eva?" Dad asked.

Eva tilted her head to one side, trying to think of an answer. "I guess I want to save Mother Earth from all the damage we humans have done."

Her father laughed.

"You are already a hero, Eva," he reminded her. "Is there any chance you could have a career in the park after college?"

"I guess I could."

"That might have a greater chance of happening. Don't you think? So let me know how you feel when you get out of college. I'm still your dad. I'd like to do what I can to help you secure a position," he said.

Eva liked hearing Dad's soothing voice. But suddenly a wave of fear crashed over her. Was he saying he would not come home and retire with her mom? Was that too much for him? Was he just going to fly all over the world, partying with corporate and foreign government leaders while their mother was left home alone like an abandoned old maid?

"Of course, you're still my dad, but are you retiring with Mom? Are you staying together? You aren't getting a divorce, are you?" Eva blurted this out and tears began to form at the corners of her eyes.

"Not now, Bob," Colleen said, looking at her husband.

Eva wondered what Mom meant.

"Like I said, Eva," her father began, "we're just going to keep on like we have been for a few more years."

A waiter came and asked them if they wanted dessert.

Colleen asked for the family favorite, Carrot Cake with whipped cream. Dad only wanted more coffee. Eva felt relieved to hide in a family custom, so she chose the Carrot Cake too, and so did Judi.

After the waiter left, Eva and Judi gazed at their mother. She was the one most likely to address the issue after Eva's tears had fallen.

"We've looked at our relationship. We've talked it over," Colleen said.

"Everything is fine as it is," Bob added quickly.

"Fine?" Eva said, feeling like she could faint.

"It's fine, you see, Sis, I told you," Judi declared. "There's nothing to worry about. We should just go on with our lives."

"But, what is going on between you two?" Eva asked looking at Colleen.

"We're fine, don't worry. We're still your parents and we always will be."

It was not the answer Eva was looking for. After twenty-eight years of marriage, she thought they'd say how happy they were together. But, the fact was, they hadn't been together for years. Eva had pried into them and had found the truth. They were, in fact, just living up to an obligation. Now, it was up to Eva to accept what had become of their marriage. She was not like Judi. She would not play along. Her thoughts rushed forward to the next worrisome conclusion. Was it also possible that Dad might have another woman? Was she a woman that he might now consider more interesting than her mother? How sad. Eva suddenly felt worried about her mom, but Colleen looked undisturbed by any change that may have entered their lives.

Eva lifted her fork and poked around in the little bit of carrot cake on her plate. What had happened to the great love that they used to have? Mom used to tell them about it. The romance, the passion. What happened to it? Had real life set in and the drudgery of the years, going to work, paying the bills, making sure the children had gotten everything they needed—had this destroyed their interest in each other? This was the time Eva wanted to see them together, relaxed and enjoying their final years. It would help her believe in love and marriage. But no, they just wanted to keep doing the same old things until death disrupted their lifestyle completely.

Eva marveled at this. This complete resignation on the part of her parents toward the pattern of their lives, lived without much personal pleasure, and finalized not by a sense of accomplishment, but by a sort of breaking down and drifting apart. When she came back from her thoughts, Eva heard Judi again talking about the restaurant.

"We could call it Café Liberty."

"That's a nice name," Dad responded. "But how about Café Liberté—with an accent?"

"Or Café Liber-tea?" Colleen suggested, spelling the name out. They all laughed.

"But we serve more than tea," Judi said, rejecting the suggestion.

Eva saw a look of sadness on Colleen's face. She turned to Judi and gave her a frown.

"Well, yes, Café Libertea," Judi revised her response, "I really like that Mom."

"Does the restaurant serve wine and beer?" Dad asked.

Their friendly conversation continued about Judi's place of employment.

Eva watched them, surprised that they were, in fact, clearly content with the way their lives were going. Judi moving her way into a marriage. Mom and Dad drifting out of one. But no one was concerned. Why had they taught Eva to believe in marriage? Was it only a convention for raising children? She thought of other families she knew. She had some friends at school whose parents had never married. If Eva chose not to have children, was marriage necessary? And what did the word "love" mean anyway?

The Kaufman family finished their dessert. They paid the bill and left the dinner table the way they had arrived. Their lives moving along in pursuit of the small daily accomplishments that would soon be forgotten and hold no significance by the time their lives were over. Eva felt so sad. She got into the car and fastened her seatbelt. Suddenly she heard the chime of her cell phone. She looked at it in her purse. There was a text message from Matt Merriweather. "At a great enviro conf 2day u'd luv it! Saving Planet."

Yes, Eva thought, nothing else mattered. They must save Mother Earth.

Chapter Twenty Two

Coffee Confrontation

Amanda was racing her old car down the turnpike headed for the park. She was late for her exercise class. She decided to take the car because it was much faster than the train. When she pulled into the parking lot, she could see the other women lined up ready to begin. She greeted them and got into line.

Exercising was always difficult at first, but once she got moving, she was in the swing. When it was over, she marveled at how exercise could put a sense of youthful cheer back into a human body. If she could just remember this feeling, maybe she wouldn't have to push herself so hard to get to exercise class next time.

Exuberant now, she decided to give herself a treat. She would go for a drive through the entire park to see what else was happening there. She drove slowly and enjoyed the sights: The beautiful big gardens with their bright yellow and pink flowers—these were an accomplishment of the gardening volunteers. The Statue of Liberty raising her torch above the harbor. The people riding bikes and pushing baby carriages. Joggers were running down Freedom Way. Fishing poles held lines extended into the deep blue water while senior men and women kept their eyes on the bobbers hoping for a bite. Life was wonderful when you had a sunny day in the park.

Amanda was feeling confident.

As she drove along, she began to think of Barbara Harrison. Her office was not far from the park. Driving along Freedom Way, Amanda thought about the reports that Sally had secretly acquired for the

Friends' financial expert. The Foundation was having some financial problems.

"I should just go over there and pay Barbara a little visit," Amanda thought. "I'll pretend that I'm offering the olive branch of peace. I'll ask her to join the Friends and support our plans to preserve nature on the new land." Amanda laughed. It was a splendid idea.

Yes, take the initiative. Just act like you know that you are right and they are wrong. Give Ms. Harrison an opportunity to make the better choice. Isn't that how they always do it in the business world? Just go over there and turn the tables on the Foundation. Yes, this would work. Amanda slowed the car, set the turn signal and drove to the office of Barbara Harrison.

When Amanda entered the Foundation office, she saw Sally at the front desk working as the receptionist.

"Amanda, how good to see you. Who did you want to meet with here today?"

"Sally, what a nice office you work in. You were lucky to get this job."

Sally smiled brightly and cast a cautious glance toward a door across the room. "Barbara is on the phone right now," she whispered.

"Ah, so she **is in** the office," Amanda replied, beaming.

Sally smiled and nodded in the affirmative. She whispered, "Let me see if she would be willing to see you today. She's in a board meeting right now."

While Sally sent a message to Barbara, Amanda sat down and peeked through a slit in the door. She could see Barbara Harrison churning in her chair, crossing and uncrossing her legs as the Board of Trustees discussed their plans.

Suddenly the intercom buzzed, and Barbara made a request. "Sally, come here. Bring me the files on the sports complex and, while you are up, prepare coffee and bring it in for us."

Sally picked up a clear plastic folder that displayed a collection of brochures and put them under her arm then she went into the board meeting.

After a few minutes, she came out and went to the little kitchen in the corner where she prepared the coffee. She took a silver tray and cups out of the cabinet. She set up the three small aluminum coffee pots and began brewing several flavors of coffee.

"Three pots of coffee?" Amanda asked.

"Yes, three board members, three pots of coffee. None of them likes the same flavor," Sally whispered.

Amanda watched as Sally came back to her desk, made some adjustments on her computer, and then signaled to Amanda to stay quiet. They leaned toward the conference room door and listened in hopes of hearing what was being said.

"They are looking at the brochures again," Sally whispered to Amanda.

"What brochures?"

"The ones with the pictures of big yellow machines. They're called earth-movers and they can lift huge piles of dirt or large trees."

"Move trees?" Amanda asked, wrinkling her brow.

Suddenly, the door snapped shut.

There was nothing more to hear.

"So what have you been up to?" Amanda asked.

"I'm back in the habit of feeding the kitties. I learned my lesson. If I don't bring food for those kitties, the mother cat is forced to bring in bunnies and little birds. I'm going again tonight. You know, Peter is out of town. He went on a job interview in Chicago."

"Oh, I didn't know," Amanda responded. She wanted to ask how Sally felt about Peter being gone so far away. She had hoped marriage was in their plans, but now she wondered if Sally would ever give up the cats for Peter.

"You should see the kitties," Sally said smiling. "They play like little lions, clawing at me all the time, leaving deep scratches on my hands. See?" Sally held her hands out showing many red lines on her hands and wrists.

The intercom buzzed again.

"Sally, where's the coffee?"

"Oh, yes, Barbara, I'm bringing it now."

Sally leaped from her chair, went to the kitchen and set the three small coffee pots on the tray with plenty of cups. She added spoons, sugar and several different types of milk and cream. She carefully lifted the heavy tray and carried it through the conference room door to the board members.

Amanda waited and listened. After a few minutes, Sally returned and sat down at her desk. The conference room door snapped shut again.

"Oh, Amanda, I'm so tired. Barbara just drives me crazy," Sally whispered. "The board members seemed really agitated today. Something has them very worried. They were looking over the brochures and signing important-looking papers. They call it Stage Three."

"Stage Three?"

Amanda was beginning to worry that her visit was possibly not the best idea. What could Stage Three mean? What were the other stages?

"Have you ever tried that new coffee with hazelnut and marshmallow?" Sally asked.

"Oh, no, I haven't."

"I wanted to give it a try. The vendor that provides our coffee gave me a free sample, but it makes too much for me to drink alone. Hey, I could fix it now and we could have a taste. What do you think?"

"Oh, ah, ok, sure. That sounds like fun," Amanda replied.

Sally got up and began making the coffee in yet another pot.

Amanda watched Sally while she listened to her own thoughts rumbling like thunder inside her head. If Stage One was the plan, and Stage Two was the announcement, Stage Three had to mean they were taking action. But doing what?

Suddenly Amanda wondered why she had come here today to this office. Oh, yes, she wanted to extend the olive branch. She wanted to do away with the bickering and competition between the two groups. She wanted them working together, united for the improvement of the park. But really, would it ever be possible for Amanda and Barbara to talk together like friends? Now, Amanda doubted it. So what was she doing here? Stage Three. Could she have a chat with Barbara and discern what Stage Three meant?

Sally watched the hazelnut coffee as it brewed. She set out cups and then filled them.

"Here's yours," Sally said as she placed Amanda's serving on the small table next to where she was sitting.

Amanda looked down at the cup and decided to wait for it to cool. She wasn't much of a coffee drinker.

"Mmmm, it tastes good. I like it," Sally said with great satisfaction.

Amanda gave it a quick taste. She did not want to disappoint Sally, but the hot fluid tasted like boiled mud.

"Yes, well it is nice," Amanda said and set the cup down on a side table. "How much longer do you think this meeting will go on?"

"Oh, you know how meetings are, they can go on and on."

Amanda wondered if she should just back out now, while she had the chance. That was it. She should gulp down this awful coffee and bid Sally good-bye.

"Yes, I like this," Sally said, but she was stirring in additional sugar.

"Let me try some sugar in mine," Amanda said, adding a couple of spoons to hers.

Coffee was a drink that Amanda usually avoided. It always made her feel so jittery. She drank just enough from the cup to make it seem she was enjoying it. She placed the cup and saucer back on the small table. "I guess I'll have to be going now. I didn't realize they would be tied up in a board meeting all day."

"Oh, sorry you didn't get to speak to Barbara," Sally said. "Should I let her know you were here?"

"Oh, no my dear, don't bother. I'll come back some other day, and I'll call you to be sure she's in and not too busy."

"Ok," Sally responded.

Suddenly the conference room door clicked open. Several of the board members came out.

"Ok, our work is done. We've signed the contracts."

"Good work, board members, now we'll meet again in three weeks and review . . . . Oh, oh, we have guests. Sally, why didn't you tell me we had a guest?" Barbara demanded.

"It's only Amanda, you know, she's from the Friends of Nature. She just stopped by for a moment and was about to leave."

"Why did you stop by?" Barbara asked directly of Amanda.

"Oh, I was hoping to speak to you, but I see you are very busy. Never mind, I'll stop by some other time."

"Oh, no, stay," Barbara said. She flashed her bright smile, the one she used in the video.

"Ok, Helen, I expect to see you and the full board in a few weeks. Bye."

Barbara signaled to Amanda to cross the room to her private office.

Amanda followed her and entered.

Barbara's office was decorated with tapestries on the walls in Mexican prints. Large brown and orange vases stood in corners holding tall tan dried grass. Small yellow vases posed on the corners of end tables. In these were more tall grass dyed red and orange. To Amanda, the colors of the décor seemed to speak of the coming autumn and the colors of changing leaves, but she knew that in the Mexican culture, orange and red were symbols of the hot desert sun.

"Amanda. How are you? Have a seat," Barbara said, smiling.

"Fine, I just thought I'd pay you a visit to see how you and the Foundation are doing." Amanda said smiling back at Barbara.

"We're doing just fine," Barbara declared. "Shall I order some coffee to be brought in? We have some nice cookies here too." Before Amanda could respond, Barbara continued, "Yes, let's do that. I'll tell Sally to bring in some coffee."

Amanda cringed. "Well, I have had a cup already."

Sally must have heard them speaking because she instantly stepped through the door with the tray, cups and the remaining hazelnut coffee.

"We're trying this new coffee that the vendor gave us," Sally said.

"Oh, we are?" Barbara asked, lifting an eyebrow in disapproval of Sally's assertiveness.

"It's hazelnut. I tasted it. It's great."

Barbara looked doubtfully at the pot of hazelnut coffee.

Amanda wanted to ask for tea, her nerves were now rattling out of control, but a request for tea would put Sally through extra effort. Amanda decided to take the cup, but set it aside. She wasn't here for a coffee klatch; she was here to carry out her plan of action.

"You know, Barbara, really, I think it is possible for the Foundation and the Friends to work together on the new land. Don't you think it's at least possible?"

Barbara sweetly agreed.

Amanda continued, "Both of our groups are concerned about benefiting the community."

"Yes, we have that in common," Barbara replied.

"We also have a certain obligation to keep costs moderate."

"Yes, but we want the best for our community," Barbara assured her.

"So with this in consideration, I've come to suggest that you and I find ways to amicably plan what actions should be taken in regard to the new land."

"How nice of you, Amanda."

"Yes, well, there is just no need to be at odds with each other." Amanda smiled pleasantly. That first cup of coffee was beginning to make her head spin.

"That is very true," Barbara said. "Amanda, you know in your heart that this community would deeply appreciate the improvements it will receive with the Foundation's plans for the botanical garden. Amanda, I know you love flowers. Wouldn't you enjoy a botanical garden?"

"Yes, I would enjoy that, but does the community want that or does the community want simple flower beds that seniors and children can participate in planting?"

"A community doesn't always know what it wants. Do the seniors really want to do all that work? Are you sure, Amanda? I believe that people will say "Aren't we lucky to have such a wonderful botanical garden to visit in our community.""

"But it costs so much money to build and operate a botanical garden," Amanda countered. "After it is built, how many people from this community will be able to afford a visit? Will enough people visit so that the garden can sustain itself on entrance fees alone?"

Amanda watched as Barbara looked up at the ceiling and considered the critical aspects of her argument.

Barbara moved beyond the garden to her next strong point.

"There's our idea of the sports complex. The children in this community will have a brighter future if they have a sports complex. Don't you agree?" Barbara looked at Amanda "They could practice their sports and learn to become professional athletes. You wouldn't want to deny them this opportunity, would you?"

Amanda was losing her sense of civility. Obviously, Barbara was not willing to give up the original game plan of the Foundation. Amanda wondered if Sally had been telling the truth about the Foundation's financial woes. Would they stick to their original plans in the face of money shortages?

"But, Barbara, where will the youth get jobs in this community working as professional athletes?"

"It's an opportunity," Barbara declared, looking at Amanda as if she were foolish not to recognize this.

Amanda sipped some more coffee, not because she wanted it, but because she needed something to do with her hands while she thought out her next move. Fear was growing inside of her. She had made a big mistake coming into Barbara's lair without preparation. Amanda decided to give voice to her next strongest argument.

"You have to admit, Barbara, that the hotel is not necessary. We have so many in town now."

"But this will be a new one, it will be totally environmentally sound, efficient with no waste of electrical energy. We'll use solar panels. The building will be structured to process waste and bottles through a recycling system. It will have bird-proof windows so that no bird will strike them and die. Reflective materials will be used to block out the sun's heat so that air conditioning will not be necessary. There's a new awakening in the building industry that we must build things GREEN, that means with a sensitivity toward nature and the environment."

"Well, that's nice, especially now that this country has just finished a building boom based on old technology." Amanda sneered, "We're going to build everything over again, I guess. That will certainly boost the economy."

"Amanda, I understand where you are coming from. You are getting older and it is difficult to keep up with the many changes in our modern high-tech environmentally conscious society."

Amanda snorted. "Getting older and not able to keep up with the changes?"

"Yes, that is why you want to keep the new land as it was. But that land is toxic. You have to understand it needs to be remediated. We can revitalize our community with the botanical garden, the sports complex and the new hotel. All that your Friends offer to this community is to maintain that old weed patch as it is. It is full of invasive weeds. You want to take schoolchildren there and call it a wildlife area? What a shame."

"What? That is not at all that we are doing."

Amanda was furious. Barbara was telling her that she was an old goat trying to save a weed patch. Her head was buzzing and whirling.

"Well, let me just tell you, the Friends have a financial expert. We know that your proposals cannot stand up in this economy. You will fail, Barbara Harrison. You and the Foundation will fail. I, for one, do not want to see beautiful land destroyed to put up buildings that are too expensive to operate. These buildings will be filled only with the empty promises the Foundation has made. Otherwise, they will be standing there empty and of no use to the community."

"Oh, you have an expert, do you?" Barbara leaned forward in her chair. "I'm glad you have an expert. The Friends are going to need an expert. You will need as many experts as you can afford. As a matter of fact, your little group will run itself into bankruptcy trying to pay off enough experts to prove your point. You're going to need more fundraisers than that party you had. A little bird told me you only raised twelve-thousand dollars. That won't be enough." Barbara sat back with a smug look on her face.

"The state will never rule in your favor," Amanda warned her. "They will realize how financially risky the Foundation's plans are. Just remember my words. You are the one who will be facing failure very soon."

Amanda emptied the coffee cup. The bitter taste of caffeine filled her mouth. Suddenly she realized that she had just told the Friend's secret to Barbara. Gary had commanded them to keep it quiet.

She began to stutter, but then she stopped. What would happen to their campaign against the Foundation now that Barbara knew of the expert? Amanda bit her tongue. Finally, she tried to speak again.

"I am sorry I came to this office," she said. She realized that she really meant that—in more ways than one. "I wanted to offer you the olive branch of peace. I guess we are still at war." Amanda picked up her purse.

"I'm so sorry you can't see the advantages of our plan," Barbara responded. "But let me tell you this, the B & L Foundation is ready to roll. Nothing, not even that lazy government bureaucracy is going to stop us. When you see what we can do, you may want to change your mind. Let me tell you, we will forgive you—because **we** are the ones who represent what the community wants."

"Oh really?" Amanda glared at her. She turned and opened the door. When she looked back, she saw Barbara Harrison sitting at her desk with a big evil smile.

Amanda hurried out to the alcove. She waved good-by to Sally as she walked past her desk and through the heavy glass front doors.

The sun, which was now low in the western sky, slapped Amanda's face with a hot hand. Amanda felt shame and bowed her head as she walked to her car. She had given away the Friends' secret.

Chapter Twenty Three

More Secrets

"I'm back from the environmental conference."

Eva read the text then responded, "That's great. How was it?"

"I'll call you with the details."

She and Matt were communicating frequently. He had introduced her to all the latest environmental issues, legal actions and upcoming tours and events. Eva never realized before that there was a global community of environmental activist that she could join in their efforts to save the earth. Some of them were local people like Gary Russo, who did more than conduct Friends of Nature meetings. Eva had found him leading a workshop online. Some of the activists were from distant lands. Many activists were locked in contradictory battles for jobs in the chemical factories, while opposing the damage unscrupulous greedy industries would perpetrate on pristine lands and native peoples. Eva doubted that her mom or Amanda knew of these incredible conflicts. People in other places were not just fighting for a park, they were fighting to save their lives. It made Eva want to move on to more demanding issues, but she had to prove herself at the park first.

Soon she and Matt were talking on the phone. He gave Eva a report on the conference then asked, "Have you found the nest of the yellow-crowned night heron yet?"

Matt sounded so hopeful. Eva wanted to give him good news.

"No, I've been looking for it all summer. It will be migrating south soon. Maybe the fire chased it away."

"Could be. Listen, I'm free this afternoon. Let's get together and wander through that part of the park again. The herons make large nests, if there was a nest, it should be visible by now. The leaves are falling from the trees. The nest should be easy to see. Let's go have another look."

Eva doubted that the bird had nested in the park, but she liked the idea of getting together with Matt. "I can meet you there early this afternoon."

"Ok, I'll see you. We'll meet at the opening in the fence."

Eva put her phone away. She looked up at the photo on the wall of herself and Judi. It did look nice. She walked across the living room and looked out the window. One of the trees on the street was already turning yellow.

Eva thought about the classes she had started at the local state college. Thanks once again to Dad for providing the funds. College was such a challenge. Eva had to succeed. She wanted to be on the same level as her friends, Matt and Curtis. How could she be a true environmentalist without a degree? After lunch, Eva got her jacket and headed to the park. It was a cool sunny day in September.

She walked up the trail and saw Matt standing outside the opening in the fence. It was much larger now, due to the activity of the firefighters.

"Let me show you the area where we've been doing the plant study," Eva called out. She ran toward Matt. He gave her a hug and a quick kiss on the top of her head. Eva liked this but was unsure what it meant, if anything. They pushed through the tall grass and began wandering the narrow secret trails that led into the new land.

They worked their way to the taller trees and peered into them. "I've kept an eye on these trees all summer when I was here doing the plant identification project," Eva explained.

"Let's go over there," Matt suggested.

They strolled off in the other direction.

"I've learned, while bird watching," Matt began, "that they seem to nest, not where the books and brochures suggest, but in some unbelievable cranny or corner. They could be in a tree that leans over the fence to this property and not really be located on this property."

"Birds and animals like to use old fallen-in human structures too," Eva added.

"That's because there are no big old trees like there used to be long ago," Matt explained. "During an ornithology hike I was on in Alaska, we joked that the moment you give up is exactly when you see the spectacular bird."

They laughed together.

"So, we can't give up yet," Matt said. "Let's try that stand of trees over there."

They walked off again across another field toward some other trees.

"The first time I saw the yellow-crowned night heron nest," Eva said, admiring Matt's strong hands as he held his binoculars, "it was out on a limb. I don't know why, maybe because tree limbs have more branches to hold the nest toward the ends of the limbs."

"That's exactly it," Matt agreed.

"So we should be sure to look at lower limbs that reach out far. Like that one reaching out over the marsh over there."

They made their way to the marsh and studied the trees with extended branches. Nowhere did they see a cluster of sticks or any structure that could have been the remains of a nest blown apart by the wind.

Matt sat down on a fallen tree. Eva sat next to him. They looked out across the cattails of the marsh. The red-winged blackbirds had accumulated in large numbers and were making such a racket.

"They're getting ready for the migration," Eva explained.

Suddenly the birds lifted up like a cyclone that circled into the air. Matt and Eva stared up at the swirl of black wings. After flying in wider and wider circles above the tops of the trees, the whole flock poured off through the sky toward the late afternoon sun.

"Was that incredible?" Matt asked.

"Incredible," Eva responded.

Then another voice came from behind them.

"It certainly was incredible, but if you want to see something incredible, you have to follow me."

Eva and Matt turned toward the stranger's voice.

It was Dan Murphy. He was standing behind them in the grass; his scruffy beard helped him to blend in with his habitat. "I'll share something with you two, but you have to promise not to tell," Murphy said.

"That's not a fair deal," Matt responded. "You have to convince me that what you've found is worth sealing the deal."

"Murphy, what are you doing here?" Eva called.

"I'm almost always here," Murphy grumbled. "This has been my sanctuary for years now. What are you two doing here? Oh, don't tell me, a little mating dance?"

Eva felt like hiding. Why wouldn't he believe they were there for an environmental study?

"We came hoping to see some proof of nesting by the yellow-crowned night heron." Eva responded.

"Ha, you still haven't found it?" Murphy scoffed. "I got some great shots of the nest this summer. I even have some photos of the young in the nest."

"What?" Eva gasped, "You knew it was here and you didn't tell anyone?"

"You can't give up the secrets of the sanctuary. True birders don't tell."

"But we needed to know about that bird to help save this park," Eva explained.

"Did you post your pictures on the internet?" Matt asked.

"Nope, I didn't let anyone know," Murphy responded.

"So is that the secret you were going to share if we promised to keep it?" Eva asked.

Murphy waded through the grass until he stood before them.

"I don't know if I should tell you. You'll go running off and tell the Friends of Nature. They won't do anything about it. Besides, the law protecting endangered species exists, but it's not enforced very well. So what good would it do? I decided I would protect the nest. That's what I did all summer. No one disturbed the herons."

"I was working on the plant identification project near here for weeks," Eva said. "I looked at all the trees every time I came here."

"You might as well have been a hundred miles away," Murphy bragged. "You would have never found it."

Eva looked at him and then looked over at Matt.

"Ok," Matt said. "On my scouts honor I promise not to tell where the yellow-crowned night heron nested—not that it means much now. The chicks have fledged and are in the Caribbean by now."

"Yeah, really Murphy, there's no harm in knowing now," Eva added.

"But what about next year? The birds will come back. They had a very successful summer this year."

"Ok, on my scouts honor, I promise not to tell," Eva said, surrendering to Murphy's demands.

He took a step forward. You see over there."

"Where?"

"There." Murphy pointed with his arm extended. Eva stood behind him and looked down the length of his arm.

Matt lifted his binoculars and looked in the same direction. "That cluster of sticks on the end of that branch—way over there?" Matt asked.

"Yes."

"Where?" Eva said in panic. "I don't see anything."

"Come on, let's go closer," Murphy said. He led them around the marsh, through a grove of red maples, over to some gray birch. There on the end of the limb was the nest.

Eva and Matt ran closer to the nest and looked up at it.

"How do we know it's the nest of the yellow-crowned night heron?" Eva asked. She remembered that the nest she had seen several years ago was like this one, made of sticks and balancing out on the end of a low branch.

"What else would build a next in this location with this structure?" Matt asked.

"I have the pictures to prove it. Look right here," Murphy said. He pulled some dog-eared prints out of his pocket. Eva turned and looked at the glossy images of a yellow-crown night heron sitting on the nest. She looked up at the site again. The pattern of branches around the nest were the same.

Murphy then showed another picture where he had pulled back from the nest. Now they could see the nest, the tree and the wind turbine in the background. He had clearly identified the bird and the location.

"These would make great pictures for a court case," Matt said.

"You promised not to tell," Murphy growled.

"We promised. We'll keep our promise," Eva said. "Wow, Murphy this is great. You found it. I can't believe that I didn't. I put so much energy into trying to find this bird. I just stumbled upon it a few years ago, but for me to find it again. I just didn't."

"Thanks for showing them to us," Matt said. "These are great shots. But Murphy, if the bird is threatened by activity on this land, you have to speak up. You can't just keep this a secret." He handed the pictures back to Murphy.

"I'm hoping the Foundation and the Friends get locked in some court battle that goes on for years," Murphy grinned, "Then I'll be able to enjoy my sanctuary until I die. I only have a few more years left of this life."

"That's your strategy?" Matt asked.

"Murphy, you hold on to those pictures," Eva advised. "If it becomes necessary to protect the bird, you must give them to your friend Amanda. She'll know what to do with them. Do you promise you will do that?"

Murphy looked down at the ground and scuffed a stone with the toe of his boot. "I guess I could do that."

"That's the only way we can keep the promise," Eva said.

"But I have the pictures, you don't," Murphy reminded her. He hurriedly put them back into his coat pocket.

Eva knew she needed to keep Murphy's trust. "Of course," she said. "We'll never say a word to anyone about the nest."

"Good, you keep your promises," Murphy said, looking first to Eva and then to Matt. "I've got to be going now. Don't get into any trouble in here, you sweet young things. I'll see you later."

Eva and Matt laughed and glanced back and forth at each other. Then they stood and watched Murphy make his way through the bramble to the distant gate.

"So here's the nest," Matt said.

Eva pulled a small camera out of her pocket. "Let's take a picture of it."

She took several close-ups and then stepped back to get the wider angle that looked similar to Murphy's picture with the wind turbine in the background.

"The problem is," Matt said, looking thoughtfully, "we don't have the bird in the shot, nor do we have the chicks."

"I know," Eva said. "All we have is a picture of a lot of sticks out on a limb. It could be a blue jay's nest for all we know."

"No, it's not a blue jay's nest, but it would take an expert to prove it was a heron's nest."

The sun was on the verge of setting. The treetops were still catching the light but the fields behind them were being lost in the dusk.

"We'd better get home," Eva said.

They turned and walked a path toward the burned area of the land. It was open now and easy to cross. From there, they went to the opening in the fence.

"Oh, Eva, let me send you some information. I think you'll like it. Have you seen the Everglades? Or a rain forest? You have to see this directory. There are trips planned for every interesting site on the planet. It's my goal to see as many of them as I can. I've already been to Alaska. I saw the Fairweather Range. You can only see those mountains in clear weather. I've been to Hawaii and saw the volcano Mauna Loa, the biggest on earth. I want to go to South America next. I want to see the Amazon rainforest. Eva, if you want to be an environmentalist, you ought to travel. You need to experience the world's many beautiful treasures."

Eva looked at Matt. His eyes were sparkling with joy and fascination. His excitement tempted her to seek new adventures.

Chapter Twenty Four

Amanda's Shame

Amanda sat in her car with her arms drooping over the steering wheel. What had forced the secret from her lips? She had told Barbara Harrison the Friends' secret. She had let the enemy know about the expert witness. That was the most powerful weapon that the Friends had in defense of the park. And now, Amanda had given the secret away. How would she explain to Gary Russo what she had done? What could she do now to correct the error she had made?

Amanda reflected on the day. It had been a beautiful day. She had done her exercise that morning. She had felt so good. Then she got the crazy idea to visit Barbara Harrison at the Foundation office. She wanted to win Barbara to the Friends' plan for the parkland. Now, in the late afternoon, sitting in her car, she felt so sick. Sick from the coffee and sick from Barbara Harrison's remarks—and worst of all, sick from knowing that she had given away the Friend's best strategy for winning a bigger, better park. All that they had collectively been struggling for was ruined because of her own loose tongue.

Where had she gone wrong and why? Amanda played the visit through her mind again. She had gone there with a clear desire to bring the two groups together. Why should it be so hard for the Foundation to work with the Friends? Ah, it was a mistake to go there on impulse. She had not thought it out, or worse, she had not discussed it with anyone. Now that Barbara knew the Friends were going to rely on an expert, she would line up ten against the only one that the Friends could afford to bring to the state hearing.

Amanda had always thought of herself as someone with great self-control. She thought over every word of the discussion with Barbara. Where had she lost control? Was it when Barbara insulted her? Insinuated that she was an old goat in a weed patch? Was this what drove her to give away the Friends strongest tool? Was it pride? Had she felt it necessary to slam Barbara with something greater, something that would truly ruin her plans?

Amanda stared across the parking lot and watched as Barbara left the building and got into her car. She was probably head to a restaurant for a late lunch. For Barbara this was just another workday. It was just a job. But for Amanda, this was the cause that she had promised everyone she would defend to the death. How could she have done this? Now she realized she had even failed to keep her promise to Stephanie.

Suddenly it occurred to her: **Who had told Barbara about the twelve-thousand dollar fundraiser?** Was Sally sharing secrets to both sides? Was Sally no longer trustworthy? Amanda felt confused and defeated. Her head was buzzing. The caffeine was still making her so sick that she feared to drive.

"What I need is some food to counter this caffeine."

She thought of the Hungry Fish. "I won't have to drive far. I'll go there and have some lunch. I'll visit with Colleen's daughter, Judi." Amanda started the car.

As she drove past the new land, she looked, hoping to see signs of recovery after the fire. Surely, the rain of the past few weeks was awakening re-growth in the burned-out area.

What she saw was not what she expected. There was more blue sky pouring through an opening that had never been there before. Where were all those tall cottonwood trees? Where were the eastern white pines? Instead, two large yellow machines were lifting their mighty steel hydraulic arms and dropping tree trunks into the back of a large red truck. The shock of this vision caused Amanda to veer her car off the road. She stopped short of a ditch.

What could possibly be happening?

Another large truck came out of the field and drove onto the park road. Dirt fell from under its tarp-covered load. **The destruction of the land had already begun.**

A feeling worse than the caffeine tremors now came over Amanda. The B & L Foundation was not waiting for the state's hearing. It was moving ahead. If the land were already altered, the Friends could do nothing to preserve it.

Amanda raced to the Hungry Fish Restaurant.

"Judi, I need some lunch, just get me something to eat quickly before I collapse."

"Amanda, nice to see you here today. How about our lunch special—a cup of chicken noodle soup, a cheese sandwich and a small bowl of fruit?"

"Anything will do. Listen, there are bulldozers up there on the new land. I've got to call Gary and let him know. The Friends have to do something to stop them."

"What?"

"I'm calling your mother and Gary. We've got to do something to stop them. But I really need something to eat, please, hurry."

Judi rushed to the kitchen and soon brought Amanda the chicken soup special.

Amanda left her message on Gary's phone and then picked up a spoon and began to eat. As she ate, she remembered seeing that wicked smile on Barbara's face.

Barbara knew they were already altering the land. The government hearing would be a farce. The financial expert that the Friends had hired would give testimony that may prove true, but it would do nothing to stop construction that was well on its way.

Amanda sat at the counter and physically shook from head to toe with rage. She angrily bit into the cheese sandwich. As she ate, she started to feel calmer. Maybe the calcium in the cheese was calming her nerves. She slowly realized that telling the Friends' secret to Barbara was now probably of no consequence. For a moment, she felt relieved, though she still felt guilty. The changing events had saved her. Unfortunately, these events were the worst things that could have happened to the park.

From her call to Gary, the word went out. By the afternoon, a huge crowd was standing near the site of the bulldozers. Everyone watched as the machines knocked down more trees and carried them away. The big machines took bites out of the surface of the land until the holes grew big enough to hold the machines themselves. Then, the machines crawled down inside the holes where they continued to chomp away at the earth.

"We've got to do something," one supporter of the Friends cried out to Amanda.

"We're doing a press conference here today. Gary is getting it set up. He'll be here soon. Please stay and show your support."

Amanda waved to some newly-arriving members of the Friends. Then she turned and saw Murphy. It felt good to see an old soldier of the struggle.

"We need to do more than a stupid press conference," Murphy growled. Ed Wilson was standing next to him.

"The Friends do what we can," Amanda replied.

"I agree with Murphy, more needs to be done," said Ed Wilson as they walked along. The two men pulled away from Amanda and headed closer to the machines.

"Amanda! Here, I brought some protest signs," Colleen said. She was carrying some signs that she had just made. Amanda was glad to see Eva was with her.

Soon Gary came with reporters and camera crews trailing behind him. He started a speech. "The state has not made a decision on this. The Foundation is acting illegally. They do not have the right to move soil until all the tests have been done and until the state determines the use of this land."

Amanda went over to him and waited.

Everyone turned to watch as another big cottonwood tree came crashing down. The crowd moved closer to the excavation site.

Amada watched as Eva gave out the last of the signs and then joined the growing crowd. Other people arrived with their own signs. The camera crews scanned the crowds who cheered and held up their signs.

Across from the crowd, on the other side of the immense hole that the machines had dug, Amanda saw Murphy and Ed Wilson standing with their hands on their hips. Anger twisted their faces. They were looking down at the machine operators and yelling. Their voices challenged the noise produced by the earth-moving machines.

"You get out of here. Who said you could do a thing like this?" Murphy called.

"You scab non-union. You just do whatever your boss tells you to do, don't you?" Ed shouted.

The crowd pushed angrily toward the torn land and the broken trees.

Soon the park police arrived and pressed them back away from the edge of the hole that was growing ever deeper and wider.

The crowd roared with opposition to the police presence. Amanda turned and saw Colleen and Eva caught up in a train of people, connected arm in arm, coming out from behind the police line. They moved through the woods to another area of the pit. They stopped at the edge and began singing, "We will not be moved."

The bulldozers pushed forward. The backhoes reached up and bit at the earth near the feet of the crowd. Amanda felt a fury rise in her. She screamed and ran to join the line. "We are not leaving here. We do not want to see another tree go down. If you kill us, the blood will be on your hands."

"The sap will be on your hands, too," some comedian in the crowd yelled.

People laughed but then began an angry chant and pushed again toward the machines.

Amanda looked over at Eva. She then lifted her head and pulled her shoulders back, as if to say to Eva, 'This is the way to do this. See!'

More people came and joined the crowd that roared with satisfaction as it moved closer and closer to the edge.

"Stop the digging, stop the holes, save our land from the Foundation moles," someone chanted and the crowd took up the chant.

"Who do these Foundation people think they are?" one asked of the other.

The crowd looked to the other side and saw Ed Wilson dropping into the pit.

When the backhoe paused to lift again, Ed climbed onboard. He punched the driver in the shoulder. The man leaped off the machine to get away. Ed then sat down and put his hands on the levers. He backed the giant yellow machine away from the edge where the protesters stood. He turned the machine around and lifted the big heavy bucket.

"Get out of here or I'll smash the cab of your truck," he screamed to the dump truck driver. The driver threw the truck into reverse and backed out of the hole.

The backhoe followed the truck, holding its bucket menacingly high.

The crowd cheered and watched as Ed stopped the equipment at the top of the dirt ramp and then he shut down the machine. The park police rushed in to grab him. But no, they were held back by the crowd. The news reporters tumbled over each other to get coverage for the evening news.

Soon the crowd ran past the machines and down into the hole.

"We took a stand. It's our land."

The chanting went on. Police reinforcements came from the city. They captured protesters who tried to enter at the gate and hauled them away. Other protesters formed a line along the road and held up signs.

Amanda watched as Eva ran back and forth with a big smile on her face. "She's having fun," Amanda said to Colleen. "Who would think this is fun?"

"I can't believe it myself," Colleen said. "We've all been acting a little crazy today."

"Mom, you're really getting into this," Eva yelled.

Gary Russo ran to catch up with them. "This protest really showed a lot of support for saving the land; I hope the media shows the truth of what happened here. This is great."

Smiles covered the faces of the protesters as they celebrated their accomplishment.

"We stopped the bulldozers. We saved the land."

Gary went to the edge of the pit and climbed onto the yellow machine that Ed Wilson had parked. He stood next to Ed and addressed the crowd. Media cameras looked up at them and reporters plunged microphones into the air to catch Gary's words.

"This is a victory," Gary announced, "but we're not done yet. We need all of you to come to the state hearing so we can win this battle, once and for all."

Amanda looked over at Colleen and Eva. She felt proud to see a mother and daughter in the battle to save the park. It brought tears to her eyes. All around her, the people were happy. Amanda knew that for today, they had shown their power to defend the park.

When Amanda got home that evening, she checked the media. There was already another headline: People's Park—Power to the People. Spectacular pictures of people holding signs filled the screen. The crowd standing on the edges of the pit. A video showed Ed Wilson climbing onto the backhoe and punching the driver. Amanda read through the article. She was surprised and impressed by what she saw. She gave Gary a call.

"So what did you think of the news coverage we got?" Amanda asked.

"I liked it," Gary said. "I think our petition campaign has brought us recognition. More people are aware of the issue. They showed up for the rally. I think we are beginning to turn the corner on this battle. But that's just between us, Amanda," Gary said.

"Of course, we can't slack off now and think the battle's over."

"Back to work," Gary said.

"You know it," Amanda sang, "it's back to work we go."

Amanda sat in front of her computer gazing at the pictures. The Friends of Nature had a kind of power that came from the people of the community. Amanda could feel it, like she used to feel it back in the days when she and Murphy had tied themselves to the trees on Main Street. Together, the people had done something that they didn't really believe they could do. They stood up to a corporate entity and its foundation and stopped it from carrying out its plans. In a society that held the corporation in higher esteem than the community, there was always a feeling of weakness in each individual. Now, having stopped a corporation, the community was experiencing a startling revelation. For Amanda, it was a sweet accomplishment.

Chapter Twenty Five

The Hopeful Winter of Waiting

The first winds of October were making their way through every gap in every window of the Hungry Fish restaurant. Eva looked through the window glass at the park beyond. She hadn't been to the park in weeks. Some of the trees still had orange and yellow leaves, while most were already bare. She tugged on the sleeves of her big wooly Norwegian sweater and looked across the table at her mom. Colleen was also staring out the window with her fingers wrapped around a hot cup of tea. They were waiting for the Friends of Nature meeting to begin.

"Were you able to get your research done for your biology project?" Colleen asked.

"Yes, Mom, and I've got the first draft written. Matt and Curtis have both been answering my questions and sending me links that are helpful."

Eva thought about the daily messages that came from Matt, who was working all day teaching school in the suburbs. Curtis, who was still working at the park, was taking it easy during fall-winter season. He had no summer seasonal workers to train, no weeds to pull, no garbage to monitor, only a long list of broken benches and picnic tables to mend before spring.

Eva watched as her sister Judi came toward them. She was carrying a tray of orange-colored Halloween cookies.

"Want to try a cookie? I baked them. I am so busy," she said. "We're already taking reservations for holiday parties. But I can't complain, I'll be making a lot of money this year."

Eva smiled. She knew Judi was happy with that. Her relationship with James was going well too.

"Speaking of money, how are your funds from the summer park job holding up?" Colleen asked, looking at Eva.

"Fine, you know I don't spend much," Eva said.

The door opened and Gary Russo stuck his head in. "Are you the only ones here?"

"So far," Colleen said.

Gary sat down. Judi brought him a cup of coffee. They waited.

Eva looked up and saw Amanda coming through the door. "Amanda, we're glad to see you again."

"Eva, I haven't seen you since the rally. What have you been up to?"

"Going to college, studying chemistry, biology and all that stuff so I can be an environmental scientist of some sort," Eva explained.

"Keep up the good work," Amanda said. She took off her coat and hung it up. "Oh, it's chilly in here; let me put that back on."

A few more members came and joined them at the table in the back room. Gary called the meeting to order. "I'll start with my reports," he said.

Eva stirred another spoonful of honey into her tea and listened.

"The court case for Ed Wilson has come to an end. He'll need help paying his fines. He was charged with assault and theft of equipment. His heroic acts didn't impress the judge. He begged for mercy from the court, so they let him off lightly—no jail term. Luckily, the guy he punched was not seriously hurt."

"We were all impressed by what Ed did," Amanda said. "We have so many park heroes and we must come to the defense of every one of them. We'll pass the hat and begin fund raising to pay his fines."

Eva smiled at Amanda. No one mentioned it, but Amanda was a park hero, too. Eva wished she could donate money, but her funds were low. She watched as Colleen tossed a large donation into the center of the table. "Here's my family's contribution." Others followed in smaller amounts.

Gary smiled and then went on with his report. "In all fairness, the judge sought to keep a balance. She also ruled against the Foundation, charging them with failing to have a permit for excavation. They will have to pay a fine for that. Unfortunately, the Court chose to overlook the fact that the Foundation moved ahead with their plans before the state hearing. So the Foundation was not punished for the damage they did to the land."

Gary paused and looked around.

"That's not right," Amanda grumbled. Eva smiled at her. You could always count on Amanda for a comment.

Judi came to the table. "Anyone want anything else?" She looked at the pile of money in the center of the table. "What's this for?"

"It's for Ed Wilson's court fines," Eva explained. Then she laughed and said to Judi, "You weren't expecting a tip of that size from the Friends, were you?"

"How about another one of those blueberry pies?" Amanda asked.

"All in favor, say aye," Murphy called. Hands went up.

"Ok, another blueberry pie," Judi said. "But you better leave me a good tip."

As she left to get the pie and more coffee, Eva watched as Colleen got up and walked with Judi to the next room. What was going on between them? Eva wanted to leave the table, too, but Amanda caught her attention.

"I saw some beautiful pictures of the yellow-crowned night heron," Amanda said.

"Oh, you did? I'm glad," Eva said, keeping an eye on the door.

"I was given a copy of the pictures to keep," Amanda said and winked at Eva.

Eva turned and looked at Amanda. This was good news. It meant that Murphy was trusting Amanda to take action if needed.

"Enough," Murphy said, tapping Amanda on the shoulder. She laughed.

Soon Colleen came back and laid a check on the table. Eva looked at it. It was from the Hungry Fish bank account and it was a hefty donation toward the fines. Everyone looked at the check and smiled.

Other members of the Friends made short reports on various subjects. As they gave their reports, the blueberry pie was delivered, divided and devoured.

Finally, Amanda stood up and thanked everyone for coming to the meeting. Gary made another plea to get them to come to the government hearing. "We need every one of you there."

Sitting in the room, with all the talk and decision-making, Eva became impressed with the importance of the hearing. She wanted to see what it was all about, how it was handled and what the government officials who accepted their petitions were like. She turned to her mom, "I don't have any classes that day. I could go." Colleen nodded approvingly.

However, by the date of the hearing, everyone's enthusiasm cooled under the gray winter clouds and falling rain. The response was so sparse; there was no need to obtain a bus to take the supporters. Eva began to secretly wish that she had not offered to go, but the sense of importance and the need to show that there were supporters obligated her to stay involved. Gary and Colleen drove their cars and gave rides to the small group that made the trip to the state capitol.

When they arrived, they entered through the tall marble columns of the government buildings. Inside, Eva looked around at the high ceilings and gigantic marble scrolls and scales that impressed upon her the power of government that dominated their everyday lives. The Friends of Nature went into the hearing room and sat together on big wood benches under dim somber lights. They looked around at the deep mahogany wood paneling, large desks and oak podium of the state hearing room.

Doors opened and in came the authorities. They led a very formal, tedious procedure. Eva thought it was quite a contrast from the angry crowd that was protesting the bulldozers weeks ago. Here in the government halls, not one angry voice erupted. The state police stood watching. The contenders were each allowed a set amount of time and a set number of experts to address the issue.

Eva slouched down in her seat on the bench as she watched Gary hand over the signed petitions to the commissioner. He explained the strong community support for preserving the land as a wildlife area. Curtis submitted maps of the plant communities and the value they offered in detoxifying the soil. The accountant, Burt Martinez, addressed his qualifications and the actuarial advice he had obtained in creating the financial assessment of the Foundation's plans.

The Foundation brought forward their experts, including a real actuary, not just an accountant, like the Friends had. Barbara Harrison gave a glowing picture of the advantages the community would gain through development of the land that the B & L Foundation was donating. The Foundation's tax advisor spoke about the advantages to the state that the Foundation's plan would bring. He addressed "rateables," income flow and jobs. Eva looked toward Amanda and saw a deep frown on her forehead.

After the formal process and the submission of all their reports, the hearing came to an abrupt end without a cry or scream. Gary inquired and found out that the decision would not be made until the next summer. They bowed their heads and looked at the floor.

Eva couldn't understand why. Her mind was bubbling with questions. Why would it take so long for a decision? Why did the people have to wait? Couldn't the state make the decision quicker? She felt enraged. It was not fair. Didn't anyone see that this could give the Foundation more time to break the rules and push their plan further along? Eva complained to her mother, but Colleen just shrugged. All the adults accepted it, even Amanda. Why was Amanda being so quiet? She always had an opinion. Eva wanted to get up and scream at them, but she knew they would only think she was being childish. She too had to accept it. What could they do but wait?

All parties to the matter shuffled out of the room.

"Let's go to a diner and get a bite to eat," Gary suggested. "There's a good one just around the corner." This lightened their mood. They turned their steps in the direction of the diner and went in. Amanda pointed to a booth. They went there and sat down. After they ordered their food, Eva decided to make an attempt at opposing their acceptance of the delayed judgment.

"How do they expect us to go through the whole winter waiting?" she asked.

"It's all part of the struggle, I guess," Colleen said.

"I've waited many years for decisions of this sort," Amanda offered. "It's always a long slow process."

"It's called "due process," Gary explained. "That's what democracy is about. Both sides of the argument are considered. It is not up to the bureaucrats to make all the decisions. The state has to hear our point of view and seriously consider it."

Eva sighed. It made sense, but still she felt more should be said or done.

After the meal, the most active and determined Friends of Nature climbed into their two cars and rode home in silence. It was all a matter of time.

When the Thanksgiving holiday came, it was a great relief for Eva. She tossed the books aside and helped her mom and Judi with the feast. Typical of the Kaufman family that knew no true holiday obligations, they had to have their dinner on Friday instead of Thursday, because Judi had to work the holiday and the weekend serving Thanksgiving dinners at the Hungry Fish.

Again, Dad would not join them in person, but his happy face would greet them from a computer screen early Friday morning. In spite of it all, they bought and prepared the turkey, sweet potatoes, and pumpkin pie to mark the tradition.

With Dad's morning visit finished, Eva thought she might like to take a walk.

"Judi, I'm going to the park this morning for a couple of hours, want to go with me?"

Eva watched as Judi cast her eyes about trying to decide what she should do.

"Ok, sis, I guess, let's do that. We haven't had a good talk together in a long time."

The two young women put on their winter coats. Eva got her bird guides and binoculars. They walked down to the train station, past big quiet houses and leafless trees.

From the train station, they walked into the park. Eva looked into the treetops hoping to see some birds. Her sister Judi chattered on about working at the restaurant and the first adult love of her life, James. Eva hardly heard a word of it. The gray skies made her feel sad and hopeless.

The hedges and shrubs had turned a dark and dirty shade of green. The tall grass was tan and gray. A pin oak still held some bright red leaves, but by the end of November, most of the trees had dropped their yellowed leaves to the ground, defeated in their attempt at imitating the sun.

Eva looked about and remembered the many people she had worked with and had seen almost daily in the park during the summer. Where were they all now? Only a few dedicated joggers passed them on the trails. None had familiar faces.

Eva looked into the shrubs at the side of the trail.

"Oh look, here's a late fall migrant. See that bird," Eva said to Judi.

"A bird where? I never see them. If I didn't come with you, I'd probably never see a bird in this place. You know, Eva, I'm not much of a bird watcher, but James says I have a good eye for interior decorating. He liked my ideas about some new tables and chairs for the restaurant. He also liked my suggestions for changing the menu."

Eva sighed with boredom, but Judi continued. "Can you believe this, we had more people reserving tables for Thanksgiving this year than last year. You know, the tradition is changing. More people are going out to restaurants rather than staying home for the holiday. Remember how Mom used to cook all that food and invite all our relatives? You remember, the old ones we saw only on Thanksgiving?"

"It's a kinglet." Eva said, lifting her binoculars to have a look.

"Oh, Eva, what a magnificent bird," Judi said.

When Eva put down her binoculars, she realized that Judi had not even looked in the direction of the bird. Eva shook her head, "You are missing so much when you don't see the natural world around you."

Judi shrugged, "I like the smell of the spices in pumpkin pie."

Eva sighed again. "Judi, let's go see the area where the Foundation's machines dug the pit this summer."

"Oh, why? What's there to see?"

"I want to see how it looks over there now, so many months after the fire and bulldozers."

They hurried along until they arrived at the opening in the fence. It was very wide now, the gate posts had been knocked down by the bulldozers. They walked through the gap and followed a path until they stood at the rim of the hole that the machines had dug. A small pond had formed. Ice covered the surface. They watched as a great blue heron flew up and over the tops of the bare trees.

Eva turned to study some burnt pine branches that were lying on the ground. She kicked a burnt cottonwood log with her foot. A small creature popped up and fled into a tattered and leafless berry bush that still held fruit for the winter birds. Eva moved closer.

"It's a winter wren," Eva said. In the shrub, the little brown bird flitted around, holding its tail straight up in the air. It stopped for a moment to gaze up with its tiny brown eyes, and then it jumped into a small green pine tree at the edge of the burnt area and hid.

Eva smiled, "Judi, just think, this winter wren has no idea how this location had been overrun by angry humans during the summer. Right now, this is what it will call home for the winter. A quiet place out of the wind," Eva explained with satisfaction. The wren flew out of the small pine tree and landed on a fallen branch where it began picking the bark for beetles.

"James and I are getting along so well. I really love him and he loves me."

Eva paused and looked at her sister, "Sis, is this going to be some kind of announcement?"

Judi and Eva looked at each other.

"Well, Eva, he did say that I have made a great contribution to the business. His parents like me a lot too. We did discuss marriage."

Eva stood in silence. The possibility that her sister would be a restaurant owner, a managing partner as the result of a romantic pursuit—this sent laughter bubbling out of Eva.

"Judi, I can't believe you. You had this in your head from the beginning. You met James; you pursued him. He hardly had a chance to think twice."

"What do you mean?" Judi protested, "I was only hoping. He could have been as ugly as a troll and as mean as a crocodile. But as it happened, he turned out to be quite a charmer and will inherit his father's restaurant."

"That old bait shop and burger place?" Eva scoffed.

"I've persuaded them to turn it into a café. They listened to my idea and they are going to do it."

"A café?"

"When the New Year comes, we're going to rename the place the Bay View Café. Well, that's what James wants to call it, but I want to call it Café Libertea."

"Oh, the Bay View Café? I guess you lost that battle, huh sis?" Eva snickered.

"I am actualizing my dreams, dear sister. Now tell me about your dreams. Have you seen Curtis lately?"

"What makes you think that Curtis is my dream? We are friends, just co-workers at the park. I don't even see him anymore. I'm busy with school."

Eva marveled that Judi had completely forgotten about Matt Merriweather, someone Eva had been in communication with for months, someone who had become a regular in her life—at least on the internet. But then again, Eva hadn't talked about Matt. This was just something she didn't want to share with her sister or mother. It was fun having a secret like this.

Judi stopped on the trail and looked at a large red bird in a tree in front of her. "Oh look, Eva, there's a cardinal. I thought cardinals always flew south for the winter."

"Well, I'm proud of you Judi, you can recognize a cardinal. You're beginning to gain an eye for nature," Eva replied.

The two young women followed the narrow overgrown path back to the main part of the park. From the opening in the fence, they strolled along the smooth wide sidewalks that framed the great lawns where concerts had been held during the summer.

Eva looked around. Some small black geese, called brant, were waddling along, picking at the grass. Eva noticed how they stayed so close to each other, as if they were frightened of the possibility of being alone.

"These brant nest in the Canadian tundra," Eva explained to Judi. "This park is one of the few locations in our country where you can see them. They're seen in England and Ireland too."

The brant cooed softly, and then, alarmed by a passing dog and its owner, they suddenly lifted from the ground. Their wings whistled in the air as they passed over the heads of the two young women. Flying in unison, the brant went east and raced out to the wide-open water of the harbor.

As Eva and Judi sauntered further down Liberty Walk, a flock of Canada geese came down from the sky in "V" formation. They cupped the air with their large brown wings, pushed their feet forward and then splashed into the icy cold water of the north cove near the Columbus monument.

"I love the honking sound of the geese," Eva said.

"You are in love with nature, sister. I can only take so much of it."

Eva looked at Judi. "Strangely, what I've learned in college is—parks are not habitat. They are not really good examples of nature."

"Not good examples? How can you say that?" Judi gasped.

237

"Parks are manipulated, grass is cut and sprayed to reduce the amount of fleas, trees are trimmed to suit the human eye, not the needs of the birds. They put out poison for the rats and it sometimes kills the wild hawks instead. They plant non-native species of flowers from all over the world because people want flowers that are big and showy—but these flowers have no nectar or pollen and so they aren't even useful to butterflies or bees."

Eva looked sternly at Judi. It was time for her to make an announcement of her own dreams.

"Right now, I'm considering going to Peru next winter to see the Amazon rain forest. I want to see what real nature looks like before it is destroyed. I want to see the true, wild nature that has not been so infringed upon and tampered with by humans."

"You want to go to the Amazon rain forest? It's dangerous there. There are all kinds of poisonous snakes and plants. There are diseases like malaria and dengue fever. Eva, you are too much into this environmental stuff. What will Mom say? She won't want you to go that far from home. The Amazon is nothing like the woods that we went camping in as kids. Mom will be opposed to this."

"Do I need her permission?" Eva asked.

Judi did not answer. They continued to walk along the trail in silence.

After a few minutes, Judi lifted her head to speak, "James and I have talked it over. We want to give ourselves a year. This way we can get the Bay View Café completely remodeled. It's like we'll be rebuilding the café for our wedding. We're going to plant a huge flower garden and put in stone walkways at the back of the restaurant."

Eva saw the excitement in her sister. Her blue eyes sparkled like ice in the sun.

"If all goes well," she continued, "I'll be wearing an engagement ring soon. I'm not going to ask Mom if this is ok; I'm just going to say "yes" when James places it on my finger. Eva, I'm going to cry."

Eva laughed. "I guess we really are moving ahead in life."

Judi was crying now and wiped a tear from her eye.

Eva looked away at the treetops. It was difficult to accept these sudden changes in life. First, they got jobs. Now, they were planning marriage and travel. How would Mom take it? Certainly, they would stand up for each other's right to make independent decisions, even if Colleen did not approve. But what might happen next?

"Let's go further down Liberty Walk and see what's happening in the nature area behind the Statue of Liberty." Eva suggested.

As they walked, snow started to fall. The Statue of Liberty lifted her torch into the swirling cloud of big white flakes. Soon, the snow filled the air so intensely that the Statue of Liberty disappeared. After a minute, it stopped snowing and the view was clear again.

Eva and Judi walked on until they passed the picnic tables now covered by snow as if covered by white tablecloths. Pine trees were decorated with snowflakes and ice crystals. The snow-covered dried flowers of the rudbeckias marked the locations of last summer's gardens.

Eva saw another bright red cardinal and some gray mockingbirds hopping around plucking the bright red berries of the hawthorn trees. She was glad to see that the park was providing them with food. Goldfinch appeared wearing their drab gray and black winter feathers. They flew over the open fields in search of thistle seeds. A red-tailed hawk circled low over the ground in search of rabbits. Eva was amazed to see that nature had claimed the park that people had abandoned to winter.

From Liberty Walk, the two young women turned toward the south cove. The winter sun struggled to brighten the cloudy day. Near the water's edge, Eva identified rafts of ruddy ducks, with their bills tucked under their wings and their tails sticking up making them look like a row of sugar bowls with spoons. Meanwhile, little black and white bufflehead ducks appeared and disappeared in the water as they dove for food. Red-breasted mergansers leaped forward and then dived deep and disappeared for several minutes. Eva marveled that they could play in water so cold it would kill a human in an instant. Two hundred years ago, the New York harbor had been a winter sanctuary for millions of ducks and geese. Now only a token population came to their traditional winter waters.

As the sun began to set over the south cove, the two young women turned toward the long trail to the train station. Suddenly Eva saw something move swiftly and quietly through the corner of her vision. She looked up and saw a large white blur, like a ghost, moving above the surface of the snow-covered field. It was an owl. In its talons, it was carrying something.

"Oh my dear, Judi, look! It's a snowy owl. They only come down from the tundra at rare times when there is a food shortage up north. This is incredible."

Eva signaled to Judi to hide with her behind a large bushy pine. They watched as the owl pulled apart its prey and choked down pieces of flesh. When it was satisfied with its meal, the owl lifted into the air on its large white wings and silently flew away.

"Come on, let's go see what it was eating," Eva said.

"I really don't care," Judi responded. "I'll stay here. You go look."

Eva walked up to the site where the owl had devoured most of its meal. There in the snow were drops of bright red blood, a few bones and some remaining fur. Eva pushed at the remaining fur with the toe of her boot to examine it closer. She tried to figure out what the creature had been. The fur was calico. "It was a kitten."

The snowy owl was preying on Sally's poor kitties.

"We can't let Sally know," Judi whispered.

"I guess we won't," Eva replied, "Nature is too cruel for her."

The weather was getting worse. Now, the snow started coming down fast in smaller flakes that blinded them.

"We have to find our way back," Judi screamed. Her voice drifted out across the empty field. Nothing could be seen now but total whiteness.

"I think we go that way," Eva said.

"You are being punished for saying that parks are not really nature," Judi replied.

"I take it all back. Parks are a place of nature. Nature is everywhere," Eva said.

"There's a sign," Judi yelled and pointed. "Look, yes it's pointing to the train station. Let's go."

When the two young women finally made it home, they hung up their snow-covered coats to dry on the coat rack. They hurried to tell their mother about the adventures they had experienced in the park.

The smell of Colleen's traditional dinner filled the air. She listened as she put on gloves and checked the turkey in the oven.

"We saw all kinds of birds," Eva announced cheerfully.

"The park was beautiful, as always, but cold," Judi said. "Let me set the table."

Eva sat down at the table and began a scientific assessment of the park based on her college studies. Colleen listened and smiled. Eva continued to talk as her mom went to the oven and pulled out a loaf of bread. She placed it on a rack to cool.

Judi put the plates on the table, and then she whispered to Eva. "What do you think? Should we tell Mom about our future plans now?"

"Not now, Judi, let's not bring it up now," Eva said. "Mom seems so happy, let's not have any emotional discussions at the dinner table, we can wait until after."

The meal was delicious, the conversation friendly but directionless. From time to time, the two young women would look up from their plates to see Colleen beaming with joy.

Eva cleared the dishes. Judi set the table for dessert. The two young women sat down then nodded at each other.

"We have some things to tell you, Mom," Eva announced.

Colleen looked at them with curiosity.

Eva paused and in doing so, lost her chance to speak. Judi jumped right in.

"Mom," said Judi, "I just want you to know that James and I are seriously considering marriage. If everything works out well, we'll be married in the Bay View Café during the month of roses, June." She sat back in her chair with her chin in the air proud of her announcement.

Colleen laughed. "I knew that was coming, dear. Of course, I'm glad for you and for all of us. I think James will be a wonderful husband."

"Ok, Mom, then here's what I have to say," said Eva. Colleen turned toward Eva with a look of concern.

"Mom, our biology professor is leading a field trip to Peru to see the mountains and the rain forests. I'm going because I want to see what real wilderness looks like. All I've ever seen is park land and camp sites. I want to walk through a jungle and see where the migratory birds go when they leave us behind in winter."

Colleen gasped. "Leave it to you, Eva, to spring something on me. You always take me by surprise. Of course, I'll be worried, but what can I do? I don't want to stand in your way."

Eva and Judi looked at each other.

"Isn't Mom great," said Judi. "She's so good at letting us grow up."

"Well, I have some news for you two," Colleen informed them. "Don't think your mother is going to sit at home and cry. I have a life of my own and now that you two are leaving the nest, I can do new and different things with my life as well."

The two young women looked at their mother. Worry filled their eyes.

"Gary Russo called me today."

"Oh, no Mom, Gary Russo is too young for you," Judi squealed.

Colleen gave her daughter a look of doubt.

"Judi has a one-track mind," Eva laughed.

Colleen laughed, too. "As I was saying, Gary called and said they need a new face in the leadership of the Friends of Nature. He wanted to know if I'd be willing to run in the election for his position. He wants to move on."

Eva smiled. "Go for it Mom. It sounds great."

Judi sputtered, "Oh, what am I going to do? Two dedicated environmentalists in my family. You two will drive me crazy."

"What are your chances of winning the election, Mom?" Eva asked.

"Well, they put out a call for candidates. If I'm the only one that responds, I'm in by acclamation. If someone else responds, then we will need to hold an election."

"So that's it?" Judi asked.

"Yes, I'm going to run for president of the Friends of Nature," Colleen declared.

Eva laughed. "Well, Mom, I guess we didn't see that one coming."

Colleen smiled and said, "I'm excited. I really enjoy what I'm doing in the Friends. Let's celebrate. Oh, the turkey!" She ran to the oven and pulled it out before it scorched any further.

Judi sighed but then smiled in acceptance. "We Kaufman ladies are losing our domestic skills."

"I'm sure the turkey will be fine," Eva assured them.

"It's fine," Colleen announced.

"Well, in spite of that, we have a great dessert." Judi stood and went to the kitchen cabinet where she brought forth a box. On the side was printed "The Bay View Café." She set it on the table and lifted out a blueberry pie.

The three women talked to each other about their hopes, dreams and plans. Then, when the time together ended, they cried and hugged. It was time to make something important happen in their every-day lives.

Lying in bed that night, Eva thought about all that had occurred during the holiday.

This coming year, Judi would be making plans for her wedding and married life. Colleen could soon be president of the Friends of Nature. Eva was steadily working on her degree and wondering what flying to South America and seeing the rain forest would be like. Matt had told her about the trip. He was planning to go. Should she really go? It could be dangerous. Eva rolled over in bed. She must get to sleep. But her mind could not let go. It moved on to the next worry, "What decision would the state make about the new land for Liberty Park?"

Chapter Twenty Six

Nature's Balance

"You understand, don't you, Amanda?"

Amanda felt like the floor was collapsing beneath her. All the years she had been active in the Friends of Nature and now here was Gary Russo trying to talk her into letting Colleen run for President of the Friends.

"We'll still keep you in your paid position with the Friends," Gary said in a kindly tone. She knew he heard the anger in her silence.

It was a relief to know they weren't going to take the money away from her. She counted on that to buy groceries. She swallowed hard. It's not that she disliked Colleen. Colleen had become a great friend. They had spent many hours collecting signatures for the petitions. It had been a good chance to really get to know each other. Oh, maybe she doubted that Colleen could handle the position, deal with the media, and put up with cantankerous members like Murphy. It just seemed to Amanda like she herself had, all these years, been moving in that direction. Anyone could have seen that. But now, they wanted to give the position over to Colleen.

"We'll find another important responsibility for you, Amanda. A better one really."

"I would like being president of the Friends of Nature," Amanda stated.

"Listen, Amanda, I'm moving on and where I'm going, I could put in a good word for you."

Amanda listened. "What do you mean, Gary?"

"We'll be working together in other ways in the future. I'm thinking about a new position we can create for you. Colleen, I'm sure, will be in favor of it, once she gets the presidency. So, if no one runs against her, she's in. Once she's in, we'll work on what we can do with you."

He said it like she were merely a piece on a game board. Amanda felt like she had somehow become a problem in their big plans and now she was someone they had to squeeze in somewhere. Colleen and Gary were about the same age and she wondered now if there had been something going on between them that she had missed. How could she have missed anything? She always felt Colleen had been sincere with her. If Colleen was interested in a personal relationship with Gary, she would have said something to Amanda. Wouldn't she?

"Amanda, can I have your word? Will you consider supporting Colleen's campaign to be president of the Friends?"

Amanda waited. She thought. Then she spoke, "Give me time to consider it. But I could still run myself, if I decide to."

"Please seriously consider supporting Colleen," Gary said.

"I will consider it," Amanda promised.

"Now, we need to do some cleaning and sorting of the Friends office. Our landlord wants us out. We don't know where we're going to go, but we need to sort, toss and clean to be ready. In the meantime, I'm looking into other space for our organization. Amanda, can you go over to the office and get things rolling on that?"

"Sure," Amanda responded. Maybe while she was cleaning out the office, she could think about whether to run for president.

Outside a gray and rainy spring day awaited her. She put on her raincoat and headed out the door. Her car had broken down. She could not afford to fix it. Fortunately, she could take the train. As she made her way to the station, she marveled at the many gardens people planted in front of their homes. Iris in yellow, purple and white were blooming everywhere. There were flower pots on porches with pansies and geraniums.

The Friends office was in a building just outside the park. They shared space with a used clothing store, a woodcraft workshop and an animal shelter. The office was very small, consisting of one desk, a chair, a phone, an outdated computer and a closet with some supplies. There were boxes lined up against a wall that were full of forgotten things that no one ever looked at. The only person who had spent much time in the Friends of Nature office was Gary Russo. No one else wanted to go near it.

Arriving at the office, Amanda saw Colleen sitting at the computer diligently working.

"Oh, you're here?" Amanda said. Colleen's bright smile drove all the resentment out of Amanda.

"Good morning, I'm working on updating the database. We're going to move it to a better computer. Gary wants me to go online and make some changes to the web site as well." Colleen lifted a bottle of cranberry juice and took a sip.

"Gary asked me to do some sorting and cleaning," Amanda explained. "I guess I'll start with these boxes here." She began lifting the lids and looking into the boxes.

"Good luck with your task there," Colleen said. She turned back to the computer screen.

Amanda thought as she poked around. So, this is what it had come to after years of participation: Colleen had the computer skills needed in this high tech age. Old goat Amanda was only useful to do the cleaning. Amanda burned inside. For the first time in years, she was mad at Gary. If Colleen could do the computer work, then Amanda could be president. She had the experience, social skills and face recognition in the community. How could they set her aside like this?

Amanda reached into another box and found a smaller box full of old yellowed crumbling newspaper clippings. There were pictures of herself and Murphy from years ago. "I think I'll just take this box home and sort it out there," Amanda muttered.

"Be careful, there are roaches and other bugs in this place," Colleen advised. "You might want to quarantine it for a while before taking it into your house."

Amanda laughed. Colleen was funny. Well, of course, why wouldn't Gary pick Colleen for president? She was intelligent, had a job and money and was still young enough at forty-five to keep up with the pace.

Again, anger and disappointment boiled in Amanda. She liked Colleen a lot, but the position was rightfully hers. Besides, how was Colleen going to have time to represent the Friends in public? Gary knew that Amanda had time available to go to meetings and be ready to do those spontaneous press conferences. Amanda was the best candidate for the position. What could have made Gary change his mind?

Oh, what was she thinking? Maybe Colleen had suggested it to Gary. Colleen looked so knowledgeable sitting there tapping away on the keyboard like she knew what she was doing. And she was going to update the web site too? Amanda shook herself. She knew what she had to do; she had to talk to Colleen. After all, Colleen was her friend.

"Colleen, how are you doing these days?"

"Fine," Colleen responded still gazing into the computer's screen.

"It looks like you are really sharing the workload with Gary these days." Amanda stated.

"Oh, yes, I'm checking the email now. This keeps me busy and keeps me from worrying," Colleen admitted.

Amanda looked at Colleen with curiosity. Colleen had two beautiful daughters who were likely to succeed in life. They had good health, education and jobs. Colleen was doing well on her nursing job, too. What could she have to worry about except the park?

Amanda sighed. "We're all so worried about the decision the state will make in regard to that parkland."

"Oh, Amanda, to add to my troubles, I'm worried sick about Eva."

"Eva? I would think she was the least likely to give you any worries."

"She wants to go to Peru to learn about the jungle. I can understand that she wants to experience the true wilderness. I just don't know why she has to go so far away. Why couldn't she focus on local forests? We have plenty of wilderness left in our country."

Amanda heard a tremble in Colleen's voice. It touched her. It was the fear that she might lose a daughter.

"Your worries are valid. My Stephanie took a trip like that once and never came back. You can never know what will happen in your life and the life of your children. I think, as Americans, we feel everything should go well for us, but sometimes it doesn't. And when it doesn't, we just don't understand why."

Amanda began to look at this conflict of mother and daughter and wondered if she could find a reason for Colleen to turn down the presidency. Suggesting that Colleen should step aside just because Eva was planning a brief trip—this was clearly so self-serving, and Amanda did not want to look like that. She valued her friendship with Colleen and her daughters.

"I'm sorry, I shouldn't have mentioned my Stephanie. I don't want to fill your head with my worries. I don't want you to be like me. Eva has to go and be true to herself. There's nothing a mother can do."

"No, Amanda, I understand what you are saying. I feel sad for you that you lost your daughter. But my problem is, I often worry so much. It consumes my life and because of it, I have failed to do more with my life than I could have. It's part of why my husband is leaving me. I just could never get over my fear of traveling. He loves to travel, but for me, I struggle with this terrible fear. I've struggled for years—every time there was a vacation trip, a drive to visit distant relatives. And now, Eva wants to travel. I suppose she has her father's love of it. She has no fear. But the Amazon rainforest? Why does she have to go there?"

Colleen lifted her hands, rung them in anguish, then put them back on the keyboard. "I'm trying to change my life, Amanda. I'm trying to deal with my irrational fear." She stopped talking and let her fingers run along the keys as if to run away from the struggle within her.

Amanda looked at Colleen. Here was a woman who had the life that Amanda should have had with Stephanie. Yet this woman with not one, but two healthy, happy and potentially successful daughters, felt her own life was a failure. She was struggling to redeem it. Amanda was amazed. She could not believe that Colleen had any problems.

Colleen finished her task before shutting down the computer. She lifted her juice bottle and turned to look at Amanda. Amanda watched as Colleen's eyes drifted over the surface of her own face, as if Colleen were trying to understand in the wrinkles and lines what age was and how to cope with it.

"I'm sorry, Amanda, for being so consumed with myself. I know your life has been full of struggle, compromise and acceptance. You are right, we always expect so much more from life. I am lucky to have two daughters that are both alive and doing well."

Amanda smiled.

"You are truly lucky. I only had one and she's been gone for over ten years." Amanda leaned against the wall and gazed up at a poster on the opposite wall about saving the trees. She did not want to compete with Colleen. She really wanted Colleen as a friend.

"And to think back on it," Amanda continued, "I almost didn't have Stephanie. When I was seventeen, I was going to marry Murphy. But he was so set against having any children, I couldn't marry him. I felt I would always be missing out on something important in life. So I married George, had a daughter and, in her sixteenth year, I lost her. And I lost any chance at grandchildren as well," Amanda said. "Life is strange. We build sandcastles and the powerful waves of nature wash them away."

"We do the best we can with the life we get," Colleen said.

Amanda looked at Colleen with respect. That next generation wasn't as crazy as everyone thought, Amanda decided.

"And speaking of doing the best you can," Amanda said, "I've heard that you may be running for office. Do you want to be the next President of the Friends of Nature?"

Colleen set her bottle down and looked at Amanda.

"Gary did talk to me about it."

Amanda saw before her a tall, thin, middle-aged woman who was still afraid to take on responsibility outside of her home and family. Amanda knew she could easily say a few simple words that would discourage Colleen. All she had to do was dwell upon her fears, belittle her limited experience. Amanda could dissuade her, but she did not have the meanness to do that.

"Amanda, I'm glad we are here alone together." Colleen said. "I wanted to get the chance to talk to you about it face to face. I know you have dedicated so much of your life and time to this organization. I know you still want to give more of your time to it. I have my own doubts about myself. My usual fear grips me. I liked the Friends because it's right here in my own town and my own state. I don't want to fly off to conferences half-way across the country. I can play a big role right here. But Gary says we need to link up with other environmentalists, even those around the world. It's stupid, I know, but all I want to do is work here in my community. Why is that such a problem? Why am I perceived as a neurotic just because I don't want to fly all over the world?"

Amanda listened. She tried to put herself into Colleen's dilemma. She tried to think of living with those fears and limitations. If Colleen did not like to travel, why should she have to? Send Eva on those trips representing the Friends of Nature. Or, maybe, better yet, Amanda could take some of those trips for Colleen. They could share the responsibility.

It was an interesting idea, but it needed more thought. She lifted the lid on another box. It was full of banners for a protest against the creation of a new highway. Oh, yes there was a time when they wanted to put a superhighway through the park. The community had stopped that as well.

Amanda waited, holding a box lid in her hand. She did not want to suggest her idea of working together before she had enough time to think it out. She looked at Colleen who was now sorting through a stack of paper newsletters that had been sent in from around the country.

Amanda thought, and in thinking, she only stared into the open box. This woman, Colleen, was new to the organization. Amanda had recruited her just last year when she volunteered with the gardens. She was younger and had more energy, but she lacked Amanda's experience. Maybe, maybe it would be better if Amanda could work in the background, help Colleen. Let her go before the cameras and talk to the media. Amanda could be the "brains" behind it all. Yes, that could work, Amanda could be Colleen's assistant. It was a brilliant idea.

"I think you should do it," Amanda announced.

Colleen jolted in her seat.

"What?"

"Yes, I think it's great. You should run for president of the Friends of Nature."

Amanda looked at Colleen. "But I'll tell you what, it's a big responsibility. I'll help you on your election campaign. I could also be your assistant in every other campaign we take on as the Friends of Nature. Let's do it."

Colleen looked at her with a smile before stepping over to Amanda and giving her a hug.

"I must say," Amanda continued, "I did think Gary should have offered it to me. But really, I'm tired of being the warrior. I've fought so many battles and I hope I'm scoring my greatest victory with the state deciding in our favor. I don't think I have the energy it takes to be in leadership. But I can't give up my life's work. So I'd like to be an assistant and help out. I'm glad you are running. We can work together."

"Well, Amanda, you do have a lot of experience. When Gary asked me, I thought it was funny, me? When I told my daughters, they were surprised and thrilled. They were proud of me. They convinced me. But you know how it is, a leader is only as good as her supporters. I could certainly use your support. We can be a good team and get much more done."

"The election is at the end of June," Amanda said.

"That's close to the time when the state will make its decision," Colleen said. "It will be a busy month. Hopefully, I'll be put in office by acclamation. Otherwise, we'll be doing an election and a campaign to get the public to support the Friends' plan for the park."

"As easy as it would be to gain your position by acclamation, Colleen, it looks better if you win an election." Amanda could see, yes, Colleen was a novice. To win an election was a show of strength. A leader needed that. On the other hand, it was more important for the Friends to focus on winning the state's approval and not get bogged down in elections for a new leader in the midst of this battle.

"What a busy time it will be," Colleen exclaimed. "And that's when they're going to start remodeling the Hungry Fish Restaurant."

"Remodeling the Hungry Fish?" Amanda asked.

"Judi and James are becoming quite serious with each other. You know, James' dad owns the Fish. After they renovate the building, they are going to plant a large flower garden next to it," Colleen explained. "Judi and James will be the first to get married there next summer. Oh, yes, and they're changing the name, it's going to be the Bay View Café—well Judi wants to call it Café Libertea, but she's learning. She can't always have her own way. I'm looking forward to their special day with happiness," Colleen said. "That's one thing I'm not worried about."

"It will be wonderful, I'm sure," Amanda said. She smiled at Colleen. Obviously, Colleen was going to need a lot of help. Amanda was feeling better now, thinking of herself as an assistant, maybe consultant sounded better.

"Look at this mess. We have a lot to do today. Gary says we have to be out of this office by the end of the month."

They began sorting through the supplies and checking the phone messages, a package arrived and a guest stopped by for a chat. Afterward, Amanda swept the floor while Colleen made some calls. Then they locked up and left the office. Colleen gave Amanda a ride home.

After waving good-by to Colleen, Amanda decided to go to her backyard and survey what gardening work she needed to do there. The sky had cleared and the sun was coming out. She looked at Stephanie's flowerbed. Some butterflies, called Mourning Cloaks, were crowding around the edges of a puddle that had formed there. Amanda admired them, amazed that they existed here in her backyard.

"Making some garden plans for this spring?" came a man's voice from the garden fence.

Amanda turned to see Murphy peaking over at her.

"No, just thinking in general."

Amanda walked over to Murphy. She winked at him. "Here's some news for you. Colleen Kaufman is running for president of the Friends of Nature. And here's another surprise, I'm helping in her campaign."

"Oh yeah, who's running against her?"

"Well, no one yet. We're in the nomination process. I'm going to be her consultant."

Murphy laughed. "I should run against her. That would guarantee she'd win. Who would vote for an old lazy dog like me?" Murphy snarled, then winked.

"She could win by acclamation. Murphy, if we need you to run as a spoiler, we'll let you know, but please don't even think about running."

Murphy laughed.

"Hey, did you see the big blue jays I attracted to my backyard? I've been putting some peanuts and corn out and I finally got them to come. They like that white pine tree in the corner there."

"Oh, very good Murphy, you just keep an eye on those birds," Amanda said and then she waved goodbye. She went into her home and closed the door. It had been a beautiful day.

Chapter Twenty Seven

Earth Day Returns

Eva was so glad that spring had arrived. During the dreary days of winter, she had experienced her first year in college. It had been a constant struggle to stay awake in class, complemented by long agonizing hours trying to write her papers and the anxiety of preparing and taking tests. She was glad to have the support of Matt and Curtis as they sent reassuring text messages and emails answering her questions.

Being the naturalist that she was, she watched the weather reports to see what time the sun was rising and setting each day. As always, just when it seemed most hopeless, the earth tilted on its axis and brought change. For the Northern Hemisphere, spring was in the air. Her first year of college would be finished. Eva was excited and hopeful.

She thought about working at the park again this summer. She was not sure if that was what she wanted to do. It meant another summer of telling people to keep their dogs on leashes, to put their trash in the garbage cans and to stop feeding the pigeons. It was a shame that people needed to be told repeatedly. Yet, when Curtis sent the job offer, she could not refuse. She got her uniform out of the back of the closet and arrived for her first day at work.

For some strange reason, this spring, the park patrons were complaining constantly about the goose droppings on the sidewalks.

"There's entirely too many geese here," one park patron stated as he stood in the park office filing his complaint.

Eva tried to explain that before Europeans came to this Hudson River estuary, it had been the winter home to millions of birds; humans had destroyed their beautiful habitat.

"What do I care about that?" the park patron said. "These goose droppings are all over the playground. This makes it unhealthy for children to play in the park."

Eva knew she could not argue. She reported the complaint to the superintendent. Still, she hoped the migratory geese and their avian friends, the Atlantic brant, would hurry up and go north. They seemed to be lingering. Their late departure was increasing the park patrons' hostility toward them. Meanwhile, the resident geese were already looking for nesting sites along the park pond. Their population would soon expand. Yet, Eva knew, when the little yellow fuzzy darlings popped out of their shells, everyone would be in love with them.

Eva headed out to walk the trails. Ahead, she saw a woman relaxing on a bench, gazing up at the sky as a new flock of Canada geese came flying in from the harbor to graze on the lawn. Eva saw a smile on the woman's face, so she greeted her with a matching smile.

"I really love the geese," said the woman, looking at Eva. "That's why I come to the park. I love to watch them eating the grass and honking. They are such kindly creatures."

Eva smiled, "I know, I really like them too."

Eva did not want to tell the woman what she had over-heard as a park employee. The Park Service was discussing the possibility of hiring a company with specially trained dogs to chase the geese every time they landed in search of food. The superintendent explained that it was the only way to keep peace. On one side were the park patrons who hated the goose dung and on the other were those who hated the brutal practice of harvesting. Eva hoped the park patrons would soon begin thinking about something else.

Earth Day was coming. Events like this meant that all park employees would have extra tasks in preparation for the big day. The park's community center, where all the events were held, needed a thorough cleaning. Floors had to be swept, more garbage cans needed to be installed, tables needed to be set up. Vendors, environmentalists and scouts would soon bring in their displays. Earth day was a time to educate the people on the splendor of nature and how it could be experienced in the park. Eva had already been told that Curtis was in command of the cleaning and set up. On Earth Day she watched him take charge.

"Many people still have not learned the lessons we are trying to teach," he explained to a small group of newly-hired summer helpers. "We'll just use some of last year's exhibits over again. This year, Eva, I want you to do the botany table. Can you get a volunteer from the Friends to help you?"

"I'll do that," Eva replied.

During the day, Eva found it rewarding to be an experienced employee. She was trusted more now and she was allowed to guide the new hires in what to do. She spent more of her day talking and less doing. In spite of that, she was glad when the work was completed.

Walking back from the train, she remembered she was to get a volunteer to work with her at the botany table. When she got home, she discussed it with her mother.

"Well, dear, since Amanda recruited us into the Friends, let's recruit her to help you with the park's Earth Day table. I'm sure she'd love to do it." They called Amanda and she agreed.

On Earth Day, Eva and Amanda sat at the table greeting guests and handing out information about "biotic succession." Eva knew all about it and explained it to anyone who listened. "This is nature's way of re-establishing plant communities on bare land." Eva said, watching their responses. When they didn't seem to understand the importance of it, she added, "It's a source of hope for the return of the forests that once covered the eastern half of this country."

Even with this message of hope, there were long stretches of time when everyone avoided their table. Eva stared into the crowed.

"Amanda, how could we help people relate to nature?" Eva asked. "The forces of nature govern humans as well, but they don't see it. The way the land heals itself with biotic succession is, in many ways, like the way the body heals itself from cuts and burns."

"What, my dear?" Amanda responded. Eva laughed.

The roar of the growing crowd became deafening. Eva wondered if their effort to educate was useless to people in urban settings who rarely saw trees or grass around them.

"So, I hear your sister is engaged to marry James, the owner of the Hungry Fish?" Amanda screamed over the roar of the crowd. "How do you feel about that?"

"The owner of the Café Libertea, do you mean? You watch, the name will change as a result of my sister's powerful influence. Oh, yes, she's planning on a wedding next year. If she's happy, I don't mind."

"And what are your plans for the future? Is it going to be a double ceremony?"

"Oh, no, I'm still in college. I'm totally committed to a career in protecting the environment." Eva saw a look of pride on Amanda's face and it made her feel good.

"My daughter Stephanie wanted to do the same thing. I think what you are doing is great, Eva. We need more young women in this field so they can help save the earth. You are truly our hero."

Eva thanked her for her praise. "It's a hard life, though. I need to learn more. I need to travel and see the world in all its magnificence. I can't let anything stop me."

"Oh, I know, my dear. You can't be afraid. Take the bull by the horns. Last year, I put my suit on and I went into the media office and set them straight. You do what you have to do. And you, Eva, you'll be an expert. I was just a lowly citizen with an opinion."

Eva looked at Amanda and smiled with admiration. Amanda nodded with glee and began telling a tale of her youthful rebellion. Eva laughed as she listened. The older generation was so funny. They would tell you to obey the rules and be good, yet the best moments of their youth came when they were themselves the most rebellious.

The Earth Day event swirled around them. Companies handed out brochures telling the residents how to reduce their use of heating fuel, how to reduce their use of electricity, and how to compost paper and table scraps. Meanwhile, musicians sang songs about saving the earth, and puppets pointed fingers at children who dropped litter. The whole event spun its message for everyone to hear and do.

As the afternoon passed, Eva and Amanda decided to put a new spin on their message. Eva patiently explained how plants clean carbon dioxide from the air and produce oxygen for people to breathe. Amanda flagged people down and directed them to the table. "This is Eva. She's our park's guardian angel. She knows a lot, so just ask her a question."

Eva laughed. "Amanda, please."

"Well, ok dear, let me do some explaining." Amanda put her chair in front of the display table and sat down.

"Come here, children. I want you to understand something."

Eva watched as Amanda drew a small audience around her. "You all know automobiles cause a huge amount of pollution. It's terrible. Car exhaust causes asthma and cancer in children. Our Earth is plundered to produce fuel for these gas guzzling, oil leaking monsters. The entire world is paved over with cement so automobiles can go faster until they run over someone. I wish automobiles had never been invented. Let me tell you, my daughter was killed in an automobile accident."

She looked at the children gathering at her feet. "These automobile monsters came and took my Stephanie away. I want all you lovely children to be safe. Be careful when you cross the street. Don't ride with careless drivers. More people are killed in car wrecks than in war—did you know that? And no one protests that! But we should. We need a safer way to get around. I curse those automobiles, even though I am forced to use one sometimes, I hate it."

Eva saw in Amanda's eyes a passion and fury that made her seem a little eccentric. Yet Eva could not argue against her. The audience broke into small conversations where individuals agreed, yet no one saw a way to solve the problem.

"You certainly have good points, Amanda," Eva said in a gentle tone.

"I guess I got carried away, but you know what? When you get older, you don't care anymore what people think of you; you just want to speak the truth." Amanda picked up her chair and moved back behind the table next to Eva.

A musical band climbed onto the stage and began a new round of nature songs. Eva watched as more Earth Day revelers approached the table. One wore a big ball around her belly that was painted to look like the earth. Her husband was in a globe that looked like the sun. Their little boy was wearing a slightly dented moon around his waist. Amanda and Eva laughed at the sight.

Eva was amazed how the day rolled from serious to humorous and back again. She was thankful for the opportunity to sit with Amanda, but felt like she was wasting the chance. Surely there must be something they needed to discuss. She searched her mind.

"Oh, Amanda, I've been so busy in college, I almost forgot. We're all still waiting on the state's decision. Do you think they will agree with the Friends' plans for the park?"

It was all Amanda needed to hear. She dived right into the subject. Eva listened and was happy to get the update. After several minutes, Amanda brought it to an end. "No matter what happens, your mom and I have decided to work as a team and fight for what's right for the park and our community."

"I'm sure you will," Eva said. She felt glad knowing that Colleen and Amanda would be there protecting the park that had helped her find her career and identity.

"So tell me, Eva, your mom says you're planning a trip. Why do you want to go so far?"

"Amanda, I want to go to the Amazon rainforest. I wanted to see a part of the earth that is pristine, untouched by human hands. So, I signed up for the trip. I'll be traveling with a team of biologists and environmentalists. But what a surprise! In class, I learned that humans have been cutting trees and changing the Amazon for tens of thousands of years. Scientists believe that the Amazon forest had been smaller during the glacier age and then grew larger over time. Parts of Alaska may have been part of the Amazon rain forest, but it moved northward on the tectonic plates. The whole earth changes and it always will. What I've learned in school is that we can't be sentimental in our understanding; we have to be scientific."

Eva saw a look of amazement on Amanda's face. "What's really important is, we have to have a balanced approach. We have the knowledge and technology to make human life comfortable without destroying the earth." Eva said. She thumped the table in front of her. "I truly believe this, but we have some obstacles. It's going to take more than just recycling a few bottles, but that's a start."

"You seem so excited about this," Amanda said. "Promise me, Eva, you will stay active all your life. A lot of damage has already been done by the selfish and greedy. We environmentalists must take charge and not let the damage continue."

"Of course," Eva said.

"Don't give up the fight, Eva, you are a necessary part of it."

Eva was about to tell Amanda more about the Amazon rainforest when she saw Sally and Peter walking by.

"Hey, what are you two doing here?" Eva called.

They came to the table.

Eva looked up at Sally—and for some strange reason, she remembered how the snowy owl had feasted on one of the kittens. This made Eva laugh.

"You are working in the park again this summer?" Sally asked.

"Oh, yes, I must be crazy, but it is a good job."

Sally smiled back at her. "Remember when I worked here? I used to sneak off and read a romance novel under the trees."

"Yes, I remember, and you left the tourists to fend for themselves."

"Oh, those cranky, demanding tourists. The jobs I get are always terrible. Now, I hate my job at the Foundation. Just between you and me, that Barbara Harrison is so difficult to deal with. She's a maniac. If the state opposes the Foundation's plan, I think Barbara is going to go crazy."

Eva and Amanda laughed.

"I'm telling you, I don't want to be there if she has to face defeat," Sally continued. "We're all still waiting for the state to decide."

"Yes, we are."

"I'm hoping the Foundation wins," Sally said to them, "then Barbara will be happy and I can keep my job. Maybe I'll even get a raise. You guys ought to support this stuff. What's wrong with having a botanical garden? A sports complex? Everyone loves sports."

Amanda and Eva looked at each other.

"We have to get going," Peter said. He took Sally's hand. "We want to see the other exhibits."

"Oh, yes, do see the other exhibits," Amanda said. She and Eva waved good-bye.

"I just hate listening to her push her boss's agenda," Amanda whispered to Eva. "Even while she hates Barbara so much."

Eva laughed. "Poor Sally, she doesn't know what she's doing. She just wants to keep that paycheck coming no matter what." Eva said, "So let me tell you about the birds in the rain forest."

Amanda chuckled and leaned back in her chair.

"I was amazed to learn that so many of the birds that stay the summer in our area migrate to Peru for the winter. One out of every five birds on this earth lives in the Amazon rainforest."

Just as Eva was getting deep into her favorite subject, Curtis stopped at the table. He greeted Amanda. She welcomed him and invited him to take her chair.

"I'm going to stretch my legs," Amanda explained. She turned and disappeared into the crowd.

Eva was surprised. She felt puzzled. Had she begun to bore Amanda?

Curtis grabbed the back of the chair, spun it around and sat backwards in it resting his arms over its back.

"So rumor has it your sister is getting married to a business man, James."

"Oh, yes, she is."

"Well, that should be a marriage made in heaven—the marriage of business and environmentalism. Usually business destroys nature, but maybe we are living in a new time where business can be good for nature."

"Or nature can be good for business." Eva said laughing. "I'm tired of being told how business is now beneficial to the environment. I don't believe it. Did you know that every major city is surrounded by garbage hills where our precious junk is buried?"

"I see you are on your soap box today, Eva. This is a good time and place for it."

Eva laughed. "Well, I believe my sister has made a good choice. James is a good guy. He gives money to the Friends of Nature. I just hope life is not a constant compromise."

"Sorry, it's a compromise all right." Curtis said and frowned. "He's playing his cards right. He'll look like an environmentalist and build his market base from that. I'm just wondering, how will you feel if your sister marries him and she becomes richer than you are? How dedicated are you to the cause, Eva?" He laughed.

"Money isn't everything," Eva said. She thought of how Judi was always focused on money.

"You'll have to find a job once you get out of college. I'm just saying, you may have to make a compromise and end up working for a mining, oil or gas drilling company as an environmental advisor, one of those types that paints the company's goals with green paint. Or, I'm suggesting this now, you could come work for the Park Service."

"I'd love to work for the Park Service."

"Yeah, but even that's a bit of a compromise. Anyway, your sister is marrying a smart guy. He's hedging his bets. That is what savvy business people do. Either way he wins. As for the park, we need people like him—people with money. We need people like you, too."

Eva was stunned. What was Curtis saying? Needing people with money?

Amanda returned to the table. Curtis stood and let Amanda take the chair.

"I'll see you later today, Eva," he said, and then he wandered off into the crowd.

Soon Judi and James came by. Judi was wearing the pink rose dress she had worn to the B & L luncheon. She smiled and showed off her engagement ring. "My wedding will be the first wedding at the new Café Libertea, in the beautiful garden we are planting this summer." She began handing out some flyers announcing the grand opening of the Hungry Fish under its new name. I love roses and they will be blooming on our wedding day in our tea rose garden." Judi said, turning her head and smiling at each one of them.

James smiled at Amanda, and then seeing some of his friends in the distance, he raised his hand and waved. His friends waved and came to the table.

"You're going to marry this lovely lady?" one asked.

Judi lifted her head with pride.

"Sure, she's better at the business than I am," James said, then winked.

Eva rolled her eyes and laughed.

The community center was now wall-to-wall people. The warm sunshine had brought them out. Everyone and every group was represented. Eva was amazed. But no. Someone was missing. Eva looked around. Of course! **Barbara Harrison and the Foundation were not present this year**. Eva nudged Amanda and pointed this out to her. "What could it mean? Could it be they are running out of money?"

"It's a good sign for our side," Amanda whispered.

They pondered this quietly and smiled.

By late evening, the Earth Day crowds began to dwindle. Amanda and Eva helped with the clean-up.

As Eva rode home on the train, she thought about her sister's wedding. The advantage for Eva was that Judi would soon be out of their shared bedroom. The entire room would be Eva's. She looked forward to the days when she would no longer have to listen to her sister's philosophy on how to succeed in life. What was success anyway? Running a silly café near a park?

As the train rolled along, Eva contemplated her life. She knew she wanted to do greater things. Amanda was right; there was a whole world out there that needed to be saved. She could not make chasing money the sole purpose of her existence.

But Curtis was right too; Eva had to live in the real world. She had to earn a living. How much money would she earn being an environmentalist? Would she take a job working in the park? That job had its aggravations. Even now, she was disappointed in the amount of money they paid her. She had to buy schoolbooks and pay for transportation. The spring weather was already getting hot, making work in the park much more challenging. A big national holiday was coming soon. As an experienced employee, Eva would have more responsibilities. She wondered what Independence Day would be like this year.

Chapter Twenty Eight

Independence Day

The American Revolution's declaration of independence from the tyranny of the King of England in 1776 was about to be celebrated once again all across the country. Eva knew that the Fourth of July was the most important day to the entire Park Service. All park employees would be needed to prepare the parks for this national event.

Every American flag in the park was inspected and, if torn, replaced by another American-made American flag. The grass was cut, the trees trimmed. The picnic tables were given a fresh coat of paint. The ferries to the Statue of Liberty had their engines tuned and were lined up at the docks, ready to carry the huge holiday crowds. On these ferries people from around the nation and around the world would travel to the Statue of Liberty to honor the American dream of justice and liberty and gaze up at the torch of Hope.

The city and park police were on alert to prevent terrorist acts that might sabotage the greatness of the day.

Declaration Day, as it was also called, held a special significance this year for the Friends of Nature. Today, the state would declare its decision on the land that had been donated to Liberty Park. The divided community of the B & L Foundation and the Friends of Nature focused on the media for word on the state's decision.

Having prepared the park, the park employees went to work on the Fourth braced for the thousands upon thousands of people who would come.

As the sun rose over the Hudson River, the multitudes, tired of work, looking for a holiday and hungry for barbeque, made their way into the park by car, by train, on foot and by ferry. They eagerly began their search for the perfect picnic table.

"Go to Liberty" a voice called across the park radio.

"Liberty, we need foot patrol down here to help answer questions and direct the people to the picnic sites."

"Liberty copies. We're sending them now. Liberty out."

Eva picked up her canteen and lunch pack.

"Eva, we're assigning you to McBride Gate. Don't let anyone go through that gate without an official park pass," Curtis explained.

"Ok, I'm ready."

The foot patrol moved out. It was now late morning on a bright sunny day, but in the western sky there were some deep purple clouds. Judging from the wind, Eva believed the distant storm might just keep moving north.

Though it had been a sanctuary of quiet in winter, the park was now filled with the cries of babies, the yells of eager young boys and the scolding commands of parents. Dogs came and went, on and off leashes as if they, too, knew this was a special day. Radios filled the air with songs and advertisements, while smoke filled the air with the scent of hickory and burning fats. The lawns of Liberty Park took the people into its big green hands and gave them over to joy and celebration in the summer sun.

Eva arrived at her command post and climbed the stairs. From high in the guardhouse at McBride Gate, she could see most of the park lawns. She saw the Friends of Nature gathered around their picnic site. They leaned toward a large radio in the center of one of their picnic tables. They were eagerly awaiting the announcement of the state's decision.

Eva waved to them from the lookout tower. She could see Gary Russo, past-president of the Friends, strutting back and forth like a sergeant ready to give orders to move the troops ahead. She could see Amanda sitting at one of the picnic tables talking with the new president, her mom, Colleen Kaufman. They were so engrossed in their conversation that they did not see Eva waving. She continued to wave at them, but they did not wave back. Sitting next to them was Murphy. Eva saw him point toward her and speak to them. They looked up with big smiles on their faces and waved back.

Eva watched as more and more people came into the park. There were people from Mexico and India; there were Jews and Palestinians sitting next to each other. There were Arabs looking like they had just stepped out of a Bible story. Past immigrants and current, they were all celebrating Independence Day.

Eva cast her gaze out over the New York harbor. The ferries were loaded with people going to see Ellis Island and the Immigration Museum as well as the Statue of Liberty. The water had so many sailboats and motor boats; that it looked frothy and white. Just as the park patrons had vied for the best picnic tables, the boaters were looking for the perfect place to drop anchor in preparation for viewing the fireworks this evening.

Eva looked with concern to the west. The purple clouds had moved closer, but the wind was still blowing north, a direction that should guarantee good weather in the park. She hoped for the best.

At noon, Eva pulled her sandwich from her lunch bag. Everyone was eating barbeque and she was having a vegan sandwich—a mix of beans, peppers and onions. As she ate it, she thought about Sally who had persuaded her to try a vegan diet. Maybe Sally was right. Maybe people shouldn't eat animals, at least not so many of them. Eva smelled the chicken cooking on the distant grills. She tried to console herself. There were supposed to be health benefits from eating a purely vegetable diet.

By late afternoon, Eva noticed that the Friends were all hovering closer to the radio. She watched them for signs of joy or anger.

Eva looked at the sky. To the east, big white fluffy clouds sailed along, but to the west, there sailed an armada of angry gray cumulonimbus.

Eva turned back around to see the Friends of Nature jumping for joy.

Colleen came running to Eva.

"We won. It's going to be a nature area, a bird sanctuary. We'll have more gardens. The state voted for our plan and against the Foundation's plan."

Eva let out a scream. It had happened. The people had won. The environmentalists had succeeded at making their point. They had saved the land and she had been a part of this victory. Eva sat now at her station and reflected on this happy outcome. The park would be even bigger now, with more land preserved for wildlife. The children of the county would have an opportunity close to home to hear songbirds and watch turtles lay eggs in the sand.

"We won!" Curtis said as he came to relieve Eva from her duty. She was now free for the day. "Go see the Friends and get some barbeque."

Eva had satisfied her appetite with her vegan sandwich, but when she got close to the picnic and smelled the chicken sizzling on the grill, she lost control. She grabbed a plate and took a piece of chicken. After all, it was a time to celebrate.

Then Eva saw Sally and Peter coming through the crowd toward the Friend's table. She quickly gobbled the last of her chicken breast. She was wiping her hands as they approached her.

"Hi, I guess you heard the good news?" Eva called.

"I heard it," Sally said. "And here's some more good news; I'm quitting my job. I'm not staying there. Barbara Harrison will go crazy."

"We're making other plans," Peter said. "Sally, tell her the other good news."

"Guess who's getting married next?"

Eva looked at her, "Not you and Peter?"

"Yes, of course. I want to move on with my life; I can't take care of kittens forever. I want children. I want to learn how to be a real parent. I can give my children what I never had."

It was good news for them, but Eva felt sad; it seemed like everyone was getting married. She shrugged and looked at Sally and Peter. "Whatever makes you happy. Congratulations."

"We've got to go," Peter explained. "We've got a lot of people to talk to."

Eva watched them disappear back into the crowd. She stretched her arms and legs, and then she gazed up at the sky. A thunderstorm was now seriously approaching. Eva realized they would soon have to pack up and leave. Her gazed dropped down to the grill where the food had been cooking.

Another piece of chicken was still on the plate next to the grill. Eva hated to think it would be thrown away in the rush to clean up. She cautiously moved toward it. She looked around and, seeing no one nearby that showed any interest in it, she scooped it up and put it on her plate.

As Eva ferociously bit into her chicken, Gary Russo stood among the Friends to summarize their battles against the Foundation.

"We made the best arguments. The state saw a risk in investing in the Foundation's plan, especially in the hotel. The sports complex was not likely to draw the kind of crowds it needed to pay the bills. So the weaknesses of their plan were made visible by our efforts. We also showed that the community really did not want the Foundation's plan. This being an election year, they had to listen to what the community had to say. Our serious, hard-fought struggle brought us a victory."

Everyone cheered.

Amanda came and sat down next to Eva.

"So we scored a victory. Now Eva, there is work for you to do to save the earth right here in our community. I'm happy with this."

"I'm looking forward to it," Eva said.

Murphy joined them at the table. "I was extremely doubtful that the state was going to rule in our favor. They always rule in favor of big business." He looked into Eva's eyes. "You know the real reason they did this? The corporations are in a bind right now. They got all kinds of loans going bad. Money is disappearing. Our economy is sliding into an abyss. The state saw too much of a risk in what the Foundation wanted to do. That's the real reason we won a victory."

"Oh, Murphy, don't be so negative," Amanda scolded.

"Amanda, I'm telling you, it's true. The economy is faltering. The bad economy gave us our biggest chance of winning."

Gary Russo joined them now at the table. "You see what people can accomplish if they just work together and stay focused," he said. "It gives me faith in this country. It's still a democracy. A victory like this helps the people understand. As I see it, the United States is still a social experiment. In reality, we are all still fighting the revolution to make a just and fair society."

"Ah, stop with the patriotic stuff," said Murphy.

"Hey, man, it's Independence Day, that's what it's all about," said Gary. He patted Murphy on the shoulder in a friendly way. "Oh, there's the media, come on Colleen, we've got to talk to them."

Eva looked around at the Friends who were weaving in and out between the tables, their paper plates loaded now with dessert. For the people, it was the perfect day. But for nature, there stood at the edge of the park, the towering purple cumulonimbus ready for attack.

The winds were shifting. Eva felt a strange gush that seemed to be blowing up from the ground.

The park police were out with bullhorns announcing that a severe storm was approaching.

"We should pack up," said Amanda. She began grabbing supplies and leftover food and shoving them into boxes and picnic baskets.

The wind blew stronger. Trees were bending as if assaulted by an invisible hand. Plastic bags scurried across the lawn and jumped into the river. People hurried to their cars.

Suddenly big splats of rain pelted those who were left in the picnic area.

Eva saw the Statue of Liberty lifting her torch into the gray swirling clouds. Lightening pierced the darkened sky. She helped Amanda load the last of the food into her mother's car, and then they climbed inside for protection.

"Where is Mom?" Eva screamed.

"There!" Judi said pointing.

Colleen came running with the news reporters chasing after her, their microphones and cameras in tow. Everyone jumped into automobiles.

Heavy rain now pounded the rooftops. Colleen started the engine and turned on the windshield wipers, but they were of little help against the blinding rain.

Lightening flickered across the sky as park police directed throngs of cars out of the park. Slowly, Colleen's automobile joined the flow of vehicles that were lining Freedom Way eager to escape the storm.

"I'll take you home first, Amanda," Colleen yelled over the rumble of thunder.

"Oh, thanks, Colleen, and why don't you come in and visit my home for a while. Maybe the storm will pass. In the meantime, we can have ourselves a little party. I have some vegan cookies that Sally made and a couple bottles of wine. There's some herbal tea, too."

"Oh, that's a good idea," Judi cheered. "Let's visit Amanda's house and have a party."

Colleen and Eva needed no further persuasion. Colleen steered the vehicle across town and turned into Amanda's driveway.

"Let's take the shot cut through the front door to get out of this rain," Amanda advised.

Judi and Eva grabbed two baskets of leftovers from the trunk. They ran to the steps and onto the porch. Colleen parked the car and then joined them.

Blocking their entrance to the door was a big furry calico cat.

"Who is this?" Eva asked.

"Oh, her?" Amanda replied, "Sally found her a couple of weeks ago in Stephanie's garden amidst the marigolds. So, we named her Marigold. You know how Sally is; we had to adopt the cat and feed her."

As they turned to enter the door, Judi nudged Eva and then pointed to a box on the porch with a soft blanket inside.

"Yes, she's been staying on the porch ever since," Amanda explained.

As soon as the door opened, Marigold shot inside.

"Oh, no, I didn't mean for her to get in," Amanda wailed.

"Cats rule," Colleen said. "She's the queen."

They all laughed as they entered the house.

Inside the women looked around. Amanda showed them where to hang rain soaked jackets and where to put their wet sandals and shoes.

"Here, bring the food into the kitchen. I'll get out the vegan cookies."

Eva looked around at the living room. It was small, but cheerful, with draperies in a print that looked like yellow asters with green leaves. A big old stuffed sofa was opposite to the fireplace with a large wood-carved coffee table between. Marigold realized the comfort available on the sofa and immediately invited herself to curl up there for a nap.

As Eva entered Amanda's kitchen she viewed the pale green wallpaper in a design to look like the leaves of mint and other herbs. Amanda certainly liked images of nature.

"We'll sit here at the kitchen table. I don't know why it is, but I think women do their best thinking at the kitchen table, don't you?"

They all sat down on the chairs that matched the table. The bright maple wood varnish gave the room a country kitchen look.

Amanda reached into the matching wood cabinets and pulled out two boxes of herbal tea and two bottles of wine.

"This wine is supposed to be organic," she proclaimed. "My neighbor Murphy gave it to me. He only drinks beer and coffee.

She soon had the table set with wine glasses and teacups. She placed green glass plates on the table and set out the picnic leftovers and desserts.

"Here's to our victory at Liberty Park," Colleen declared as she lifted a glass of wine.

"To our victory!"

"The people will have a bigger park with more gardens and a bigger wildlife preserve," Amanda stated proudly.

They lifted their glasses and cups and cheered.

"And to you, Colleen, for stepping up and taking the position of President of the Friends of Nature. I don't know why my neighbor Murphy ran against you, but you beat him down. So let's drink to your victory too."

Again, they lifted their wine glasses and teacups and cheered.

"And here's to the future marriage of Judi and James," Judi said.

"For goodness sake, you don't toast to yourself," Eva chided her.

"I do. I was very successful this year. I had a plan and I put it into action. I persuaded James to marry me. Now we are planning the wedding."

Colleen laughed. "My daughters are going at it again. You two are two very different people; you are going to have to accept your differences."

Eva sighed with indignation.

"Last week, we finished planting the tea rose garden where we are going to be married," Judi announced. "Now we'll wait for it to grow."

"Oh, Judi, a garden wedding surrounded by the park. That's lovely." Amanda said and smiled at Judi. Eva and Colleen smiled up at Amanda.

"Take a cookie," Amanda said as she held out the tray of vegan cookies. They surveyed the cookies with doubtful expressions on their faces.

"These cookies have lots of good things in them" Amanda assured, "bits of apple, some pumpkin and sunflower seeds, along with some raisins, but no eggs, of course—oh, and there's peanut butter to hold them together. Sally made them, but I'm still trying to decide if I like them." She watched as everyone took a cookie and bit into it.

"Speaking of weddings," Amanda continued, "you probably all know that Sally and Peter are planning to get married. When they do, I'll be here alone again."

"Well, it looks like you'll have Marigold, at least," Colleen responded.

"But I don't want to be without people in the house. I love nature, but I'm really a "people person." I also need the income that I will lose when they both move out. Now, I guess I'll have to get some new tenants."

"I'm sure you'll find someone," Colleen assured her.

"It's just that Peter was family and I grew to care about Sally. Is there anyone in our park community who would want to move into these little rooms?"

"Little rooms?" Colleen said, "These are nice rooms compared to the Friends' office."

"That's it," said Judi. "Make this house the Friends' new office. Amanda could live here and keep an eye on things."

"That's an interesting idea," Eva responded. "She'll get plenty of visitors."

They munched on more of the vegan cookies, poured more wine and tea, and then discussed it further. Colleen got up and peeked into the other first floor rooms. There was, of course, the kitchen, living room, bathroom and one bedroom. From the living room, near the front door was a stairway that went up to the top three rooms.

"Amanda, you could live down here and offer the upstairs as office space. I'm not trying to push you into this; we're just day-dreaming, but, you know, this idea could work. Can we go upstairs and see?"

Amanda was excited by the possibility. Her house, which had become such a financial burden to her with the heating bills and taxes and the need for repairs, could actually be a gift to her favorite organization, the Friends of Nature.

"Well, yes, let's go upstairs now and I'll show it to you."

They stood and followed Amanda up the stairs to the rooms that still held Sally and Peter's belongings. Their doors were closed.

"All the rooms are the same size as this one, but this one is the most charming. It was my daughter Stephanie's room. She's the one who got me involved in the park. See. This room overlooks the backyard."

They went into Stephanie's old room.

There were the dolls, large and small, still sitting on the bed. The china tea set, with its rose covered cups and saucers ready for a tea party. From the tops of the lavender curtains, pink fuchsia blossoms draped down over the three panes of window glass.

Eva stepped in and looked around at the cherry wood furniture: a vanity and stool, the bed board and dresser. She slowly walked to the window.

"Oh, what a nice little garden down there. Look Mom."

"That's my daughter's garden. She planted it with her own hands." Amanda explained.

Colleen stepped into the room and took a look outside. The backyard had two old Adirondack chairs next to a large flowerbed lined in stone. Large trees shaded the lawn that extended back away from the house.

"What a beautiful yard. We could hold private fund raising parties there," Colleen said. "If we get those two rooms and they are about this size, they will make a nice office for the Friends."

Eva looked at Amanda. She was smiling.

"We need to do this. We will do this," Amanda said.

"We could get some grant money," Colleen suggested, "and do some educational work. Our group will grow. Oh, Amanda, I'm so glad you are offering your home for this use."

"This is exciting," Eva announced. "This could work very well."

"It will work," Amanda declared. "Let's consider what we have to do next."

"We need to bring it up at a Friends' meeting," Colleen said. "Discuss it with Gary Russo. I think he'll like the idea."

"Let's give Gary a call now," Amanda said. "Come on downstairs. I'll get him on the phone."

Now standing in the living room, Amanda leaned on the fireplace mantel, holding the phone to her ear. Colleen sat down in the stuffed chair and looked up at Amanda. Judi and Eva sat down on either side of Marigold on the sofa. The newly acquired cat continued to pursue her late afternoon nap as though nothing were changing in the world around her.

"He's not answering. I wonder where he could be."

"Let's check the weather," Eva suggested.

They turned on the weather report and watched as the storm moved on. The media then gave a quick announcement about the state's decision on the new land for Liberty Park.

After the report, the television gushed out a few advertisements intended to lure the public into purchasing more automobiles. Then a woman reporter came back on the screen to make another important announcement. "Please everyone, the rain is over for today, don't miss the fireworks."

"Hey, the park is re-opening for the fireworks," Eva yelled.

Amanda's phone rang. It was Gary returning her call.

"Gary, we're over here at my house. Listen, we've got a great idea. Let's set up an office for the Friends at my house."

Amanda gave some details. "What? Come back to the park? Ok, sure, we'll be there for the fireworks."

Amanda ended the phone call and then turned to Colleen and her daughters. "He says it will work. We can do this. But we have to have an official vote at the meeting."

The women cheered.

"Another glass of wine," Amanda suggested.

"No, no," Colleen advised, "we need to have some herbal tea so we can drive back to the park at sunset and see the fireworks."

"Of course, and come on, you have to help me eat all these vegan cookies. I can't eat them all."

Eva looked out the kitchen window. The sky was clearing. They would soon be in the park celebrating their victory with their entire group of Friends.

As Amanda poured cups of tea and pushed the tray of cookies toward them, Eva sat down at the table.

"Well, sister, there have been a lot of changes to celebrate," Eva said to Judi.

"Yes, I'm going to be a married woman with a business."

"Ah, my sister, always focused on herself. What I mean is, we proved that people can change the world. We can solve our problems and make amends for the damages done to Mother Earth. It is an exciting time to be alive."

"I'm glad we're still able to see the fireworks," Judi responded smiling. "I'll call James and let him know I'll be back at the park."

Eva reached over and snatched the last cookie from the tray. "Ok, Sally's cookies are gone; let's go to Liberty."

"Yes," Colleen said, "Let's go to Liberty Park and celebrate democracy."

They put their teacups in the sink and locked the door behind them.

In the window sat Marigold awaiting their return.

*   *   *

Awaiting a return. Eva pondered how strange it was that no one had any way of looking into the future. No one ever knew what would happen next. Would life continue or would there be no return?

She looked across the airport waiting room. There stood her mom Colleen, her sister Judi, and the woman who had inspired her, Amanda Walters. They had tears in their eyes as if Eva were going away, never to return.

Eva looked around at her fellow travelers, all of them students. They were future scientists, botanists, ornithologists ready to board a plane for Peru. They were eager to see one of the world's greatest places, the Amazon rainforest.

Eva wanted to take this trip. It was so important to her education, her natural world experiences. How could she save Mother Earth if she was not fully aware of the wonders of this planet? Eva felt sure now that she had a mission to fulfill. She knew she would return. She turned and waved good-bye to her mom, sister and Amanda as the line of students began to board the plane. Once seated, she pulled out her phone. There was a text message from Matt. "Looking forward to seeing you in Peru." She was ready.

www.ingramcontent.com/pod-product-compliance
Lightning Source LLC
Chambersburg PA
CBHW030423290526
45786CB00001B/105